THE NEW AMERICAN DREAM MACHINE

THE NEW AMERICAN DREAM MACHINE

Toward a Simpler Lifestyle
in an Environmental Age

ROBERT L. SANSOM

ANCHOR BOOKS
ANCHOR PRESS/DOUBLEDAY
GARDEN CITY, NEW YORK
1976

ISBN: 0-385-07439-5
Library of Congress Catalog Card Number 76–2818
Copyright © 1976 by ROBERT L. SANSOM

CONTENTS

PREFACE

As the environmental movement enters its second five years, it faces a challenge of maturity: to set its course toward a distant objective that reconciles ecological protection with economic growth and energy needs. This book is motivated by my concern that the integration of growth policy, energy policy, and environmental protection has not occurred. Thus, this book constitutes a framework for such an integration.

My concern about the inadequate formulation of long-term environmental goals developed while I served as the U. S. Environmental Protection Agency's assistant administrator for air and water programs from 1972 through early 1974. Previously I had been EPA's deputy assistant administrator for planning and evaluation and before that a member of Dr. Henry A. Kissinger's National Security Council staff. These experiences made me particularly sensitive to the impact of the overt break between Richard Nixon's White House after the 1972 election and the EPA, run by William D. Ruckelshaus. The nation was denied a coherent policy reconciling environmental and growth goals. Even energy conservation was an anathema to Richard Nixon. Little has changed between President

Ford's White House and Russell Train's EPA. EPA ploddingly and successfully holds industrial pollution at bay. But, without White House support and leadership, it is helpless in gaining public recognition that cleanup in America depends not just on industrial compliance but on how all types of growth are managed, particularly automobile use, energy consumption, and land use.

At EPA just over five years ago, a major and largely successful effort was launched to force industry to clean up. This book, based on firsthand experiences, records the difficulties and consequences of that effort. It describes how big business tried, working primarily through the White House, to stop EPA. It attempts to analyze why EPA prevailed. Then in a series of chapters on energy, transportation, land use, and technology the book assesses the new environmental problems linked to America's profligate lifestyle. Very simply, every American, not just industry, must reform if these problems are to be managed and the environment saved.

This is, in short, an agenda for retuning the U.S. economy, or American Dream Machine, to conform to newly recognized ecological and energy limits. The emphasis is on practical solutions, not wild-eyed concepts. The basic facts and policies on energy, the environment, technology, and growth are presented. My hope is that, from the integration of these key aspects of the future, the reader can understand how America's lifestyle causes pollution and what to do about it. Innovative and politically arduous growth, energy, transportation, and land-use policies must be implemented to provide America with a safe and livable human environment.

The first environmental campaign against industry took five years. The campaign for lifestyle reforms will unfold over a generation—until the year 2000. There is no time nor any excuse for delay. We are capable of implementing these policies now.

THE NEW AMERICAN DREAM MACHINE

1.

INTRODUCTION:
LIFESTYLE POLLUTION

To most Americans pollution is a belching smokestack or a pipe discharging filthy wastes into a river or stream. Such an image of ecological abuse was the target of the environmental reforms of the 1969–73 period, encompassing eight pieces of far-reaching legislation. But it is evident now that there is still another form of ecological abuse: lifestyle pollution. It is not easy for us to admit we cause pollution. It is difficult to concede that America's lifestyle is the culprit. It is simpler to finger the oil companies, the electric utilities, and Detroit's automobile manufacturers. But we, like they, pollute the environment.

Even if Detroit can produce ultraclean cars with practically no emissions, there are so many Americans owning and driving cars that we will still pollute many major metropolitan regions of the United States. We use land foolishly. Our indiscriminate clearing and paving of the landscape has destroyed the important and efficient natural ecological cleanup processes. When we pave the land or cover it with concentrations of buildings, the water cannot seep through and be cleaned. When we drain and fill in wetlands, they cannot cleanse pollutants. Neither the water table nor the wetlands can be replaced once destroyed. Our lifestyle also requires the use of so much energy that even the most environmentally conscious energy producers and transporters using the best techniques and great sums of money cannot satisfy our appetites without causing serious ecological damage.

We prefer a "devil" theory of pollution; we feel more comfortable if there is someone to blame for our ills. With industry we have had such a culprit. Now that industry is cleaning up, lifestyle pollution is surfacing as a threat to our often-stated environmental goals. Reform comes home.

Few have seen, in the uncertainty and chaos created by the energy crisis, a mandate for reforms in America's lifestyle. Resounding clashes with the conventional wisdom, like the energy crisis, have a way of leaving us shell-shocked, shorn of our cherished assumptions, somehow inadequate in our comfortable habits, and leaderless. Moreover, there are always a few who try to take advantage of public and political confusion. Today some industries are trying to overturn decisions, even reverse the course of the environmental reforms which they have long and unsuccessfully opposed. Thus, reform-minded people interested in the environment and in promoting environmental lifestyle changes must guard their flanks and rear against opportunists who want to renew industry's license to pollute freely.

ENVIRONMENTAL PHASES

The new environmental era of lifestyle changes is revolutionary because it affects us all, requiring changes in how we live, travel, relax, and work, going right down to such details as the number of blankets we sleep under at night.

This new environmental reform should be distinguished from the first, which was a direct confrontation with business, and its impact on industry's thinking and actions. We can think of the environmental periods as phases. Phase I, *the confrontation with big business,* ran from 1969 to 1975. Its central task was to force industry to stop polluting. In 1975 we entered Phase II, a period of *lifestyle change,* which will run until around the year 2000. During this period, lifestyle pollution must be eliminated. Lifestyle changes will be necessary on the part of more than 200 million Americans, not just several thousand companies, although the companies too must change their business styles.

From now until the turn of the century, mass-consumption habits in America will change from those based on the frontierlike abundance of environmental and material resources. Among the newly emerging consumer attitudes will be ones reflecting the need to conserve environmental resources such as urban and coastal lands and the air over our major cities, and to prevent serious damage to our major rivers caused by mine drainage and oil spills and filth-bearing storm runoff from paved urban and industrial surroundings. We will use energy less lavishly in our homes and for travel, and use less of such energy-wasting commodities as glass. In cities like Denver, Washington, D.C., and Atlanta, we will drive less and use public transit more. When we drive, our preference will shift to smaller automobiles. We will cease filling in our wetlands and building homes on every scenic promontory, riverbank, and ocean overlook.

After this period of changing our way of life, we will enter a period of *environmental growth*. This Phase III will witness a moderation of America's economic growth rate. Reduced economic growth will occur in part because of environmental constraints, but primarily because growth will be directed toward ends other than the need to feed and guarantee prosperity for a growing labor force. Because zero population growth birth rates have already been achieved, by around the first decade of the next century environmental demands will also be growing at a zero rate (for reasons explained in Chapter 8). Economic growth will continue but at a reduced rate. This will cause environmental problems to recede in importance as the pace of improvements in cleanup technology comfortably exceeds that of economic growth.

Phase I (1969–75) Eventually historians will fathom why 1969 was the year of environmental awakening in America. Perhaps the country sought a way of turning its thoughts away from Vietnam and toward improving life at home—pacifism turned into environmentalism. Perhaps it was a product of the youth culture of the 1960s and its rejection of post-World War II materialism. Perhaps the signs of impending environmental disaster were too abundant to be ignored. After all, it was in the summer of 1969 that Cleveland's grossly polluted Cuyahoga River burst into flames. In terms of the public's awakening, however, the January 28, 1969, Santa Barbara oil spill, which oozed onto the front pages and evening TV screens for months, deserves the most credit. The dying birds caught in the Union Oil Company's black tide symbolized the helplessness of life overwhelmed by pollution. And in smog, city dwellers have their own black tide. The greater Los Angeles area's ongoing smog alerts, increasingly duplicated in a score of other U.S. cities, were further evidence to many Americans of the need for action to curb pollution.

A river in flames, oil-soaked gulls, smog alerts—all had a common ecological theme. Long-lethargic political bodies and leaders were spurred to action. In 1969, after seventy years, the 1899 Refuse Act, which prohibits waste discharges into navigable waters with a U. S. Corps of Engineers permit, was given an administrative rebirth. Few of the 45,000 industries spewing wastes into our rivers had ever sought, and even fewer had ever received, a permit. Suddenly, permits were to be required for all dischargers.

President Richard M. Nixon captured the spirit of this awakening with his announcement on signing the National Environmental Policy Act on January 1, 1970: "The 1970s absolutely must be the years when America pays its debt to the past by reclaiming the purity of its air, its waters, and our living environment. It is literally now or never." Such a strong statement seemed to trumpet the arrival of environmental reforms.

The spirit of this first official presidential act of the decade of the 1970s was widely shared. Witness the following eight major pieces of environmental legislation that passed between 1969 and 1972. Congress enacted the National Environmental Policy Act (NEPA) in 1969, establishing the Council on Environmental Quality and giving it review authorities over the environmental impact of federal actions. The Clean Air Act and the Resource Recovery Act passed in 1970. Congress labored hard in 1972, producing the Federal Water Pollution Control Act Amendments, the Marine Protection Research and Sanctuaries (Ocean Dumping) Act, the Federal Environmental Pesticide Control Act, the Noise Abatement Act, and the Coastal Zone Management Act.

After the energy crisis of the spring of 1973, Congress slowed its reform pace. Long-pending legislation to control the introduction of potentially dangerous chemicals got stuck in a House-Senate conference committee. Legislation to control strip mining passed, only to be twice vetoed by President Gerald Ford. The Land Use Bill was thrice voted down. It took evidence that cancer may be caused by contaminated public water supplies to gain passage of the Water Supply Act in late 1974, and an outbreak of kepone poisoning in Hopewell, Virginia, spurred Congress to pass the long-delayed Toxic Substances Act in 1976.

The major pieces of legislation passed from 1969 to 1972 are evidence of a far-reaching commitment to clean up America. They have survived the environmental hesitation caused by the energy crisis in 1973. The task of carrying out these laws was made more achievable by the establishment of two organizations. The Council on Environmental Quality was established on January 1, 1970, as required by the National Environmental Policy Act. Its function is to advise the President on environmental matters. It is also chartered to review the performance of government agencies in preparing environmental impact statements. No major government action with potentially adverse environmental consequences is allowed until the full environmental implications have been delineated and aired in public. The second environmental institution was proposed by President Nixon on July 9, 1970. He centralized the executive branch's environmental regulatory authorities in a single agency, the Environmental Protection Agency (EPA), brought into being on December 2, 1970.

Phase II (1976–2000) The year 1975 marked the transition from Phase I to Phase II because it was the year of recognition that lifestyle changes are necessary to achieve environmental goals. These lifestyle changes are not well understood. What will be the consequences of reduced automobile use, energy conservation, and more careful land-use policies? How much will they cost society? What role will new technologies such as mass transit play in reducing societal cost and inconvenience? Will society, by changing its mode of living, reap benefits other than a clean environment such as a more stable and richer community life? To what lifestyle goals should society realistically commit itself? When will the transition to an environmental lifestyle be complete? Will it be a never-ending descent to a static, pastoral existence at lower per capita incomes or will it result in a dynamic society and culture and increasing wealth?

Underlying Phase II's requirements is the issue of altering America's growth psychosis, its obsession with a "more is better" lifestyle. In the economic field, "cowboy economics" describes our propensity for increased material wealth without regard to the external impacts (societal "bads") of rising individual consumption on society's limited environmental and material resources. Now "spaceship economics" needs to eclipse cowboy economics. One man's back yard is another's front yard.

One thing is certain. As the United States enters Phase II, a new political impetus must be found for environmental reform. In pressing for industrial compliance during Phase I, a tiny minority, albeit a powerful one, was forced to institute technological reforms wanted by the majority. But now it has become evident that more is needed if air and water cleanup and other environmental goals are to be achieved; the majority will need to change its energy, transportation, and land-use lifestyles. It might have been expected that, realizing the sacrifices it has to make, the majority would reassess the desirability of attaining the environmental goals themselves. Congress initiated this reassessment in June 1973 and continued it with vigor through early 1976, when it completed redrafts of the Clean Air Act that recognized the necessity for lifestyle reforms.

In short, the commitment of America to lifestyle changes requires a major upheaval in national values. Political and environmental leadership can help (1) by making understandable the need for lifestyle changes if environmental goals are to be reached, and (2) by setting out realistic but challenging goals to which lifestyle changes can be directed and against which progress can be measured.

THE ENERGY CRISIS: A HARBINGER OF LIFESTYLE CHANGE

The energy crisis provides the most vivid and tangible example of the significance of Phase II. When it became acute in 1973, the first reaction of our national leaders was to ask if environmental reforms had caused the crisis. Only later, in 1975, was it accepted that energy conservation, an effort wholly consistent with preserving the environment, was called for as a departure from our wasteful energy habits.

Even in 1975 energy conservation had been embraced only rhetori-
cally by our politicians. When the U. S. House of Representatives
was confronted in June 1975 with the opportunity to curb wasteful
energy use through an automobile gasoline tax, it was resoundingly
defeated, 345 to 72. It is probably a fair appraisal that in this vote,
80 per cent of our representatives voted the lifestyle politics of the
mid-1950s; only 20 per cent understood the energy and environmental imperatives of the mid-1970s.

Subsequent installments of the energy crisis, like an insistent turning of the screw, brought added pressure to slow down the environmental cleanup effort. The winter of 1973–74 came within a few
strokes of congressional pens of being the undoing of four years of
prolific cleanup gains. The White House anxiously sought to overturn major pieces of environmental legislation directed primarily at
big business. Not many realize how close an era of accomplishment
came to being scuttled. And the pressure did not let up. By March
1974, Environmental Protection Agency administrator Russell Train
was threatening to resign if the White House followed through with
its plans to weaken the Clean Air Act, the bedrock environmental
law, with a long list of amendments designed to ease the energy crisis
and dirty the air. The Nixon White House was relying on what it per-
ceived to be the public view: the energy crisis had an environmental
lineage. Congress accepted this verdict. It voted in mid-November
1973 to exempt the trans-Alaskan oil pipeline from further environmental review. Congress's action set aside another basic environmental law, the National Environmental Policy Act of 1969.[1] NEPA
requires the preparation of an environmental impact statement. President Nixon, in a letter to the Speaker of the House, supported congressional efforts to suspend the requirement that the pipeline undergo careful environmental scrutiny.

After a headlong rush to rectify long-neglected environmental ills,
the energy crisis of 1973 and after caused many citizens and their
politicians to pause. Should Americans be skeptical of future warn-

[1] Senate and House passage of the basic pipeline law, which granted the pipeline a wider right-of-way and exempted it from NEPA, was overwhelming—by
80 to 5, and 361 to 14 respectively. The House amendment to drop the NEPA
exemption section from the right-of-way measure failed to pass by 198 to 221.
A similar provision in the Senate narrowly failed by 48 to 49; a Senate tie was
broken by Vice President Agnew, long an opponent of the environment.

ings from the environmentalists because of this experience? In 1969 we accepted the environmental message that pollution associated with energy production and consumption is a serious ecological threat. But should we have also foreseen that the environment is the most important energy problem? Have environmental regulations wrecked our economy? Should our key environmental agencies like the EPA be forced to modify their course to respond to the energy crisis, and for that matter the economic recession? In particular, had the country made a mistake in agreeing with the environmentalists and failing to develop the oil reserves of Alaska's North Slope as rapidly as possible?

Oil from the North Slope Alaskan reserves would have made the difference, some thought. Winters of doubt, energy-related unemployment, and precipitously rising energy prices would, instead, have been winters of comfort and only moderately rising energy prices.

Long delayed, the Alaskan pipeline offered potential relief to a nation starving for oil and striving to avoid dependence on Middle East supplies. National decisions on the pipeline demonstrate the inseparability of energy and environmental issues. One environmentalist has written: "If the Nixon Administration had gotten its way, the trans-Alaskan pipeline would have been almost completed by 1972."[2] It is America's bad fortune that in this instance Mr. Nixon did not get his way. The pipeline promised to deliver 2.0 million barrels of crude oil per day. In 1973 U.S. consumption was 17.0 million barrels per day, 4.7 million barrels of which was imported— about 2.0 million directly and indirectly from the Middle East. Alaskan oil, had it not been delayed by environmentalists, could have helped fill this gap, giving the United States a boost toward energy independence.

The implications of U.S. energy dependence on the Middle East for an independent U.S. foreign policy became manifest in October 1973 with the outbreak of hostilities in the Middle East and the imposition of the oil embargo. The United States, in helping to establish a ceasefire, had to be responsive to Arab concerns; otherwise, the oil embargo would have been continued.

[2] George Alderson, legislative director of Friends of the Earth, in *Nixon and the Environment: The Politics of Devastation* (Village Voice Book, 1972), p. 125.

Some Americans may have failed to see or to appreciate the link between environmental actions on the one hand and the national security and harsh economic consequences of energy dependence on the other. But millions had personally experienced the energy-environmental connection. Their automobiles had suffered deteriorating fuel economy because of equipment installed to meet environmental standards. For example, 1974 automobiles suffered a 10 per cent fuel penalty compared to their pre-1968, non-emission-controlled counterparts. The American people knew society was paying an energy price for cleanup.

Some Americans were tempted during the energy crisis to overlook what the environmental movement had accomplished. In just the four years from 1969 to 1973 so much had been done that the environmental reform movement ranks with the New Deal reforms of the 1930s, labor reforms of the 1940s, and the civil rights reforms of the 1960s. The confrontation with big business became intensive in the early 1970s, when industry exerted a concerted effort to oppose environmental legislation. After half a dozen tough laws passed anyway, industry adopted new tactics. The White House was pressured to undermine, and the Congress to reverse, the abatement program. Again industry failed. The credit, however, goes to a few good men, particularly one Republican EPA administrator, William D. Ruckelshaus, and one Democratic legislator, Senator Edmund S. Muskie, who was strongly supported by Republican Senator Howard H. Baker, Jr. These men had to combat both an executive branch determined to trample environmental obstacles and a confused and erratic House of Representatives searching for the energy-crisis villain. After the episode had passed, industry had to accept environmental requirements as a new way of doing business.

The failure of industry's efforts to undermine environmental reforms during Phase I was extraordinary: The automobile, steel and energy industries demonstrated political impotence. Although the institutions of environmental reform have been narrowly sustained, they remain under siege. The gains made are insecure because they are not yet a part of the accepted way of life in America. Realizing this, particularly in 1973 and 1974, after Ruckelshaus had left the EPA, several industries renewed the attack to gut key environmental laws. They saw the propaganda opportunity offered by the consequences of the Arab embargo. One corporate approach was to appeal for an environmental reversal by reinforcing the consumer's dissatisfaction with automobile fuel-economy losses caused by emission controls. Especially prominent was the Mobil Oil Company's "$66 Billion Mistake" advertisement, trumpeting the energy cost of automotive cleanup. It dealt not with fuel-economy penalties already incurred, for that would have lacked block-busting appeal; rising vehicle weight and increasing use of accessories had played a role equal to or greater than that of emission-control devices in causing declining fuel-economy performance. Rather, the Mobil advertisements decried the then-upcoming and tougher 1975 and 1976 emission standards and concluded that even larger fuel penalties were in prospect. No retractions were issued by Mobil when General Motors announced in the summer of 1974 that its 1975 catalyst-equipped cars were showing fuel economy improvements of about 13 per cent. This gain was achieved by all automobile manufacturers while meeting 1975 standards which were far tougher than those for model-year 1974 cars. In 1976 the gain reached 24 per cent.

Mobil's propaganda initiative was followed, in the midst of the 1974 energy turmoil, by the American Electric Power Company's multimillion-dollar advertising drive to persuade Congress to defeat EPA's efforts to install costly emission-control devices, called "scrubbers,"[3] on about one-tenth of all U.S. power plants. Full-page advertisements appeared in major newspapers and magazines arguing that the only thing standing between America and an energy superabundance based on coal were a few outrageous EPA regulations. Don't remove the pollutants, American Electric Power argued; pipe them through "tall stacks" to disperse them "harmlessly" across the countryside.

With these outbursts directed to the people's concern about the energy crisis and its effect on their pocketbooks, it became imperative to strengthen environmental defenses. But the beginning of the energy crisis also had a deeper significance for environmental prospects than reminding us again that big business still hopes for a reprieve from Phase I environmental reforms. This significance has not been grasped by the American public or our politicians. Fleetingly, it ap-

[3] See Chapter 3 for a description of the scrubber and the complete scrubber story.

pears in the debate over energy policy measures such as the gasoline tax to reduce driving. The overlooked issue is lifestyle pollution.

Reducing pollution from energy-producing sources like coal mines and power plants or from energy-consuming devices such as automobiles can go only part of the way toward the environmental goals the country has adopted. The cleanest car, the best-controlled power plant, or the best-reclaimed strip mine is not good enough if there are too many of them. And there are, or will be, too many of each if energy consumption continues to grow at the rate we have recently experienced. California's beaches will be wall to wall nuclear power plants overlooking a sea of offshore oil rigs. Even if the risks of an individual oil tanker or a nuclear power plant accident are almost infinitesimal, as the number of each increases, risks become unbearable. The only way to limit these risks is to limit our energy consumption. A gasoline tax at the filling station pump is the archetypal lifestyle-pollution-abatement measure. Even as dedicated an environmentalist as Senator Edmund Muskie, when asked in the fall of 1974 if he could support a gas tax, denounced it. Confrontations over lifestyle pollution have yielded to hesitation.

The energy crisis has proved that reforming our lifestyles to clean up lifestyle pollution is an obscure and widely misunderstood requirement. The need for lifestyle reform grows out of the energy-environment connection, but it extends far beyond it.

WHY LIFESTYLE CHANGES
ARE A NECESSARY ENVIRONMENTAL REFORM

Other signposts pointing to the need for lifestyle reform have been raised in the course of implementing the panoply of already-passed environmental legislation. Quietly the far-reaching significance of these provisions has become evident—not just for energy, but for modes of transportation and for our long-cherished obsession with economic growth. Even the premises of America's frontier attitudes and industrial experience are being challenged.

The environmental laws were drafted to achieve clean air and water. They contained well-conceptualized and detailed provisions to force industry to clean up. But they were vague about how lifestyle pollution was to be corrected. If excessive driving caused air standards to be violated, even after Detroit produced clean cars, was driving to be curtailed? How? If new housing developments jeopardized water quality, was housing construction to stop? Congress glided by these issues in drafting environmental legislation. But in 1972 the federal courts, acting in response to suits filed by environmental organizations, pointed to the overriding commitment of Congress to clean up America's air and water, and told EPA to attack lifestyle pollution. Citing language in the Clean Air Act, the courts told EPA to manage growth where necessary to meet clean-air goals and to curtail automobile use if required.

To comply with the order of a federal judge in California, EPA proposed on January 15, 1973, regulations mandating an 85 per cent reduction in Los Angeles's traffic by 1977. In mid-June EPA announced that another thirty cities, encompassing 43 million people, had to impose traffic controls of some type in order to meet air-quality standards by 1977.

Few aspects of our society are more sacred than the affair between ourselves and our automobiles. Spurred by court orders, EPA acted bluntly, saying the law offered little leeway. Gas rationing was to be required, as were parking surcharges and tolls. Expensive pollution-control devices were to be "retrofitted" onto cars already on the road. These EPA actions, unlike earlier ones against industrial pollution sources, represented a threat to the pocketbooks, the mobility, and the lifestyles of millions of car owners.

One Salt Lake City paper labeled EPA "murderers," and an Arizona paper accused EPA of "tyranny." Congressional support for the Clean Air Act evaporated. Practically entire congressional delegations from New Jersey, California, Texas, and Arizona demanded changes in the act. Congress could blame Detroit for the high cost of gas-guzzling emission-control systems. The oil industry could be blamed for the energy shortage. But the Clean Air Act was destined to be the villain of EPA's traffic-reduction plans. There was no one else to blame.

EPA had blundered into Phase II. Automotive lifestyle changes became necessary because improved technology alone could not accomplish the cleanup job. The automobile demonstrates the meaning of Phase II perhaps more succinctly than the energy crisis. The accompanying table summarizes pollutant emissions from automobiles, past and future, assuming existing legal requirements are met. For each of the three major pollutants, the first column shows how many grams of each per mile a car is permitted to emit, and the second column shows the percentage of reduction from what cars emitted before controls were imposed.

REDUCTIONS IN POLLUTANTS EMITTED BY AUTOMOBILES

Model Year(s)	Pollutants					
	Carbon Monoxide		Hydrocarbons		Nitrogen Oxides	
	Grams/ Mile	% Reduction	Grams/ Mile	% Reduction	Grams/ Mile	% Reduction
Pre-1968 (uncontrolled)	85.0	0	8.8	0	5.5	0
1972-1974	28.0	67	3.0	66	3.1	38
1975-1977	15.0	83	1.5	83		
1978-1979	9.0	90	.9	90	2.0	58
1980	3.4	96	.4	95	1.0	82
1985	← no change →				0.4	92

The Clean Air Act requires that the U.S. automobile companies reduce emissions of the two major automotive pollutants, carbon monoxide and hydrocarbons, by 95 per cent. Nitrogen oxides emissions must fall by 92 per cent. By any accounting, these are challenging technological requirements for the automobile industry to reach in a time span of twelve years. But they are designed to protect the vast majority of cities from exposure to health-damaging concentrations of air pollutants that increase heart and lung diseases, and may play a role in causing cancer. At any one time, roughly 5 to 10 per cent of our population is directly endangered by excessive pollutants, but over the lifetimes of a given group of people, a far larger percentage is vulnerable.

These automotive emission-control standards were designed to meet the nation's health needs whatever the cost. Car buyers paid from $250 to $350 for emission controls in the mid-1970s. Over the period 1975–83, national costs of at least $41 billion will be incurred. While it is true that over the same period we will be spending about $7 billion for vinyl roofs and about $65 billion for automobile air conditioners (including associated fuel penalties), emission-control costs will be substantial by any measure.

Moreover, additional expenditures would not further reduce emissions, at least before the early 1980s, and then only if new technologies show promise. Emissions with today's technologies are approaching zero. We are up against a technological barrier. If these reductions do not reduce air pollutant concentrations to a health-protective level, the only real option is to remove cars from the streets.

As might be expected, achievement of these tough emission standards for each automobile will clean up many cities. But, because only one tenth of America's cars are replaced by new car purchases each year, the benefits of the ten-year phase-in of cars with lower emissions will not be seen until around 1985 to 1987.

In 1971, 55 per cent of the nation's population residing in fifty-eight metropolitan areas was exposed to excessive concentrations of automotive pollutants. In 1975, the benefits of the tougher automobile standards of the early 1970s reduced to 42 per cent the share of the population residing in cities that cannot reach the air standards by relying solely on new-car emission standards. In 1985, 20 per cent of the population residing in twenty-five metropolitan areas will still need to curtail automobile use to reach national air-quality goals. After the mid-1980s, unless a new automotive technology comes along to reduce emissions further, the number of city residents needing to reduce travel will begin to grow again because new cars will have about the same emissions as the ones they replace, yet there will be a net growth in the car population and increased driving per car. By 1985, automobiles will be driven 34 per cent more miles than they were in 1975.

The Clean Air Act originally charged the Environmental Protection Agency with ensuring that all cities meet clean-air standards by 1977 at the latest. Thus, even though by 1977 emissions from the car population will drop by 50 per cent compared with 1971, fully nineteen major U.S. cities, housing 66 million people, will need to curtail automobile use by 1977. Another ten to fifteen cities could be added to the list as air-quality measurements become more precise. Accordingly, reliance on the automobile must be reduced to meet the health standards in the late 1970s as well as the 1980s.

Reductions in car use needed to meet the law's 1977 requirement range from a high of 85 per cent in Los Angeles downward to 50 per cent in San Francisco, San Diego, Sacramento, northern New Jersey, New York City, and Baltimore and over 10 per cent in Boston, Phoenix, Denver, Washington, D.C., Philadelphia, and Pittsburgh. EPA reached the conclusion that only a 10 to 20 per cent reduction is feasible by 1977 without disruptive social and economic effects.[4] At EPA's suggestion, Congress changed the law to give cities needing greater reductions more time to meet the standards.

To achieve even these scaled-down goals, the auto side of our lifestyle in major cities must be revolutionized. Car occupancy rates of 1.2 passengers per car will have to rise, and mass transit will need to increase its ridership by 25 to 50 per cent or more. New buses, fast bus lanes, bans on on-street parking, and possibly other more Draconian measures such as moratoriums on construction of new parking facilities and tolls and parking surcharges may be employed.

Millions of Americans have been placed by the Clean Air Act between the rock of the technological barrier to further cleanup of the internal combustion engine and the hard spot of our automobile-dominated lifestyle. Either the lifestyle must give way or air-quality goals will not be attained.

The automobile, like energy, is a *dominant commodity*. The pain of the lifestyle changes required to put it into its proper place will be great because the changes were not anticipated. Our cities are built wrong. The highway program as implemented in our major cities was a key factor in forcing growth toward this dismal result. On the other hand, even at this late date, if we look ahead, plan carefully, and are willing gradually to alter our lifestyles, the end of the automobile era can be made more bearable. The required measures are discussed in Chapter 6.

There appears, therefore, to be a premium on looking ahead to identify other commodities that, like the automobile and energy, can

[4] See Chapter 6 for an explanation of how EPA reached this conclusion.

predetermine society's options if their impact is not foreseen and options are not developed to decrease our dependence on them.

Drawing from our knowledge of the automobile, we can identify the following factors as the characteristics of a dominant commodity.

• (1) *It is a major source of total emissions of pollutants.* The automobile emits between 50 and 95 per cent of all carbon dioxide, hydrocarbon, and nitrogen oxide emissions, depending on the local contribution of industrial sources, trucks, airplanes, and motorcycles.

• (2) *The commodity is pervasive in its use.* Industries, consumers, lifestyles, are built around it. Its "linkages" range over the entire economy. The automobile employs one out of every seven American workers and its production consumes 41 per cent of our malleable iron, 73 per cent of our rubber, 16 per cent of our steel, and 36 per cent of our glass.

• (3) *Strict emission standards and market and tax incentives to clean up will not produce acceptable emissions.* The technology cannot be cleaned up. For the automobile, a 95 per cent reduction is not enough.

• (4) *There are no close substitutes for the commodity with superior emission characteristics.* The automobile cannot be replaced, in the foreseeable future, by battery-powered cars or any other identifiable alternative in the vast majority of its uses.

DISTINGUISHING LIFESTYLE POLLUTION FROM TRADITIONAL POLLUTION

Few commodities meet all four of the tests listed above. If a commodity fails just one test, the application of traditional pollution-abatement approaches will produce the necessary environmental improvement. It might be argued that the aluminum nonreturnable can is a dominant commodity necessitating lifestyle reforms. It is accurate to say that we have adopted a throwaway lifestyle in our addiction to the pop-top can and other one-way containers. But it is possible to replace the aluminum can with the returnable bottle. This is demonstrated by Oregon's successful 1972 law banning nonreturnable bottles and cans and requiring deposits on refillable containers.

There is a "clean" substitute commodity for the throwaway. The Oregon ban, in conjunction with a two-cent incentive refund on containers reusable by more than one manufacturer, reduced litter by about 50 per cent.

Phosphate-based detergents are another example. A by-product of our clothes and dishwashing habits since World War II, phosphates go down the drain, pass through sewage plants, and cause blue-green algae to suffocate fish life in our rivers and lakes. But again, phosphates can be banned from detergents without disrupting our economy. Bans have been implemented in upstate New York and Chicago.

The fact that these commodities fail the tests of a "dominant commodity" does not minimize the environmental threat they represent. Examples of such critical environmental problems are exploding around us like fireworks on our national birthday. The necessity to implement lifestyle reforms should not detract from our efforts to solve these emerging problems. For example, studies have warned that the omnipresent aerosol can emits a gas that, through chemical reactions in the upper atmosphere, may deplete the ozone layer, which is a protective shield against ultraviolet radiation. An increase in the incidence of skin cancer could result if the earth is bathed with more ultraviolet light. The U.S. chemical industry fills three billion aerosol cans per year with almost one million tons of freon. Freon is a gas known technically as a fluorocarbon. After propelling hairspray or deodorant, freon rises to an altitude of ten to thirty miles, where it breaks up under sunlight and combines with ozone. According to one estimate, the freon already released will, when it works its way to high altitudes by 1990, reduce the ozone layer by 5 per cent. A 10 per cent loss in ozone could increase the occurrence of skin cancer by 20 per cent. Large fleets of supersonic aircraft and more nuclear tests could have the same effect on the ozone layer as aerosol cans. Control of freon is a serious problem, but again it can be banned without a serious effect on our lifestyle.

Yet another new threat is vinyl chloride, a key ingredient of many plastics. It was discovered in 1974 that occupational exposure to vinyl chloride in chemical plants can cause liver cancer. In fact, workers have died from this form of cancer. Beyond the plant gates, the general population can also suffer. This chemical can cause women to have brain tumors and miscarriages, and can damage the central nervous system of newborn babies. By 1976, however, industry was well on its way to eliminating vinyl chloride emissions in response to Occupational Safety and Health Administration and EPA regulation. Even so, as many as sixty-six organic chemicals similar to vinyl chloride have been found in the New Orleans water supply. Some of these elements are suspected carcinogens. Traces of other such chemicals have been found in the water supplies of seventy-nine American cities. Of the three hundred to five hundred new chemicals introduced each year, only a few have been fully assessed for their cancer-causing potential.

In 1974, 355,000 Americans died from some form of cancer, 5,000 more than the year before. In 1975 the death rate from cancer rose at more than twice any previous year's increase. Research work at the National Cancer Institute suggests that 60 to 90 per cent of all human cancers are caused by environmental factors, including cigarette smoke. Your chances of dying from cancer are about one in six. Pollutant-caused cancer is a more acute threat because of the latency period between exposure and malignancies. Usually, there is a twenty- to thirty-year lag. Thus far, environmental cleanup efforts have halted or reduced the discharges of toxic pollutants such as mercury, DDT, and polychlorinated biphenyls (PCBs) which have immediate or near-immediate impacts. In 1976 Monsanto, the only producer of PCBs, agreed to phase out production of that chemical.

The next task will be much more difficult and must include pre-introduction testing of new chemicals as called for in the Toxic Substances Control Act recently passed by Congress. Over the next decade Americans will face the hard choices of banning or strictly controlling a variety of toxic materials. If the aerosol can is banned, we will bear inconvenience and a billion-dollar industry will be closed down. However troublesome, these measures will not challenge us as severely as the necessity of lifestyle reforms to eliminate pollution caused by the overuse of dominant commodities such as the automobile.

Commodities like the automobile and energy which meet all four of the tests listed previously represent key threats to the attainment of acceptable economic growth with a clean environment. The only way these commodities can be managed is through lifestyle changes. Since they are major sources of pollution, their utilization must be reduced and carefully managed. But, since they are all pervasive, they cannot be completely purged from our economy or lifestyle without catastrophic consequences. Acceptable substitutes cannot be found to replace them, and no cleanup technology is available to be mandatorily applied.

LAND
AND A NATIONAL GROWTH POLICY

Land is also a dominant commodity. Two EPA initiatives in the mid-1970s helped define the need for changing the impacts of our lifestyle on land. These initiatives, also taken in response to court orders obtained by environmental lawsuits, addressed the issue of economic growth, attempting to affect where it takes place and, in some cases, whether it is allowed at all. By regulation, EPA established procedures to review plans for construction of new shopping centers, sports stadiums, parking lots, highways, and other "indirect sources" which might cause pollution as a result of the emissions from the large numbers of automobiles they attract. In addition, our fifty fastest-growing and, therefore, most pollution-prone cities were given two years to develop long-term growth plans, including patterns of development to minimize land use and automobile travel, to maintain air quality through 1985.

The second growth-controlling measure was issued by EPA after a U. S. Supreme Court ruling. By a 4–4 tie with one justice abstaining, the Supreme Court on June 11, 1973, upheld a lower court decision ordering EPA to establish regulations to prevent significant deterioration of air quality. This decision gave EPA authority its lawyers felt it did not have under the Clean Air Act. The EPA had accepted its mandate to establish regulations to cleanse dirty air to meet in 1975 the health-protective "primary" standards for pollutant concentrations. But the agency was astounded to be told by the courts that it also had to ensure that pristine air did not deteriorate. The agency was told to halt growth even if health or property damages are not at stake. In short, EPA has to monitor economic growth and land use, and curtail either if new facilities using the best emissions-control technology available caused a "significant" drop in measured air quality. Growth could be sacrificed to achieve aesthetic benefits such as long-distance visibility.

Willy-nilly then, EPA struggled to establish a national growth policy. Without detailed congressional guidance, without executive branch leadership or even support, and with outright opposition from developers, an orphaned EPA staggered from court suit to court suit. What should have been a time of challenge was a time of neglect.

Some in Congress realized EPA's difficulty. They were reminded repeatedly by EPA's administrator of the need for congressional guidance. Likewise, shopping-center developers, the housing industry, and other economic groups impacted by EPA's growth-management regulations called on Congress to show leadership. How was lifestyle pollution to be controlled? Most in Congress lacked the vision to see the problem, much less the solution. The few who did understand EPA's plight were fearful of opening any environmental legislation for amendment. They were afraid because the antienvironmental energy forces in the Congress might have been able to turn an effort to devise national growth, land-use, and transportation policies consistent with a clean environment into an effort to overturn the finest set of laws in the world for abating industrial pollution.

On June 29, 1973, in an agonizing floor colloquy, the Senate Air and Water Pollution Subcommittee made its first public concession that the Clean Air Act, the precursor of all the vigorous environmental legislation of the early 1970s, needed to be changed. Its measures to cope with lifestyle pollution had to be altered. The subcommittee shortly before, in closed session, had agreed to consider changes in the act.

CHANGING COURSE

The euphoria of the time of enactment of the Clean Air Act—which extended to companion pieces of legislation to clean up our lakes, rivers, and oceans and regulate pesticides, toxic materials, and noise—gave its drafters the strength of its vision. But its reconsideration could have been prophesied from the weak technical knowledge on which it rested. A country and a Congress that had so long neglected the environment were destined to suffer setbacks in abruptly attempting to protect it.

It is easy to explain why America has had such difficulty in responding to these developments. The issues go to the heart of a way of life. It is time for a reappraisal and an improved understanding of the interrelationships among environmental protection and energy, growth, and technology. Most importantly, it is a time for setting new goals.

A social problem also emerged in 1973 to challenge the legitimacy of the environmental movement. Events laid bare the weak political roots of the environmentalists, exposed the difficult alliance of environmentalists with the most elite and conservative elements of our society, and displayed the fuzziness of environmental thinking on the subject of economic growth, particularly its employment and other social benefits. If the institutions of environmental reform are weak in the face of the task of assuring continued industry compliance, they are inadequate to cope with the upcoming second environmental reform: the era of lifestyle changes to achieve environmental goals. Such inadequacies cannot be remedied by movement that has weak political roots and no clear perception of the ultimate goals it seeks for America.

Environmental thinking has failed to conceptualize what has been accomplished, to identify situations where compromises are needed, and to develop the strategies for these compromises, and it has failed to establish the ultimate goals of environmental achievement.

If industry is no longer the chief target of the environmental movement, the consumer is. We are the villains. And the legal confrontation tactics of the last three years have been of little value in dealing with consumers who buy heavy, gas-guzzling cars and who purchase homes that are inefficient to heat or cool. Recognition of this basic change in the nature of environmental strategy and tactics is fundamental to implementing a thorough environmental reform.

Managing the *dominant commodities* will be the decisive environmental problem of the balance of this century. The problem challenges our government institutions, environmental groups, and every citizen.

Governments must define the extent to which lifestyle changes are needed to meet environmental standards. They must inform the public and devise ways to spur lifestyle changes which recognize that the simple approach of Phase I, with firm dates for industry compliance and heavy fines or jail sentences for nonperformance, will not work. Subtle persuasion, political leadership, and carefully applied incentives are necessary—for example, subsidized mass transit fares or higher electricity rates for large energy consumers.

The environmentalists must alter their confrontation tactics to reflect the new task. Broad citizen education and involvement along with pressure for political leadership are key ingredients of a campaign to encourage lifestyle changes.

The subsequent chapters are organized to reflect the three phases of environmental reform. Chapters 2 and 3 describe Phase I, the confrontation with big business in the early 1970s and how our political institutions coped with the conflicting industry and environmental pressures. Chapters 4 through 7 lay out paths to the implementation of Phase II, lifestyle changes for energy, transportation, and land use. Chapter 8 looks beyond the year 2000 to an era of environmental growth, Phase III.

2.

THE CRISIS
IN ENVIRONMENTAL
DECISION-MAKING

In this chapter we will investigate the process by which environmental policy decisions are made by the U.S. government. I will focus on the experiences of Phase I, or the industrial confrontation, but will examine as well the flawed perceptions and abilities of our key national institutions as they address the Phase II requirement for leadership in implementing lifestyle changes. Obviously, the subjects are not the inanimate institutions that line Pennsylvania Avenue. Rather, the central characters are the personalities involved in environmental politics—the Nixons, Muskies, Ruckelshauses—and how they saw the environment as a political issue. I will also suggest reforms for improving the responsiveness of our government to environmental issues.

General public interest, concern, and action to protect and improve the environmental decision-making process is essential if there is to be continued cleanup success. Already the process has failed to set the new environmental priorities needed in Phase II. It has come dangerously close to undoing the aggressive approach to industry cleanup by failing to test completely and openly the views of those who proclaim that the energy crisis has eclipsed the environment.

Americans have had innumerable recent examples of how vital it is to the public interest for there to be effective management and public scrutiny of the federal government. Richard Nixon's abuse of power was but a highly visible and well-documented incident of a phenomenon duplicated with alarming frequency throughout the national government. The Central Intelligence Agency, even by the admission of its director, William E. Colby, abused its authority. More subtle but no less disappointing are the failures of various regulatory agencies charged with protecting the public interest but guilty of usurping it. Among these are the Interstate Commerce Commission, the Federal Bureau of Investigation, and the Federal Power Commission. Americans would be foolhardy to presume that the Environmental Protection Agency is immune to the forces that led to the "capture" of these agencies by the very industries and interests they were charged with regulating in the public interest.

Under its first administrator, William Ruckelshaus, EPA sought to honor Congress's charge. In the spirit of its legislation, EPA attempted to regulate industry aggressively. That Ruckelshaus was labeled "Mr. Clean" by friend and foe alike is testimony to some measure of success. The significance of this performance lies in how difficult it was to establish that reputation and how unlikely it is to be duplicated. For Ruckelshaus's power to prevail on environmental issues was unique. It derived from his politically potent personality and applauded integrity, from the fact that he was a favorite of President Nixon's strongman John Mitchell, and from the unique political juncture of the 1972 election, which found "Ecology Ed" Muskie, as White House politicos gleefully called him, the leading Democratic challenger to Richard Nixon.

A Republican, Ruckelshaus found from the time he formed the agency in December 1970 until President Nixon's re-election in November 1972 that his ability to regulate industry without undue interference from the White House was repeatedly tested. More than anything else, his ability to make decisions strongly opposed by the White House and still retain his job was due to the looming presence of Senator Muskie, the father of the environmental legislation Ruckelshaus was implementing and the chief Democratic contender for President Nixon's job. A President so insecure of his re-election prospects that he was willing to go the extremes of the Watergate coverup was unwilling to oppose overtly the environmental regulation of big business and thereby grant Senator Muskie a popular campaign issue.

Deep down, Richard Nixon had as much use for the environment as Alfred Krupp. After his re-election, Nixon's suppressed discontent with the environmental movement surfaced. As was so often the case with Richard Nixon, his visceral conviction on issues and his hatred for personalities who had crossed his path overtook his political acumen. He convinced himself that the environment was not a political issue of potence. The energy crisis of 1973–74 provided the occasion for a reasonably covert retreat from his previous proenvironment positions.

This "browning" of Richard Nixon when America was "greening" left EPA in a desperate position. First, several critical decisions were coming due which were essential to complete the effort to bring big business into compliance with the Clean Air Act. There was a decision on whether to ease automobile emission standards in response to Detroit's pleas. There was a long-pending decision to remove lead from gasoline. Lead from gasoline ingested as a fine airborne dust or eaten with roadside dirt by playing children was increasingly documented as a threat to infant and child health. Finally, the nation's electric power companies remained to be convinced that they had to install stack gas scrubbers to remove harmful sulfur gases. EPA survived each of these in turn. The brilliant and iconoclastic engineer Edward Cole, president of General Motors, played a key role in undermining President Nixon's position against the automobile standards. EPA prevailed on the lead-removal issue by the sheer sacrifice of its last reservoir of support at the White House. After that, Ruckelshaus's days were numbered; what had been his highly touted "independence" became to Mr. Nixon's senior staff in the White House "insubordination."

After Ruckelshaus left the EPA in April 1973 to become acting director of the FBI, his successors, briefly Robert Fri as acting administrator and then Russell Train as administrator, were orphans in the executive branch. Train survived because Richard Nixon did not. He drew his support from the Air and Water Pollution Subcommittee of the Senate Public Works Committee in resisting the Nixon White House's campaign to dismantle environmental legislation. What had been to Ruckelshaus a voice of encouragement was to Train a lifeline.

The Senate's Air and Water Subcommittee is truly a unique institution. That the Constitution provided for the possibility of such strength is another sheaf of testimony to the wisdom of its drafters. Chairman Muskie understands the power and motivation of big business as few others do. Nor is Republican subcommittee member Senator Howard Baker innocent of such matters. It was Senator Baker in 1971 who quietly but firmly told the Tennessee Valley Authority to learn how to conduct strip mining operations without harming the environment. By 1973 one could visit a TVA-funded strip mining operation near Baker's Tennessee home that met all the criteria spelled out in the strip mining legislation that passed the Congress in 1974 and 1975, only to be twice vetoed by President Ford.

The senatorial relationship between Muskie and Baker was one of enormous mutual respect. Leon Billings, Muskie's smart and cantankerous environmental chief of staff, reported that in Muskie's view Baker was the brightest member of the Senate. The Muskie-Baker alliance protected the cause of the environment from Richard Nixon. It also preserved the Clean Air Act from a House of Representatives which was panicked by the energy crisis in the winter of 1973–74.

But Congress could only defend. It could not create and lead the country into an era of lifestyle reform. This became acutely evident in 1975 when Congress stumbled in efforts to reduce energy consumption. In the early 1970s, Congress reflected grass-roots demands that industry pollution be curbed. It voted strong legislation. But there will never be a similar grass-roots movement demanding the lifestyle reforms needed in Phase II. Only strong leadership, probably presidential leadership, can provoke public support for measures like a gasoline tax to curb energy consumption or land-use legislation.

In short, the patterns of decision-making developed during the first environmental reform hold important implications for the continued success of the environmental movement. If Ruckelshaus and Muskie were the leaders of the first set of environmental reforms in this country, their traditions must survive in the Congress and at EPA if the ground gained is to be protected. Already Ruckelshaus has departed and Senator Muskie no longer dominates his committee as he once did. Institutions such as the Council on Environmental Quality (CEQ) and the Environmental Protection Agency were established during Phase I. Strong congressional oversight was a hallmark of the 1969–73 period. The courts, the White House, other executive-branch departments, the environmentalists, industry, the press, and the public all played key roles. It is timely to ask how and how well the decision-making process worked and to determine, if possible, what is needed if it is to continue to function successfully and to assume the additional burden of moving the nation toward an environmental lifestyle.

THE WHITE HOUSE

The focus of the key regulatory decisions affecting industry clean-up was the executive branch. Congress was an avid watcher and frequent contributor to the course of implementation of the legislation it had mandated. The courts were infrequent contributors, though they could direct events as forcefully as the other branches when there was doubt about the provisions of the law.

Environmental decision-making was the glamorous "in" activity in Washington in 1969, even in President Nixon's executive branch. Interior Secretary Walter Hickel, perhaps smarting from his portrayal as a frontier plunderer in his Senate confirmation ordeal, took the Administration lead. He quickly captured the press's fancy by guaranteeing that the rights to north Florida water nourishing the Everglades National Park would not go to south Florida developers. He also opposed the construction of a new Miami jetport planned to cover thirty-eight square miles within the Everglades region. Even the Nixon White House joined in that era's politically chic activity: ecology. After opposing the establishment of the Council on Environmental Quality as the ecologists' counterpart to the Council of Economic Advisors, the Nixon White House accepted Congress's mandate to do it anyway. Interior under secretary Russell E. Train was appointed the council's first chairman and was instrumental in President Nixon's order to halt construction of the Cross-Florida Barge Canal.

On the White House Domestic Council staff, John C. Whitaker was responsible for overseeing the activities of the Departments of Agriculture and Interior, and the EPA. A geologist by training, Whitaker served as an advance man in the 1968 Nixon campaign. He was a sympathetic listener on environmental issues, particularly as long as they were seen to have political potency by his bosses Nixon, Haldeman, and Ehrlichman.

But, by 1971, key White House interest in the environment began to wane. Hickel had been fired in November 1970. A crushing Nixon defeat at the hands of the ecologists came in March 1971 when the Senate voted down a federal subsidy to launch the supersonic transport; Nixon played all his political cards but lost 51 to 46. He was fervently committed to this new symbol of American power. Whitaker was soon overwhelmed by rising White House antienvironmental sentiment. He was shoved aside by Secretary of Commerce Maurice Stans, who feared the economic impact of environmental expenditures on U.S. industry. Inside the White House, ex-Wall Street investment banker Peter M. Flanigan shared Stan's doubts. Whitaker also got go-slow advice from General George A. Lincoln of the Office of Emergency Preparedness (OEP), Edward E. David, Jr. of the Office of Science and Technology (OST), and Office of Management and Budget (OMB) director George P. Shultz.

The situation was so unfavorable to the environmentalists in 1972 that their chartered White House advocate, CEQ chairman Train, was not even welcomed in inner White House or OMB circles. CEQ emerged twice a year, once to offer the President's environmental program to Congress and a second time with its annual report. For all practical purposes, the institutionalization of environmental interests in the Executive Office of the President in the form of CEQ had failed. In one instance in 1973 a top Administration official completely forgot about CEQ. In late December of that year the then CEQ chairman, Russell Peterson, formerly governor of Delaware, prepared to release a study on prices and gasoline demand. He called Federal Energy Office chief William Simon to inform him in advance. Simon, having been told by his secretary that Governor Peterson was calling, took the telephone and said, "Hello, Governor. I've been meaning to call you. We have a lot to discuss." He proceeded to urge "Governor" Peterson to reverse Delaware's law prohibiting shore-siting of refineries and other energy facilities. Peterson rejected Simon's advice. Simon hung up thinking he had talked to the governor of Delaware. The next day OMB director Roy Ash called Simon to tell him of the study the CEQ chairman planned to release. Simon called the chairman to complain about the pending release. Peterson replied, "Bill, I informed you of the release yesterday." Simon, embarrassed, apologized for not knowing the CEQ chairman.

While the White House ignored CEQ, it avoided a direct confrontation with the ecology movement. Looking over its shoulder at the distant Democratic front-runner Muskie, the White House muted its doubts about environmental reform. Taking avantage of this dilemma was another strong environmental advocate the Administration could not ignore: EPA administrator William Ruckelshaus. He became in 1972 and 1973 the chief executive-branch spokesman for the environment, in part due to the tough decisions he had to make to execute EPA's legislation. EPA-drafted regulations mandated by the Clean Air Act began to emerge in a steady stream in the *Federal Register,* the federal government's daily diary of regulations.

The White House was troubled. Cautious, reluctant operatives in the White House complained about the far-reaching EPA regulations to reduce pollution. A way had to be found to stop EPA without being so visible that Muskie could label Nixon "Dirty Dick." A way was found. To discipline the flow of regulations, a formal review process was set up and managed by OMB, not the White House. Because it controlled OMB, the White House secretly opposed tough EPA regulations while letting OMB bear the stigma of opposition. Every morning at 7:30, presidential chief of staff Robert Haldeman held a White House staff meeting. Frequently complaints about EPA's impact on industry were on the agenda. Flanigan would bitch about EPA regulation of copper smelters or power plants. Shultz would voice the concerns of the automobile industry. Whitaker and attending OMB officials were told to force EPA to "ease up."

At these White House plotting sessions, a colorful terminology was bantered across the Roosevelt Room, a few steps from the President's Oval Office. The "bird and bunny crowd" defended ecological interests. Their leader was "Ecology Ed." The phrase that caught the Haldeman group's fancy was "the quality of life." First mentioned in sarcasm, it was adopted in a moment of irony as the label for the OMB process intentionally set up to ease ecological requirements. This terminology was another example of Nixon Administration doubletalk.

THE QUALITY OF LIFE PROCESS

Through the "Quality of Life" process every concerned government agency was allowed a prepublication opportunity to review EPA's regulations. Potential economic, federal budget, legal, and energy implications of each regulation were examined. White House and OMB officials would canvass the agencies to identify any complaints against proposed EPA actions. Then Ruckelshaus was presented with a list of corrections he was to make before issuing the regulations. Ruckelshaus could see possible benefits from the Quality of Life process. It might broaden EPA's perspective, forcing the agency to do its homework. The process could inform the EPA administrator of the economic, energy, land-use, and industry impacts of environmental actions. Yet the process was also a serious threat to the independence of EPA.

Unlike a Cabinet department, an independent regulatory agency such as EPA is strictly governed by its legislation. Its laws typically begin with "the Administrator shall." The President appoints the administrator and his assistant administrators, but the President is not empowered by Congress to exercise the administrator's authorities. Muskie quickly accused Nixon and OMB of usurping Ruckelshaus's authorities through the Quality of Life process. The senator's Air and Water Pollution Subcommittee's interest in the process was sparked by the changes made at the request of OMB and the Department of Commerce in guidelines EPA promulgated in August 1971, advising the states on the development of their air-pollution abatement plans. These plans—to determine what each plant had to do to comply with the law—were to be submitted to EPA by every state in early 1972.

The regulations were proposed in April 1971, and it was expected that the final version would be issued in the summer; but it was held up in the interagency Quality of Life review process while modifications were made and did not come out until fall. These modifications removed important requirements for land-use controls to prevent the degradation of air quality in areas like the West with pristine air, and for transportation controls to reduce traffic in polluted cities. Inserted in place of these requirements was the guide that states should examine the "cost-effectiveness" and "costs" and "benefits" of their abatement regulations. On the latter point, it was perfectly advisable that states consider the most cost-effective controls to meet national standards, a position later upheld by the courts. The other changes, according to subsequent court rulings, were not in keeping with EPA's legal mandate. At the same time that the Senate pointed to unauthorized White House usurpation of EPA's authorities, Ruckelshaus was wavering on the pollution controls to be imposed on copper smelters in the West. Criticism by the Senate and by environmentalists of EPA's guidance to the states and of EPA vacillation on smelter controls stung Ruckelshaus. The flavor of his reaction is captured in his sharp response to Senator Thomas F. Eagleton in a February 1972 Senate hearing: "OMB will simply have nothing to do with the final approval of these individual 'state plans.'" He went on:

> I could have taken on June 28 those comments and that guideline draft that I had and not talked to anyone else. I could have gone down to the Potomac, I suppose, and read a book on the loneliness of command in trying to decide what ought to be done with those guidelines. But in my opinion I don't know everything that there is to know about something as important as implementing an act of this sort. Hence, I would like to get expertise that exists in other agencies of government. I welcome inter-agency review and sitting down and trying to justify what we are doing to other agencies.[1]

Ruckelshaus's tolerance of the Quality of Life process stemmed in part from his lack of confidence in the regulations which were produced by bureaucracies he inherited from the Department of Health, Education, and Welfare and the Department of the Interior. EPA was formed primarily from pieces spun off from those highly bureau-

[1] Hearings before Subcommittee on Air and Water Pollution of Committee on Public Works, U. S. Senate, Feb. 18, 1972, p. 326.

cratized organizations. EPA's inheritance had no expertise in systems analysis or economics, only air- and water-pollution engineering and health. In 1971 Ruckelshaus recruited the needed expertise. Meanwhile, his estimate of the value of the Quality of Life review process was reinforced when the final state air-pollution abatement plans were issued in the spring of 1972. The Quality of Life review had revealed a critical energy aspect of the plans. Energy was an issue of genuine and far-reaching interagency and White House interest. Aided in seeing this problem clearly by other agencies, Ruckelshaus was able throughout 1972 to encourage the states to modify their plans to accommodate energy needs. When the energy crisis broke in 1973, EPA had already set in motion modifications in state plans to minimize energy impacts while guaranteeing the achievement of vital environmental health goals.

But the advantages of the Quality of Life process were soon eroded. The pace of the corruption of the process almost paralleled the downfall of Muskie as the Democratic front-runner. The Department of Commerce began to use it to filibuster EPA's actions. At one point the department's general counsel said he would resign from the Republican party if the process were not used more vigorously to bring EPA to heel. White House cynicism grew. Soon every controversial regulation was met not by a useful, substantive critique, but by one White House staffer's remark, "What is the bottom line. Isn't the bottom line that the Clean Air Act has to be amended?" The purpose of White House intervention was simplified to "gut the Clean Air Act." The White House invited to meetings only agency representatives supportive of its views. For example, the Office of Science and Technology, charged with advancing technology's role in society, was usually represented by technicians who predicted less could be done technically than industry was willing to do. Occasionally, an invitee would get out of line. Assistant secretary of the Interior Lawrence E. Lynn, Jr., attending his first Quality of Life meeting in April 1973, remarked on EPA's proposed regulations for shopping centers: "What's *wrong* with building shopping centers so they don't violate air standards?" The White House and OMB officials, who had stopped thinking in other than antienvironmental terms, offered only a stunned silence in reply. The regulations were issued, but Lynn was never invited to attend another Quality of Life meeting.

Increasingly alarmed, Ruckelshaus made repeated efforts to streamline the review system, including several meetings with Domestic Council director John Ehrlichman. These efforts failed. Likewise, Russell Train, on the occasion of his appointment as EPA administrator in August 1973, sought to put EPA in charge of the process, but he too failed to wrench it from White House and OMB control. Train's first initiative against the process was an odd one. He fought hard at the time of his confirmation in September 1973 to have EPA call Quality of Life review meetings and hold them at its offices rather than in the Executive Office Building. He contemplated making such a request of President Nixon before realizing that a letter arguing over the proper location for meetings would hardly be an appropriate inauguration of his administratorship.

STRENGTHENING EPA

The important issue was not the existence of the Quality of Life process or where the meetings were held, but who made the big decisions. The independence of the EPA administrator from White House and other agency influence was a vital decision-making issue in the executive branch. Ruckelshaus judged the showdown would come on a few major decisions he faced. He prepared for his inevitable conflicts with the White House by instituting far-reaching reforms within EPA. He hoped these would strengthen his ability to prevail in spite of the Quality of Life process.

Not yet a year old in 1971, EPA suffered from a wide credibility gap. It claimed the costs of pollution abatement were low and dislocation impacts such as plant closures and unemployment were small. Yet it had no reliable cost or economic-impact analysis. For example, EPA first estimated the cost of controlling air emissions from nonferrous-metal smelters at $32 million; later in 1971 EPA's estimate was $87 million; in early 1972 it became $313 million; and it finally reached the $330 million to $650 million range at the completion of interagency economic-impact studies in March 1972. An agency so unable to document a defensible case was in jeopardy, facing deeply entrenched and opposing White House and other departmental interests.

Ruckelshaus established a new Office of Planning and Evaluation in October 1971 to perform independent analysis of the economic impact of proposed regulations. Economists were recruited from Dr. Kissinger's National Security Council staff, the Systems Analysis Office in the Department of Defense, and from the Agency for International Development. This EPA office took the lead in developing the joint Commerce, CEQ, and EPA economic-impact analysis which in March 1972 established EPA as an objective assessor of the impacts of its own regulations.

A second internal reform was the establishment of an executive-level review procedure, chaired by the deputy assistant administrator for planning and evaluation, to ensure that the agency's scientists, engineers, economists, and lawyers reviewed all regulations before the administrator was asked to make a final decision. Each decision paper included at least one alternative approach to the one recommended, and dissenting views were clearly spelled out.

INHERENT EPA WEAKNESS

But while the agency developed reports to defend itself against exorbitant claims of cost and economic impacts, it could do little to inform the American public of health benefits from cleanup. The agency was unable to quantify the health dangers its standards would enable society to avoid. It was impossible to remedy overnight the neglect of environmental benefits inherent in our GNP accounting system. The public was left to believe billions were being spent to protect a few sick people. EPA's health standards for the air, promulgated in April 1971, were based on studies carried out by the Department of Health, Education, and Welfare before EPA was formed. At age three, the only new health documentation EPA provided was on the impact of the removal of lead from gasoline in early 1973. Congress was forced in frustration to ask the National Academy of Sciences in June 1973 for an independent assessment of the value of health protective standards. The Academy's efforts to document health damages were no more convincing than EPA's.

Further, EPA was being forced into uncharted areas. EPA's 1973 transportation control plans exhibited the agency's most glaring technical weakness. There emerged within the agency an open conflict between its lawyers and technicians. EPA's technicians were confident in tackling the problems of applying industrial and automotive pollution-control technology to control emissions directly, but they were wary of controlling citizen behavior, such as automobile-use habits or economic development patterns, that might have an indirect effect on emissions. They argued for delays in the issuance of regulations until there was a sound technical basis.

EPA's lawyers, sensitive to repeated court rebuffs of the agency's failure to promulgate regulations by legislatively mandated deadlines, often acted without a sound technical basis. One lawyer, after participating in public hearings in Los Angeles, concluded that a 30 per cent traffic reduction was feasible for that city by 1977. When asked to respond to newly elected Mayor Bradley's inquiry on how EPA arrived at the number, then enshrined in the *Federal Register,* he replied, "I had a gut feeling after the hearings that it could be achieved."

The ultimate difficulty lay in the law. EPA was forced by legislative deadlines, often imposed on the administrator by court decisions in response to citizen suits, to act on the basis of weak technical knowledge. It sought to delay for two years the imposition of transportation controls. The district court of the District of Columbia disagreed; EPA was to act even without a sound technical basis. It failed to implement a policy to prevent the degradation of clean air because it doubted its legal authority and technical competence to act. The same court disagreed. In a third instance this court forced EPA to control the construction of new "indirect" sources, such as shopping centers that do not emit pollutants but attract automobiles which do. EPA complained it did not know how to calculate the effect on air quality of another shopping center.

Thus EPA was never in an intellectual and technical position to master its critics. Environmental issues are simply too complex, involving not just narrow technical questions but extending to every aspect of society, including the economy and social goals. The National Aeronautics and Space Administration had few credible critics of how it went about putting man on the moon. But EPA had to live with the reality that everyone is an environmentalist or an antienvironmentalist. Ruckelshaus knew this; so did the White House. The Quality of Life process depended on it for its existence.

THE BIG DECISIONS

Ruckelshaus faced the most serious challenges to his independence when in May 1972 he decided to deny the automobile industry's request for a delay in the date of automotive cleanup. He faced another challenge in December 1972 when he decided to remove lead from gasoline. His control of environmental decisions was also challenged by the energy crisis in April 1973. Russell Train was similarly threatened by the energy crisis on a daily basis beginning at his installation in September 1973.

The February 1972 congressional grilling of Ruckelshaus over the roles of OMB and the White House in seeking changes to EPA's regulations evoked the following Ruckelshaus statement on whether the White House and OMB had usurped his authority to make EPA's decisions: "It (the authority) is not being delegated to anybody else, and if anybody tried to force me to delegate it, I could no longer function as Administrator of this Agency."[2] The 1972 automobile decision tested Ruckelshaus's resolve on whether he would survive under his stated conditions as EPA administrator.

The Automobile Decision   As the public hearings for an extension proceeded, Ruckelshaus heard hours of testimony on how slowly Detroit was proceeding to clean up. Since the law allowed the EPA administrator to grant an extension only if each manufacturer had made a "good faith" effort to comply, he became convinced the manufacturers' applications for an extension should be denied. He then took several measures in an attempt to prepare the White House for a decision he accurately predicted it would oppose. He knew OMB director Shultz was on close terms with Chrysler's chairman, Lynn Townsend. He knew the White House was frequently in contact with GM's president, Edward Cole, and Ford's president, Lee Iacocca. It was likely the President would be well briefed by Flanigan, Ehrlichman, and Shultz on industry's objections. It was unlikely

[2] Ibid., p. 306.

CEQ's Train or others were able to give the President the environmental viewpoint.

John Ehrlichman was informed by his assistants Whitaker and Fairbanks of the likely Ruckelshaus decision to deny Detroit's extension request. He, in turn, told the President of Ruckelshaus's plans. Richard Fairbanks, assistant to Whitaker, drafted a short memo which Whitaker sent to Ehrlichman describing Ruckelshaus's plans and recommending White House acquiescence. Ehrlichman marked the disapproved block. Fairbanks sent another memorandum, twice as long, arguing more forcefully that the White House could not intervene in the EPA administrator's quasi-judicial decision. He spent two hours arguing with Ehrlichman, whose tone suggested his disapproval had the President's support. Ehrlichman was going to call Ruckelshaus with the message of White House disapproval. After the meeting he did not make the call. Ruckelshaus, in the meantime, had enlisted his ex-boss and sponsor John Mitchell on his behalf. He visited Mitchell's office in the Committee to Re-elect the President's headquarters across Seventeenth Street from the White House. Mitchell's office was not altogether unfamiliar territory to Ruckelshaus. He had established a close relationship with then Attorney General Mitchell when he served as his deputy in charge of the Civil Division. Mitchell got Ruckelshaus the job as the first EPA administrator, beating out the White House favorite, ex-GM vice-president and ex-Ford president Semon E. (Bunkie) Knudsen.

After hearing Ruckelshaus out on his plans to reject the automobile industry's request, Mitchell was persuaded to intercede on EPA's behalf with President Nixon. One marvels at the oddity of "Mr. Clean" Ruckelshaus working so intimately with "Dirty Tricks" Mitchell. Mitchell, in helping Ruckelshaus, was no doubt motivated by the likely 1972 Muskie challenge to Nixon's re-election. Indeed after Ruckelshaus had denied the extension request, the Committee to Re-elect the President ran advertisements before the November 1972 elections claiming that the President had stood firm in 1972 in refusing to grant Detroit a year's suspension of the standards.[3]

[3] In the course of the 1972 campaign after Muskie had dropped out of contention, White House chief of staff Haldeman came close to authorizing an attack on environmentalists as among those Vice President Spiro T. Agnew was then scolding for running down America. A *Look* magazine consultant submitted a

Once Ruckelshaus had succeeded in heading off President Nixon's likely opposition to his May 1972 decision, he proceeded with extraordinary caution to announce it. To spike last-minute big business pressure on the White House to reverse the decision, when his deputy Robert Fri received a call from the *Wall Street Journal*'s environmental reporter suggesting he had information that Ruckelshaus would grant the suspension, did not try to dissuade the reporter of his view, though he did not confirm it either. The *Journal* speculated in its May 11, 1972, edition that the automobile companies would win their appeal.

I watched the *Journal*'s reporter at the Executive Office Building press room the next day when Ruckelshaus announced his denial. As his statement began by summarizing the difficulties of the decision, the reporter turned to his Associated Press colleague and said, "See, I told you he would suspend." At that moment, Ruckelshaus announced his denial. Both reporters were astonished.

A year later a court decision required Ruckelshaus to hold another hearing on industry's request for a one-year suspension of the hydrocarbon and carbon monoxide standards. The November 1973 elections passed and Ruckelshaus realized he might not be able to preserve his independence without the Muskie threat. His plight was emphasized by a February 1973 statement Erlichman made in Detroit. He said the automobile standards were too strict. The not-so-subtle implication was that the White House favored an extension. Ruckelshaus and I briefed the White House on February 27, 1973, before the renewed regulatory hearing process began. Treasury Secretary George Shultz, Ehrlichman, OMB director Caspar W. Weinberger and Frederic V. Malek, chief of White House personnel, were there. We presented information on air-quality need for tougher automotive hydrocarbon and carbon monoxide standards. Otherwise,

---

speech for the President to give that would have alleged that there was a conspiracy or disaster lobby trying to convince America that it had an environmental problem when it did not. The White House's Fairbanks and Alvin L. Alm of CEQ rebutted the speech's allegations, only to have the writer tell Haldeman that Fairbanks was part of the lobby. Haldeman did not believe Fairbanks, who in turn got mad and threatened to resign. His offer to resign was given to Whitaker, who passed it to Haldeman. Haldeman recanted and complimented Fairbanks for his "guts."

we argued, extensive traffic curtailments would have to be imposed on major U.S. cities to meet the Clean Air Act's goals. Ruckelshaus pointedly stressed the importance of the upcoming public hearings and the need for the White House to refrain from making any statements regarding them. He implied that White House intervention of the type Ehrlichman had practiced a few days before would undermine EPA's integrity and might even reach the point of illegality. Our reception was cool. We walked out wondering, half-jokingly, in what order we would be fired. White House "hatchet man" Malek took copious notes throughout the meeting and seemed to be silently sizing us for some undisclosed fate.

Ruckelshaus was further discouraged by the fact that his ally John Mitchell had departed. He expected a White House push to dictate a reversal of his earlier decision. Only one consideration barred an effort by the White House to dictate a suspension. General Motors president Cole, when contacted by White House officials, expressed confidence that the automotive standards could be met. Thus it was possible GM would not ask for an extension. A joint memorandum, dated December 14, 1972, from the Office of Management and Budget's William Morrill and the White House's Richard Fairbanks said as much: "We are relatively certain that General Motors will not request a delay, while Chrysler may well ask for one."

GM's position was pivotal. If the White House backed an extension only to have General Motors tell the public it could meet the standards, the White House would look foolish. The denial of an extension in 1972 had dramatically accelerated GM's efforts. Cole was personally committed to solving the emissions problem. The White House wanted to believe Chrysler, but it could not ignore GM and its enthusiastic president. It is an added irony, therefore, that after he provided his December assessment to the White House, Cole was overruled by GM's chairman, Richard Gerstenberg. John DeLorean, one of GM's most promising corporate vice-presidents and a possible Cole successor, who resigned in early 1973, alluded to this boardroom power struggle in an interview in the September 1973 issue of *Fortune* magazine. DeLorean himself shared Cole's view that new emissions data available to GM in late 1972 justified the optimism reported to the White House. He and Cole urged that GM take the positive stand that with the newly developed catalytic converters its 1975 cars might meet the tough emissions standards. But GM did the opposite at EPA's March 1973 hearings, saying the catalyst was a "disaster."

EPA's 1973 decision was a compromise. The automobile industry got the more lenient standards it wanted for all states except California. Cars sold in California in 1975 had to meet more stringent standards requiring catalysts. Within a few weeks of this decision, GM again changed its mind. Cole called me at eight o'clock in the morning of May 17 in a state of euphoria. He had just returned from GM's Arizona test track with a report that the catalyst was working beautifully. He said GM would put them on all cars in 1975 if he had his way, although he cautioned there had been no "final decision" to do so.

Chrysler president John J. Riccardo never forgot Cole's role in keeping the White House from ordering EPA to ease emission standards nationwide. Because of Chrysler's close contacts with Secretary Shultz, Riccardo probably knew fully the key role Cole's December message had played. He conveyed his bitterness toward General Motors to me a few months later. On that occasion I was initiating the EPA fuel-economy labeling program. At a press conference I urged each automobile maker to voluntarily put fuel-economy labels on every new car telling the consumer how many miles per gallon it consumed. GM agreed to put them on. When I told this to Riccardo, who did not want to put labels on his cars, he exploded: "GM won't give you any trouble; they never do."

The Lead Decision The other severe test of EPA's ability to make its own decisions as required by law arose in the case of lead in gasoline. Ruckelshaus proposed the reduction of lead in leaded grades of gasoline to protect the urban public's health. In major metropolitan areas as many as 25 per cent of the children tested show excessive blood lead levels. Lead poisoning causes a few to suffer mental retardation and others to experience less severe sickness and discomfort. Poisoning can come from lead in paint, lead in dust, and airborne lead. Lead from gasoline accounts for approximately 80 per cent of airborne lead and an undetermined amount of the lead children eat with urban dust picked up on streets and playgrounds. More than 200,000 tons of lead were added to gasoline each year in the early 1970s.

The EPA proposal to reduce lead usage called for a gradual reduction in the average lead content of leaded gasoline from about 2.5 grams per gallon to 2.0 grams in 1975 and 1.25 grams in 1978. This proposal accelerated by about 40 per cent in the late 1970s the removal of lead that would have taken place anyway by 1985. Some lead reductions were taking place in accordance with another EPA regulation that required lead-free gas for all catalyst-equipped cars beginning in 1975. Lead destroys the catalyst. An additional motivation for the low-lead regulation was the possibility that engines such as the stratified charge or Honda CVCC, which might meet emission standards without lead-sensitive catalysts, would come into widespread use in the late 1970s and leaded gas would not be phased out.

When EPA's proposal was reviewed in the Quality of Life process in late 1972, the Departments of the Interior, the Treasury, Justice, and Health, Education, and Welfare objected. Interior, OST, and OEP parroted the position of the Ethyl Corporation, a lead producer, that the energy costs of lead removal were intolerably high, and advocated lead traps, an exhaust aftertreatment device, to remove lead. The oil industry was upset because investments had to be made and more energy consumed at refineries to make lead-free fuel. EPA argued: (a) lead traps were costly and could not operate with adequate efficiency to protect the catalyst; (b) the energy costs of lead removal were small, less than 0.4 per cent of total crude oil usage in 1980; and (c) the cost to the consumer to remove lead from gas was less than a tenth of a cent per gallon, and even this could be offset by maintenance savings resulting from lead removal. (Unleaded gasoline decreases spark-plug, muffler, and other car maintenance requirements.)

The Quality of Life process produced a White House–OMB recommendation that EPA not be permitted to promulgate the requirement for reduced lead in leaded gas. On a mid-December Saturday in 1972, Ruckelshaus met with Ehrlichman, Shultz, and Weinberger at the White House. Shultz was adamant in opposing issuance of the proposed health-protective regulations. Ruckelshaus said, "I must propose them because the public health case for accelerated reductions has been made; it can't be hidden." Public comments were vital to resolving the issue.

After the meeting Fairbanks and Morrill met for forty-five minutes with Shultz, who planned to get the President to reverse Ruckelshaus. Again Ruckelshaus maintained his independence as Shultz demurred, and the ultimate confrontation with the President did not take place. The meeting was disturbing to Ruckelshaus because of his isolation within the Administration. He began to have serious reservations about staying on as the Administration's environmental point man. His pro forma resignation had been submitted after Nixon's re-election along with those of all presidential appointees. If the White House had its way, he was to be given little opportunity to discuss his standing.

THE ATTEMPTED WHITE HOUSE TAKEOVER OF EPA

On December 13, 1972, I was scheduled to accompany Ruckelshaus to a meeting on energy called by Peter Flanigan in the White House's Roosevelt Room. That morning I had been called by an assistant to White House "headhunter" Fred Malek, who asked that I come to his office before the White House meeting. Malek, then in charge of White House personnel and also known as the hatchet man, was rumored to be moving to the Office of Management and Budget. I half expected to be fired. Instead, I was asked if I would be interested in talking to Malek about working for him at OMB. I replied I would first want to discuss the possibility with Ruckelshaus. I said I was satisfied at EPA and, assuming Ruckelshaus was staying, saw no reason to leave.

I walked across West Executive Avenue to the White House meeting and handed Ruckelshaus a note reporting my sudden meeting. He wrote back on the note, "You won't believe what's going on." Apparently the White House had decided to replace all but one of EPA's five assistant administrators. Only the nephew of Colorado's faithful Republican Senator Peter Dominick (now defeated) was to stay. Under Malek's new personnel rules, agency heads like Ruckelshaus were not allowed to staff their own departments. This was the White House's route around Ruckelshaus. Minutes after our exchange, a White House secretary handed Ruckelshaus a note from the White House press office summoning him to see Nixon's press secretary Ronald Zeigler.

Ruckelshaus left the room for about thirty minutes, returning visibly agitated. Zeigler had shown him a press release he planned to issue that same afternoon announcing that Ruckelshaus would stay on as EPA's head. But Ruckelshaus shocked Zeigler. He told him he had not decided to stay. He wanted assurances from the President that the Administration would vigorously pursue the cleanup program that had been launched. He also wanted assurances from Ehrlichman that the Quality of Life process would be reformed, that he would have a responsive point of contact in the White House (replacing the Mitchell channel to the President), and that he would choose his own deputy and assistant administrators. When Ruckelshaus refused to go along with Malek's tactics to make him a figurehead director of his agency by putting "White House" men under him, his courage was unique. Elliot Richardson at the Defense Department, Rogers Morton at Interior, and Richard Kleindienst at Justice permitted Malek to fill key positions in their departments.

The White House, in that heady postelection and pre-Watergate-scandal period, did not expect such audacity.[4] But it worked. Ruckelshaus was called by Ehrlichman, who apologized for the bungling. Soon he saw the President and announced at a press conference on December 20, 1972, that he was staying.

While Ruckelshaus stayed on, it was an uneasy truce. The Quality of Life process had not been reformed. Presidential interest in the environment had not been demonstrated. The President discussed politics at his meeting with Ruckelshaus, not the environment. No White House staffer's place in the sun would be protected by advocating environmental reforms. Thus neither Ruckelshaus nor his successor, Train, would have a supporter close to the President.

[4] One might even have expected the White House to fire Ruckelshaus. In *All the President's Men* Carl Bernstein and Bob Woodward have recorded a vivid description by a Texas lawyer of Nixon fund-raiser Stans's appeal: "You know we got this crazy man Ruckelshaus back East who'd just as soon close your factory as let the smokestack belch. He's a hard man to control. . . . Now, don't misunderstand me; we're not making any promises, all we can do is make ourselves accessible. . . ." (New York: Simon and Schuster, 1974), p. 56.

THE ENERGY THREAT TO EPA

After a few short months in early 1973, two developments removed the environment from the forefront of national domestic concerns: Watergate and energy. By April 1973 Watergate had taken Ruckelshaus to the acting directorship of the FBI, replacing L. Patrick Gray.[5] Russell Train found EPA beset by the whirlwind of the energy crisis.

Throughout 1972 Ruckelshaus frequently met with Flanigan, who then had White House policy responsibility for energy. The EPA administrator believed some accommodation had to be worked out when there were legitimate energy-environment conflicts. EPA had acted quickly in 1972 to permit more coal to be burned. The agency had worked closely with Flanigan and his staff on the development of the spring 1973 energy message. Ruckelshaus respected him. On one occasion he said, "We may not agree with Flanigan's concept of the national interest, but at least he's got one. He's about the only one in the White House who does." Suddenly, a few days before Watergate broke on him, Ehrlichman forced Flanigan out of the energy area. Without a presidential hearing, Flanigan's White House office was taken away and he was sent across West Executive Avenue to the majestic old Executive Office Building. Ehrlichman hired Charles DiBona and gave him responsibility to publish the message prepared by Flanigan's staff. At the same time General Lincoln's OEP was abolished and John Whitaker became under secretary of the Department of the Interior.

The departure of Lincoln, Whitaker's move to Interior, and Flanigan's exodus meant that the heavy investment EPA had made with these individuals to establish its credibility on energy matters was lost. Overnight the knowledge the Administration had gathered about the energy-environmental problem was denied those making

[5] Ruckelshaus wondered aloud if he too were to be left "twisting in the wind." In persuading him to take the FBI job, President Nixon made an emotional personal appeal. The President told Ruckelshaus if he took the assignment, his help would be forever remembered. He could have "anything" he wanted. Ruckelshaus never met with the President again. He later became deputy attorney general and resigned that job in the "Saturday-night massacre" that followed the firing of Watergate prosecutor Archibald Cox.

Administration energy policy. Flanigan understood that the origin of
U.S. energy difficulties was in the obstacles to increased oil, gas, and
coal production that removed incentives to produce or made production too costly. For example, artificially low gas prices made it
unprofitable to produce more of our cleanest fuel, and coal mine
health and safety regulations slowed deep coal mining. These problems were seen as more important than environmental obstacles in
causing the energy shortage. DiBona, by contrast, seemed to place
dismantling the Clean Air Act above these incentive and cost problems, or even energy conservation, as the solution to our energy
problem. In one of his first drafts of the energy message, DiBona had
sections that came close to dismantling the Clean Air Act. He was
going to have the President grant industry unrestrained use of pollu-
tant-dispersing "tall stacks" on power plants. In one of his last acts
as EPA's head, Ruckelshaus met with DiBona in April 1973 and
forced him to delete the unacceptable parts of the message.

Soon the White House's energy roulette game began again.
Ehrlichman resigned. Without his mentor, DiBona could not get the
support from the President needed to handle this job. Newly installed
OMB director Roy Ash began advocating the appointment of an energy "czar." Soon he won, and Colorado governor John Love
(whom Flanigan, in a remarkable reversal of his earlier misfortune,
nominated) was appointed to manage energy. But Governor Love
retained DiBona and his staff members, who continued to work hard
at convincing Love and the President that easing environmental regulations rather than cutting back profligate energy use was the key to
solving the energy shortage.

Repeatedly the President's instincts were played back to EPA
officials. DiBona was confident the President would not back the environment in an energy-environment showdown. He was right. During Train's first week on the job he attended a White House meeting
on energy. The President, undoubtedly prepared by Governor Love
to believe that the environmental regulations had to be eased to
make more dirty fuel available, opened by noting, "Russ Train is
here and he knows the value of being a team player." The President
went on to state that he had had two brothers who died of tubercu-
losis. He contended that they owed their disease to cold homes rather
than air pollution. (One brother, Harold, died at age thirty-three of

pneumonia; the other, Arthur, died at seven of tubercular meningitis.) Immediately after the meeting, the President and Love emerged to tell the press they thought environmental standards should be relaxed. Train was not informed of the press conference, nor was he invited to attend. He was told of the Administration's policy by a *Washington Star* reporter whom he called to find out what was said at the press conference.

At a cabinet meeting on October 12, 1973, the President was more explicit. In discussing the energy situation, he said that any conflict between the environment and energy would be resolved in favor of energy. Continuing to drive the point home, he said, "Russ, is Russ Train here?" (Train, not being a cabinet member, was not in attendance.) To his audience the President ordered, "Make sure Russ Train understands that." The next Monday, OMB director Ash with Energy Policy Office director Love met with Train to give him the President's instructions. Train was shaken by the clear expression of presidential displeasure and by the President's unbalanced perspective. He reminded Ash that the environment was not responsible for the energy shortage, and that as CEQ's chairman he had taken the lead in convincing environmentalists that strip mining, offshore oil development, and superports, if carefully regulated, could be environmentally acceptable activities.

But Ash had his cue from the President. His next opportunity to impress this on Train came November 21, 1973, when Train and I met with Ash, Fairbanks, and Ash's deputy, John Sawhill, to discuss the pending final promulgation of the low-lead regulation that had prompted the Ruckelshaus confrontation with Shultz a year earlier. Ash emphasized that nothing could be done that required more energy. He said, "Even public health has to wait." We pointed out that the low-lead regulations, themselves designed to protect against public health threats like mental retardation, would not take effect until 1976 and would have a negligible energy cost. We soon discovered the origin of Ash's opposition. He had talked with Transportation Secretary Claude S. Brinegar, who deployed oil industry consultants to convince Ash of the undesirability of taking lead out of gas.

No one seemed to care that Brinegar, in his previous job as a vice-president of Union Oil Company, had intervened with the White House's John Whitaker in an earlier effort to get EPA's lead-removal regulations changed. At a meeting in Whitaker's office on October 25, 1972, I had been told by Brinegar that the public health did not require the removal of lead from gasoline. EPA was not informed of Brinegar's new initiative nor allowed to review his consultants' position. Brinegar himself never contacted Train, who alone possessed the statutory authority to make the decision. The Achilles' heel of the Quality of Life process was that it sanctioned intervention of this sort. The basis for Ash's assertions would never be made public, yet he exerted almost-presidential power in opposing EPA's actions, which had been designed under intense public scrutiny after lengthy public debate and in accordance with a legislatively mandated regulatory process.

EPA went ahead with the late November announcement of its lead-removal regulation in an atmosphere of increasing bitterness with the White House. Fairbanks and deputy EPA administrator John R. Quarles, Jr., had shouted at each other in the White House's West Wing over whether EPA should proceed.

Before the week was over, the White House had sent draft language to Congress to amend the key automobile standard provision of the Clean Air Act. EPA administrator Train was not notified. This was the White House's answer to EPA's independence. EPA was no longer within the Administration. It stood midway between Congress and the White House as an independent body, putting forth its own positions and suffering from White House legislative initiatives it had no part in shaping.

What throughout 1973 had been a major difficulty for the environmentalists became, after Saudi Arabia cut off its oil exports on October 21, 1973, a desperate struggle. Energy became the Trojan horse of the antienvironmentalists in the White House. It armed them for the first time with an issue of broad public appeal. The chaos created by Watergate eclipsed any lingering hopes for a deliberate consideration of energy-environmental decisions.

Russell Train was desperate to gain an audience with the President. Never, however, in his year as EPA administrator under Richard Nixon, did he have a private meeting with his boss. His nearest moment of privacy with Nixon was in November 1973, when he was given ten minutes' notice that he was expected to accompany Soviet environmental minister Yevgeny Fedorov to the Oval Office.

Train quickly briefed Fedorov to make two points to the President: that abundant energy and a clean environment were compatible goals and that the environment was receiving high priority in the Soviet Union. Fedorov made these points, but Train hardly benefited. He later recalled, "The President didn't give me the time of day. He didn't look pleased when Fedorov made my points. He usually calls me Russ, but he called me 'Dr. Train.'" A few days later President Nixon was telling his aides to see that automobile emission-control devices were removed to make way for his energy policy.

The climax of White House efforts to sacrifice environmental requirements on the energy-crisis justification came in March 1974. After weeks of meetings at which White House and OMB officials forced EPA to consider a long list of amendments to the Clean Air Act EPA found objectionable, Russell Train and his deputy Quarles made it known to *Newsweek* and *The New York Times* that they would not support such amendments. Train thought the act needed amendment. He sought more flexibility and extended timetables on selected provisions. In a letter rebutting a March 15, 1974, *Wall Street Journal* editorial, Train summarized his position: "I firmly believe in the need for flexibility in the Clean Air Act, but I do not believe it should be gutted." He pledged to fight the amendments he opposed, though he agreed to carry them to the Hill. It was a rare position for an Administration official to take. His words were: "I want it known that I am strongly opposed to most of these proposals and I'm going to fight them to the last wire because I don't think they're necessary and I do think they'd do substantial harm."[6]

Reacting to Train's independence, Republican Senator William Scott of Virginia asked Train, at a White House meeting in the presence of Mr. Nixon, to resign, suggesting he could be appointed to "some ambassadorship . . . maybe Russia or China." Only the President's Watergate burden saved Train from dismissal. Despite Senator Scott's outburst, Nixon knew that the dismissal of Train, a member in good standing with the Washington establishment, would not improve his prospects in an impeachment showdown in the Senate. Nonetheless, some suggested that the White House's designated environmental advocate, Richard Fairbanks, was placating potential anti-impeachment conservative votes by urging the amendments

[6] *New York Times,* Mar. 11, 1974.

Train so strongly opposed. Not all senators welcomed this White House opportunism. At one point in the preparation of the White House Clean Air Act amendment package, Fairbanks tried to brief Senator Baker, the ranking Republican on Senator Muskie's subcommittee, on the planned amendments. Baker asked if Train was in agreement. When told Train was not, Baker declined the briefing.

Train's courageous stance forced the Administration to back away from four of the six controversial amendments. Among these was a provision exempting energy projects from environmental impact statements as required by the 1969 National Environmental Policy Act. Another proposed amendment would have placed economic and social criteria on par with health considerations in setting abatement requirements. This represented a return to the concepts behind the ineffectual environmental legislation of the pre-1970s.

Of the amendments that went forward, two were opposed by Train. One called for the legalization of supplementary controls relying on atmospheric dispersion of pollutants rather than permanent controls to remove them. This was the item Ruckelshaus had forced DiBona to remove from the Presidential energy message of a year earlier. The second sought to get Congress to reverse a court decision forcing EPA to promulgate regulations to prevent "significant deterioration" of pristine air, leaving such powers to the states.

REFORMING THE PRESIDENT'S ENVIRONMENTAL ROLE

The energy crisis was not the issue which turned the Nixon Administration against the environment; it merely provided an opportunity for covert White House views to emerge. The energy crisis did, however, display in full view the weaknesses of the Administration's environmental policy-making approach. The President's attitude toward the environment came out clearly as antienvironmentalist. Ruckelshaus, DiBona, Train, a variety of OMB officials, Fairbanks, and Simon all relayed the President's views. Two not-unique quotations were "The President doesn't give a damn about the environment," and "The President wants the emission devices removed." On a more subtle plane was heard, "The President wants nothing to stand in the way of energy policies, not even public health."

President Nixon, like any other President or individual, had his preconceived notions, hs prejudices. He was not an environmentalist; there was no way he could seek his own counsel on environmental choices.[7] His instinct was to side with big business. Yet in foreign policy, President Nixon had been practically the opposite of his old self in urging policies such as those toward China. Why was President Nixon so incapable of responding to the nation's environmental needs? One reason was the pathetic performance of the White House's domestic policy-making apparatus. There was no domestic policy analogue to Henry Kissinger's National Security Council decision-making machinery.

Nixon's staff served him well in 1971 and 1972 by forcing the Department of Commerce, with EPA and CEQ, to make an objective study of whether environmental regulations would jeopardize U.S. prosperity. Had he ignored these findings, which he did not, he would have had only himself to blame. In no other major controversy, from lead, to the catalyst, to scrubbing, was such a determined effort made by the White House to objectively identify the facts and options. Never again was Ruckelshaus, or for that matter his successor, Train, given the opportunity for an objective hearing on the facts before the President; rather, they were pitted by the President's staffers against the President's instincts, which on the environment were bad. The President, without doubt, was told that Ruckelshaus was determined to go his own way on the automobile decision, and he was told about EPA's plans to reduce lead in gasoline. But he was not told that the facts supported Ruckelshaus's position. The White House staffers, encouraged the "us versus them" attitude between the President's men and the departmental men. It is small wonder, therefore, that several White House staff members freely reported in early 1973 that the President did not like Ruckelshaus.

The Domestic Council was staffed mostly by young ex–political

[7] His isolation from everyday life denied the President opportunities to witness environmental degradation or others' responses to it. On a single occasion he went among the people; he took a commercial airline flight to Los Angeles the day after Christmas 1973 to avoid public criticism of wasting scarce fuel on his own plane. The pilot of the commercial plane reported his advice to the President: "I told him I was from Orange County where the smog is getting worse all the time" (*Washington Post*, Dec. 27, 1973).

operatives who had no background in their respective areas nor any mature management or analytical approach. Only the long-departed Daniel P. Moynihan had been an exception. Whitaker made a courageous effort. The others flourished merely as crisis managers. No White House official came on the scene who (a) could co-ordinate the government agencies to present an agreed-upon set of facts and options to the President, (b) had the confidence of such facts and supporting analysis to stand up against the President's instincts when they were wrong; and (c) could fashion a positive policy based not only on ideology but also on the facts.

The Quality of Life process was an attempt to recognize the need for a systematic approach to making environmental policy. But it became an instrument with which to control EPA rather than a mechanism to inform EPA and the rest of the government, including the President. As a mechanism of control rather than enlightenment, it was vulnerable to ex parte influence. EPA plans were quickly "leaked" to industry, which supplied the White House and OMB with counterarguments to use against EPA. The National Coal Association and TVA were asked to rebut EPA's views on coal cleanup technologies. Both as a Union Oil Company vice-president and as Secretary of Transportation, Brinegar sought and was given the opportunity to rebut EPA. As an oil industry executive, he should have been made to comment in public like everyone else. As an ex-oil industry executive and cabinet member, he should have refrained from intervening in the Quality of Life process.

The environment cannot be cleaned up without presidential involvement and leadership. Nor can intelligent environmental decisions be made within the executive branch unless the EPA administrator receives the advice and support of the other concerned agencies. An environmentally hostile President can weaken EPA's powers. The 1973 decision to transfer radiation standard-setting authority from the EPA to the Atomic Energy Commission is but one illustration of the President's ability to control events. The requirement for presidential involvement is made more acute by the new prerequisite for environmental accomplishment: lifestyle change. But to be successful in solving lifestyle problems, EPA must have White House help in getting the support of other agencies and setting clear goals for the public. For example, the Department of Transportation has a key support role in implementing the transportation reforms necessary to attain air standards. Yet Secretary Brinegar opposed additional spending on mass transit and never directed his department to support EPA's plans for reducing city traffic.

The Department of the Interior had a key role in developing clean energy sources.[8] It likewise has the Administration lead in land-use policy, a vital environmental issue. Similarly, the Federal Energy Administration has the power to advance energy conservation policies. Thus, however independent the EPA administrator is, he cannot be totally effective in pursuing cleanup without strong White House backing, a consideration of increasing importance as the environmental movement enters the era of lifestyle changes.

A drastic overhaul of the environmental decision-making machinery is needed. The Council on Environmental Quality has not filled the role of environmental co-ordinator. Perhaps it could if brought into the White House itself. More likely is that a new institution should be established with NSC-like powers and access. It should be charged with shaping national growth and urban policies, and co-ordinating transportation, energy, and land-use policies as they have an impact on the non-GNP measures of improvement in the quality of America life. It could be called the Council on Natural Resources and the Environment.

A second needed reform is the elevation to cabinet level of the line responsibilities for environmental management. EPA's subcabinet status does not give it the strength to cope with cabinet agencies envious of its authorities. Land-use and parks and recreation responsibilities from the Department of the Interior, in conjunction with EPA's responsibilities, would constitute such a department, leaving energy and natural resources responsibilities as a logical entity. In other words, the Department of the Interior would be split in two pieces, part lining up with EPA to form a Department of the Environment, and the rest joining with the Federal Energy Administration to become part of a Department of Energy and Natural Resources.

[8] A responsibility now assigned to the newly established Energy Research and Development Agency (ERDA).

SAVING THE CLEAN AIR ACT

The Clean Air Act has already lived up to former Kentucky senator John Sherman Cooper's prediction that it was "the most significant domestic legislation of the decade." Passed by Congress in 1969, the Clean Air Act did not and could not have anticipated the full impact achievement of clean air by 1975 would have on transportation lifestyles in our major cities, or on land-use habits in areas where the air could be significantly degraded.

Ruckelshaus in testimony before the House and Senate in April 1973 outlined two areas of probable amendment: first, transportation controls would have to be eased for cities like Los Angeles that were required to undergo disruptive traffic reductions to meet air standards; and, second, the automotive standard for nitrogen dioxide was more stringent than air-quality needs merited, incurring unnecessary energy penalties. Entire congressional delegations made similar appeals for an easing of transportation control requirements. The automobile companies chimed in to support a relaxed nitrogen dioxide standard.

The Senate subcommittee, despite Ruckelshaus's appeal, was reluctant to open the Clean Air Act for amendment. Some senators feared it would be dismantled by those who believed the environment was principally responsible for the spring's gasoline shortages or by those who believed the automobile industry campaign to ease the automotive standards.

After Ruckelshaus's departure in April 1973, acting administrator Fri made additional appeals on the same two issues raised by Ruckelshaus. What finally swayed Congress were the transportation restraints proposed by EPA on June 15. These measures brought congressmen from California, New Jersey, Utah, and other states to their feet. Suddenly it appeared the act could be more endangered by not acting than by acting.

Meanwhile, new faces appeared on the Senate committees. Of the eleven members of Senator Muskie's 1973 Air and Water Pollution Subcommittee, only four were there in 1969 when the Clean Air Act was drafted. These same four—Muskie, Baker, Jennings Randolph, and Joseph M. Montoya—were the only four of fourteen members of the parent Public Works Committee who remained in mid-1973. While the close relationship between Muskie and Baker still prevailed, Baker yielded to the pressures of the Watergate hearings, leaving Senator Buckley of New York the lead Republican. Buckley is a precise man, compelled by facts. He became disturbed that the health benefits citizens were asked to give up so much to achieve were not spelled out anywhere in terms of the population threatened or the societal costs incurred.

On June 11, 1973, acting EPA administrator Robert Fri lunched with Senator Buckley and urged that the act be opened for change. Buckley had become frustrated at Muskie's reluctance to join the issue. He told Fri he was fed up and would go it alone by asking, on the floor of the Congress, that the act be reconsidered. Apparently he had second thoughts on breaking the bipartisan coalition that had so well served the Senate in environmental matters. On June 13 he met with his subcommittee colleagues, who agreed to his viewpoint. Muskie joined Buckley in a letter of June 27, 1973, urging that EPA fund a study of health effects of air pollution by the National Academy of Sciences. An important colloquy took place two days later on the floor of the Senate. Muskie promised his fellow senators and the public that his subcommittee would identify needed changes in the Clean Air Act by the fall. He defended the act and cited Ruckelshaus's defense of it. Randolph followed, saying in response to Senator Muskie, "We have some differences of opinion which I think should be raised." He doubted the Act should force the application of the catalyst. Buckley in turn emphasized the review "is emphatically not" a retreat from the act's objectives, and added to the list of possible amendments the issue of whether the act should prevent or control growth to protect pristine air.

Muskie himself had mellowed. In private conversations he expressed concern for paper mill closings in Maine, caused in part by environmental costs. How deep his own doubts ran emerged in a remark he made at a July executive session to launch the National Academy of Sciences review. He characterized those who wanted to amend the act as wanting to know what additional damage to the population would be done if the air quality standard were raised from "0.8 to 2.0." He quoted his adversaries as saying; "All you are doing is protecting a handful of people." Muskie concluded, "I don't know whether we are or not."[9] Thus, the Academy received $500,-000 to prepare an overview health study by the fall of 1973[10] and a "cost-benefit" study one year later.

Among the Senate staff there were mixed views of the purpose of the Academy's study. Some saw it as a delaying tactic, to leave the act untouched until 1974. There were doubts that the Academy could produce anything of value by the time Muskie had promised to complete his review. Academy president Philip Handler himself doubted the Academy's ability to be rigorous on the cost-benefit study.[11] Randolph and Buckley were in a hurry; Muskie was not. All in a sense were passing the buck, asking the Academy as an independent body to perform a technically impossible study.[12] Fundamentally, the referral to the National Academy was a statement of dissatisfaction with EPA's failure to develop analysis explaining the health basis for its standards. Congress had nowhere else to turn. In the fall of 1974 the Academy issued its report on the validity of the air-quality standards the Clean Air Act sought to achieve. It found "no substantial basis" for changing the standards, although because

[9] Stenographic transcript of Executive Session of the Air and Water Subcommittee, Senate, July 10, 1973, p. 22.
[10] A symposium held in early October 1973 found the standards to be generally valid, although more research was needed. Pending further study, the Academy judged the standards should not be eased.
[11] Stenographic transcript of Executive Session of the Air and Water Subcommittee, Senate, July 10, 1973, p. 9.
[12] It was ironically the National Academy of Sciences that had told Ruckelshaus in 1972 that the advanced emission-control technologies that appeared on 1975 cars would not be available. A year later the Academy, having been embarrassed by EPA's 1972 decision, reversed its position. At the 1973 automobile hearings the Academy testified in support of the contention in its 1973 report that the 1975 standards could be met by mass-produced catalysts. The Academy's Edward Ginton was asked how the Academy had arrived at this conclusion. Was there a model? a methodology? any analysis? He replied there was none. It was the Academy's judgment and the Academy did not view its function as encompassing analysis. He informed the panel that if a methodology were available the Academy would not have been called on. This arrogance was reminiscent of earlier debates with U.S. generals executing the Vietnam War. They were confident of their views but offered no evidence to support them. Fortunately, in 1975 the Academy demonstrated it could produce a methodology, in a brilliant analysis of the problems of pollution from power plants. See "Air Quality and Stationary Source Control," a report by the National Academy of Sciences and the National Academy of Engineers, Washington, D.C., 1975.

of incomplete data it failed to show they could be justified or contradicted by cost-benefit analysis.

The tactic of delaying consideration of Clean Air Act amendments from mid-1973 to receipt of the Academy's final report in late 1974 failed to placate the act's opponents. The Arab embargo of October 1973 gave them their chance. By December the Clean Air Act was in grave danger. Its opponents in the House amended the Emergency Energy Bill to delay automobile standards at 1975 levels through 1977 and, at the administrator's discretion, through 1978. Power plants were given an additional four years from 1975 to 1979 to comply with clean-air requirements. And EPA was to be prohibited from implementing measures such as parking-space controls and use of special "fast bus lanes" to reduce automobile use in cities. Also ruled out were controls on indirect or automobile-attracting facilities like shopping centers.

Characteristic of the stampede to gut the act was an amendment offered by Louis C. Wyman, then a New Hampshire Republican congressman, to remove any requirement for emission controls in all but a few U.S. cities. His proposal to cut out the very heart of the Clean Air Act failed to pass by 180 to 210 votes. House Public Health and Environment Subcommittee chairman Paul G. Rogers was powerless to control events. He openly pled with EPA for help in stemming the tide. His effort was not aided by White House support for the Clean Air Act amendments, including those not remotely related to the energy crisis. Congressman Rogers resigned himself to defeat, comforted only by his hope that Senator Muskie would save the Air Act in the Senate.

Muskie's display of legislative acumen in November–December 1973 was masterful. He began by gaining unanimous Senate passage of a special bill giving the automobile manufacturers a one-year extension to 1976 at the level of the 1975 standards. Simultaneously, he approached the Senate's sponsor of emergency energy legislation, Senator Henry M. Jackson, with a proposal that all energy-related environmental amendments would be controlled by the Senate Public Works Committee rather than Jackson's Senate Interior Committee. Jackson agreed. He also installed Randolph, Muskie, and Baker on the Senate side of the House-Senate Conference Committee on Emergency Energy Legislation. In this position, Muskie and his colleagues reversed the House's capitulation and saved the Clean Air Act.

Muskie's carefully drafted amendments to the Air Act died with the Emergency Energy Bill because President Nixon's opposition thwarted the Congress. But in mid-1974 Muskie embodied them in another measure, the Energy Supply and Environmental Coordination Act, which went beyond limiting the damage to the Clean Air Act and actually strengthened it.

Muskie's success owes a small debt to a prehistoric oddity. Everyone knows West Virginia is a coal-producing state. Fewer know that two men in a position to ease clean-air requirements are from West Virginia: Senator Randolph and Congressman Harley O. Staggers, chairman of the House Commerce Committee, the parent committee to Congressman Rogers' subcommittee. Fewer still realize that West Virginia, unlike Illinois, Pennsylvania, and western Kentucky, has vast reserves of low-sulfur coal. Therefore, Randolph and Staggers shared an important and paradoxical reason for deferring to Muskie, who sought to impose tough air standards on the allowable sulfur content of coal that could be burned. As long as the debate over the scrubber raged and the Clean Air Act held, low-sulfur West Virginia coal would be a prized commodity.

CONCLUSION

With the single legislative stroke of the Clean Air Act in 1969, Congress with one hand had reached decisively into America's industrial past to right a wrong. With the other hand it groped for the future course of environmental reform. Action by Congress to save the Clean Air Act just four years later was more subtle. Muskie's brilliant parliamentary tactics thwarted the counterrevolution. A group of odd Air Act friends, including two West Virginia legislators, coalesced to Muskie's leadership in the finest senatorial tradition. Once the panic of the energy crisis passed, once Nixon fell, Congress would be compelled to take up the more critical task of directing the country along the path to environmental growth. To date no political leader has risen to accept this challenge.

3.

THE CONFRONTATION
WITH BIG BUSINESS

A LESSON TO REMEMBER

Silent Spring, Rachel Carson's 1962 book on the threat of pesticides to our environment, has the strongest hold on the conscience of the environmental movement. It made a compelling case against unrestrained pesticide use, documenting the destruction of birds and other wildlife. By affecting the livers of mother birds, DDT destroys enzymes essential to the production of the calcium that forms and strengthens eggshells. When Rachel Carson wrote, falcons, bald eagles, ospreys, pelicans, and other species were in jeopardy. Mothers were giving birth to birds wrapped in shell-less membranes.

Meanwhile, man's own immunity was in doubt. National Cancer Institute studies showed that some pesticides caused cancer and birth defects in humans. Despite these abundant signs of ecological tragedy, *Silent Spring* failed to produce effective government action against pesticide use. Seven years after its publication, pesticide use was up sharply. A U. S. Department of Health, Education, and Welfare commission found in 1969 that the threat of pesticides was more acute than ever. Finally, in that year, the Department of Agriculture took a small first step toward banning DDT. The reluctant defender of farmer and big chemical and fertilizer company interests prohibited the use of pesticides on tobacco, on shade trees, in households, and in most aquatic areas.

The Federal Insecticide, Fungicide, and Rodenticide Act of 1947 remains a monumental example of potentially powerful legislation which was never effectively implemented. Had this law been fulfilled, Rachel Carson's book would never have been written. The law was ineffective because it was administered by the U. S. Department of Agriculture, where large agribusiness profits, not environmental protection, are the overriding goal. One of the congressional watchdog committees that was supposed to ensure the law was implemented had been led for years by Mississippi congressman Jamie Whitten, himself beholden to cotton and corn production constituents. Whitten wrote his own rebuttal to Rachel Carson's work. He called it *That We May Live*. And while President Nixon's reorganization put the U. S. Environmental Protection Agency in charge of administering pesticide laws, Jamie Whitten was, until early 1975, chairman of the committee of the House of Representatives that approved EPA's budget. At his annual spring budget hearings, Whitten, like a country preacher, lectured EPA's top officials on the merits of pesticide use and read from the scriptures of his book.

Despite his best efforts, Whitten was unable to undermine the laws his colleagues passed. In 1972 EPA banned all DDT uses. Congress in the same year passed a stronger pesticide-control law, the Federal Environmental Pesticide Control Act. In 1974 the chemicals aldrin and dieldrin, usually used to protect corn crops, were banned by EPA. This latter decision was made after three years of litigation between EPA and the Shell Chemical Company. The presiding administrative law judge Herbert L. Perlman concluded that these pesticides pose "a high risk of causing cancer in man" and that "the entire population of the United States is continuously exposed." He noted that dieldrin "has probably accumulated in the body tissue of almost every individual" and passes easily through the pregnant female's placenta to the developing fetus and through her milk to the newborn. The outcome of this landmark "cancer versus corn" case is not the only sign that the nation's environmental awakening is being rewarded. An analysis of DDT residues in migratory birds over the period 1969–73 found that 1973 levels were only 10 per cent of those observed five years earlier (reported by David W. Johnston in

Science, November 1974). EPA reported that between 1970 and 1973 the human dietary intake of DDT declined by 86 per cent.

The lessons of these satisfying results are in the dedication it took to secure them and the nature of the opposition that made them so difficult to achieve. Not just with pesticides, but across the broad front, the environmental awakening has been answered by an outburst of opposition from industry.

INDUSTRY FIGHTS BACK

No environmental law is immune to the atrophy experienced by the 1947 Pesticide Control Act. Few have been so vigorously attacked as the Clean Air Act. Detroit's automobile manufacturers issued a steady stream of criticism, even ridicule, of the provisions of the Clean Air Act that ordered automotive cleanup. Likewise, the electric utilities proclaimed their opposition to air pollution controls. The 1972 Water Pollution Control Act Amendments irked the pulp and paper industry, and its industrial colleagues opposed measures to reduce water-polluting discharges. In the halls of Congress, in the spacious offices of executive-branch officials, and by furtive phone calls to the White House, big business confronted newly charged environmental officials with determined opposition. The press was employed; millions of dollars were spent on advertising to convince the public that excessive controls were being imposed. Some advertisements tried the hard sell, claiming environmental regulations would force widespread plant closures and bankrupt the country. Such grossly inaccurate assertions were aptly labeled eco-pornography by the environmentalists. Other companies used a soft-sell advertising approach. They portrayed industrial operations as no more intrusive than the felling of a single tree in square miles of forest.

Industry sought to weaken the stringency of regulatory measures by pointing to widespread adverse economic consequences for employment, growth, trade, and prices. Another industry argument pleaded technological infeasibility. If regulatory requirements mandated the installation of advanced cleanup technologies to reduce emissions and effluents, industry claimed the technology did not exist or adopted a go-slow attitude toward its development and application.

The confrontation itself was not unexpected, nor was it without virtue. We should expect our industries to balk at expenditures that bring little or no return. The technologies important to industries are those directly connected with increasing output and lowering cost. But likewise, the regulators' most important assignment is to create the incentive for industry to develop and employ the most advanced clean technologies. The environmental laws prescribe standards of smokestack and water-discharge-pipe quality that can be met only if companies make a major financial and technological commitment. The process of environmental-technological progress through regulation is the driving force of cleanup in the modern large-business-dominated U.S. economy. Sustaining environmental reform requires the knowledge to reject industry's overstatements of cost and adverse price and unemployment impacts. Careful work is necessary to overcome industry reluctance to advance pollution-control technology. The case for technological feasibility must be effectively made and dilatory industry tactics exposed. At the same time, technological infeasibility must be honestly confronted.

Throughout 1971 and most of 1972 the conflict between industry and newly enacted environmental legislation raged. It was a battle made more complex by disagreements and squabbles between government agencies like EPA, the Commerce Department, and the White House Office of Science and Technology. First, a dispute about the magnitude of the economic impact of environmental legislation on industry had to be settled. Then in 1972 there arose the specific question of costs of emission-control equipment to automobile owners.

Industry, not surprisingly, had powerful allies in government with whom to fight new legislation. And it was only through careful economic analysis, often done jointly by warring parties, that the battle was won in favor of environmental regulation. Secretary of Commerce Maurice Stans, President Nixon's chief fund-raiser and former accountant, verbalized the proindustry position in public on July 15, 1971, in a speech before the National Petroleum Council in Washington, D.C., entitled "Wait a Minute." It was the clarion call to battle that echoed through board rooms from Pittsburgh to Houston, to

San Francisco, and back to New York. Stans urged a slowdown in setting environmental standards and that more attention be given to economic repercussions. Meanwhile, he was working feverishly within the Administration to undercut the influence of both EPA administrator Ruckelshaus and CEQ chairman Train.

Stans had persuaded the President to establish a special National Industrial Pollution Control Council (NIPCC), to advise the White House on industrial pollution problems. Its membership roster listed 55 top executives from the polluting industries. Another 140 executives held positions throughout a maze of subcouncils on industry problems like "detergents." Not one environmentalist, university, or public-interest group was represented. In reality, this council was Stans's conduit to the board rooms, his way of receiving a private accounting of the "damage" Ruckelshaus was inflicting on industry. Secretary Stans had previously told the President at a cabinet meeting that environmental requirements were holding up many capital projects such as dams, highways, oil refineries, and power plants. He polled his business friends and sent the President a memorandum with a long list of delayed projects.

THE DEBATE
OVER ECONOMIC IMPACT

The debate within the Administration about the consequences to the economy became so intense that the White House sanctioned a special series of studies to resolve the issue. Putting aside the intense rhetoric of the raging debate, EPA, CEQ, and the Department of Commerce began studies in late 1971 of the country's fourteen major polluting industries and the national economy. The purpose of the studies was to assess the economic impact of complying with environmental requirements. On publication in March 1972, they revealed:

• None of the fourteen industries would be seriously harmed. All would remain viable and profitable. Only small and old plants in seven industries would suffer. Of twelve thousand plants, eight hundred were expected to close in the 1972–76 period even without environmental regulation. Another two hundred to three hundred would be closed as a result of environmental requirements, and all but a few of these would have closed down for other reasons between 1976 and 1980.

• Expected job losses would be 50,000 to 125,000, or about 1 to 4 per cent of total employment in the industries, or 0.05 per cent of the 1970 national work force. Between 50 and 150 small communities would experience the adverse consequences of a plant closing. By the end of 1974 EPA had been able to identify only seventy plant closings and about 14,500 job losses due to cleanup actions.

• Industry prices would rise from 0 to 10 per cent for the entire 1972–76 period, or about 0 to 2 per cent per year. Industry would pass on the cost of protecting the environment to the consumer.

• Four industries (steel, electric utilities, petroleum, and pulp and paper) were expected to spend over $1 billion for cleanup over the five years.

On the issue of national economic impacts, the study looked at the years 1972–80 and found:

• A drop in growth of 0.1 per cent per year, which could be compensated for by more expansionary monetary and fiscal policies to keep the economy's resources, particularly labor, fully employed. Of course the economy was so mismanaged that economic growth in 1974 actually fell by several per cent.

• Price increases of 0.3 per cent per year would accompany the offsetting expansionary policies. Here again events illustrated how inconsequential this impact was. In 1974 the annual rate of inflation was 12 per cent.

Only in the trade area were substantial harmful effects projected. If the United States required the installation of costly pollution-control devices on its factories and our chief competitors such as Japan and Germany did not, then our exports would suffer in foreign markets and their exports would gain a price advantage here. The result could have been an annual balance of payments deficit of from $0.7 billion to $1.9 billion. To place even this most unlikely outcome in perspective, our *monthly* balance of payments losses because of the Arab-led oil cartel, were $2.0 billion.

The completion of these studies was the beginning of the end of the economic-impact confrontation with industry. They played a key role in freeing the environmental protection effort from harassment on the grounds it was harming the national economy. It simply was not. After publication of the studies, there was an easing of White House, industry, and Department of Commerce pressure on EPA to go easy on industry in its standard-setting activities. The White House accepted the results and there were no further confrontations between it and EPA administrator Ruckelshaus on the national economic impact issue.

At this same time, key personnel changes also contributed to a waning interest in continuing the economic impact confrontation. Secretary Stans resigned in early 1972 to become President Nixon's chief fund-raiser for the 1972 election. And Stans's successor, Secretary Peter Peterson,[1] quickly backed away from his predecessor's proindusty, "wait a minute" view.

Excerpts from speeches show the contrast. Peterson spoke as follows in September 1972:

> For too long our business economy has assumed only the burden of short-term labor and material costs while shifting the less obvious social and environmental costs to the general public.

About a year earlier, Stans had said:

> Industry has been indiscriminately accused by some of ignoring the pollution problems of our times and being responsible for most of them. The charge is dead wrong and it is unfair.

Finally in 1973 NIPCC, Stans's conduit to the board rooms, came under attack from Congress. Funding for its staff and operations was deleted on the House floor by Michigan's Democratic congressman John Dingell. His point of order barring funding cited a 1909 law that bars expenditures for any council not established by law.

A few others on the "wait a minute" side did not give up so easily. Throughout 1972 William Letson, newly elevated to the position of general counsel at the Department of Commerce, sought to perpetuate former secretary Stans's position regarding disproven predictions of economic chaos. But Letson met with no success at the White

[1] Peterson did not last long at the Commerce Department. After his November 1972 re-election, Richard Nixon asked Peterson to step down and accept a vague assignment as a roving ambassador. Peterson declined and left the government.

House. He became so frustrated in late 1972 that he told White House staff members he would resign from the Republican party if President Nixon failed to rein in EPA. He did depart after the elections to become Westinghouse's general counsel.

THE PRICE OF A CLEAN CAR

The other major attack on environmental regulations was more narrowly focused. It came from a report by the White House's Office of Science and Technology (OST) and contended that EPA was placing unreasonable technology and cost burdens on the automobile. OST's attack also owed its origin to the White House unrest of 1971 over the economic implications of environmental controls. A February 1972 report released by OST director Edward David concluded that the Clean Air Act's standards for the automobile were too stringent. It found that the cost of compliance heavily outweighed the benefits air-pollution cleanup would bring. EPA contested this conclusion.

The major point of dispute was the cost of the catalyst, an emission-control device installed on cars beginning in the 1975 model year. The catalyst resembles a large tin can that has been spliced into the exhaust pipe under the front-seat floorboard. It is actually a chunk of ceramic extruded into a round, longish honeycomb and stuffed into a can. Inside, a small fraction of an ounce of platinum-palladium metal alloy has been sprayed onto the honeycomb. When exhaust gases pass through, harmful carbon monoxide is converted into carbon dioxide (soda-water fizz), and unburnt gasoline (hydrocarbons) becomes water and more fizz.

The OST estimate of how much the catalyst would cost came from information solicited from the industry itself by way of telephone conversations with Detroit officials. EPA's lower estimates were based on engineering cost calculations developed by pricing the required components with a markup. EPA estimated the cost of industry compliance with the tough Clean Air Act 1975 automobile standards at about $250 per car, in comparison with a 1967 (precontrol) car. Of this, about $150 was for the catalyst system. Early drafts of the OST report utilized figures in the range of $500 to $800. EPA objected vehemently, fearing that if the OST report were published with erroneously high numbers, the public would demand that the Clean Air Act be junked.

This issue was sorted out in EPA's favor at a meeting between CEA director Herbert Stein and EPA's Deputy Administrator Robert Fri in early 1972. The final validation of EPA's estimates occurred two months later at EPA's legal hearings on Detroit's progress toward the Clean Air Acts goals. Testifying under oath, the manufacturers gave cost estimates consistent with EPA's. Estimates by EPA were again confirmed when, in the summer of 1974, Detroit announced that the catalyst systems on 1975 automobiles would cost the consumer $130.

THE ECONOMIC BALANCE SHEET

The confrontation over economic impact reflected not just a confusion over key facts but an underlying conceptual misunderstanding of the meaning of the facts. What does it mean for the economy and society to spend more to control environmental pollution? We measure progress in our country by the GNP accounts. But that is not the full story. If pollution worsens, and more people go to the hospital with respiratory or heart problems, they expend more for medical services and the U.S. gross national product (GNP) goes up. Are we better off? Of course not. On the other hand, if pollution is controlled, hospital bills go down. But the GNP still goes up because thousands are employed in the production of pollution-abatement equipment. And, of course, the environment is cleaner. If we went too far in cleaning up, we would find ourselves with ultraclean air and water but with no goods to consume such as cement for homebuilding, steel and aluminum for appliances and cars, or paper for the newspapers we read. The confrontation does not teach us that industry is always wrong, only that industry is usually not in the best position to judge whether the costs of improving the environment are worth it. Moreover, industry is so prone to exaggerate the cost of cleanup that it is not even in the best position to assess these.

In regulating industries motivated by profits, government must demand the facts and make independent assessments. Government must weigh the damage to the health of the families downwind of a plant against the profits stockholders would lose if abatement investments are required. In the 1970s, we decided to tilt in favor of the families downwind.

Environmental programs even had an answer for the unemployed. As stated, as many as 50,000 to 125,000 were projected to be unemployed in the 1970–76 period by the closure of plants that could not operate profitably and meet environmental standards. Initially, in the early 1970s, such unemployment was of no great concern because jobs were readily available elsewhere. Later, after 1974, government's own program to finance the construction of city sewage-treatment works employed more than 100,000 in 1975 and by 1977 will employ 240,000, neatly canceling out environmental unemployment.

WHY CONGRESS CHOSE
THE TECHNOLOGY APPROACH

The story of the technological confrontation, the second major environmental struggle with big business, has a guerrilla-war character to it, unlike the massive frontal assaults that characterized the economic confrontation. It even has its Robin Hoods, maverick employees of our biggest industries—electric utilities and automobile manufacturers—who were as vigorous in applying their engineering prowess to removing pollutants as they were in using it to increase productivity and profits. Another result of the technological confrontation has been the shattering of the environmentalist view that technology is the enemy of the environment. To the contrary, achieving abatement success depends on making technology an environmental ally.

It was Congress that first saw the importance of technology in guiding the nation's cleanup efforts. Congress learned of technology's importance the hard way. Before 1969, environmental legislation had failed miserably. Some saw the reason for this failure in the reliance of previous legislation on vague prescriptions as to what industry had to do. Old laws contained vague dates when plant abatement programs had to be completed. They did not say with any precision what reductions in pollutant emissions were required. Such legislation was based on a cost-benefit concept of standard-setting. On a plant-by-plant basis, the treatment required was set at the precise level necessary to achieve the cleanup desired for the water body into which the plant discharged. This case-by-case approach was eminently logical, but it did not work.

If, for example, pollutant levels in a river were twice levels necessary to protect fish life, all dischargers were told to reduce their discharges by one half. This procedure was inadequate on two accounts. First, a community had to decide what aquatic life and uses it wanted for its stream or river. Did the community want to set water standards (criteria that describe general conditions in the water or "in stream") so that the trout rather than carp fish species would survive? Did they want to drink the water, swim in it, or simply boat on top of it? Did they want it to be industry's cesspool? The process of setting ambient water-quality standards typically was a process of agreeing to the standard industry wanted. Industry could threaten, "If you do not agree to lower standards," thus permitting greater industry discharges from plant pipes, "we will locate or relocate our plant in a community that will." In short, the old system was subject to economic threats by companies. Either industry got a community to agree to let its river be used as a cesspool or it relocated and provided jobs elsewhere.

Even if some communities set tough in-stream standards, industry used a second loophole to escape these. Technicians were unable to prescribe precisely the degree of effluent reduction necessary to meet in-stream standards. This flaw left pollution-control officials defenseless against corporation arguments that their discharges were not harming the water or that their role was not that important. A typical industry refrain was: "The other plant's or the city's own discharges are responsible for the pollution, not mine."

Previous federal water acts of 1948 and 1965 contained these flaws. These same shortcomings also crippled the nation's air cleanup effort. The prereform 1967 Clean Air Act left the states the task of setting emission limits on a case-by-case basis after weighing local air-quality benefits against the cost of control.

In short, before 1969 those seeking industry action to reduce polluting discharges had an impossible task. They had to demonstrate benefits impossible to assess on a plant-by-plant basis; often lengthy and detailed health studies taking years of work were necessary to provide data adequate to defeat arguments by high-paid lawyers hired by industry. And industry was always able to document the costs of control in excruciating detail. Since under these pre-1969 laws a new plant had to meet only locally determined environmental regulations, industries would shop around and locate where the pollution-abatement requirements were the most permissive. Each community was truly faced with a growth versus no-growth choice.

Two historic innovations were made by the 1970 Clean Air Act. First, uniform air-quality standards were to be attained throughout the nation. One town could not offer more of its air to be dirtied than another. Second, and most important, technology-based standards replaced the case-by-case approach. Now all new plants are judged by the same "end of discharge pipe" criteria. These are set to reflect the quality of emissions achieved if the best abatement technology used anywhere in the industry is installed. The two loopholes were closed. By a vote of 73 to 0, the Senate's version of the 1970 Clean Air Act, which originated this innovative approach, put the nation on a new path.

All new sources of pollution in each industrial category must achieve a uniform technological treatment standard, labeled "best available technology." A detailed study was made by EPA of each industrial process, for example of oil refineries. The average pollution-control performance of the new best plants in that industry became the standard all new plants had to meet by a uniform national date. There will be no more shopping around for plant locations in order to avoid cleaner production. Firm deadlines and high technological standards have provided a new and sound approach.

The Clean Air Act also mandated that automobile emissions from every new car were to be reduced by 90 per cent of 1971 levels by the 1975 model year (or by the 1976 model year if a one-year extension were obtained by the EPA administrator). This provision represents the most far-reaching utilization of the technological approach ever embodied in environmental law. Because this provision was the handiwork of Senator Edmund S. Muskie, the automobile standards became known as the "Muskie standards." Japan adopted them too and they are similarly termed there. Senator Muskie set a standard based not on a technology that was the best in existence, but on a technology yet to be developed. It was the only way to overcome Detroit's foot-dragging. If an industry colluded in its refusal to develop abatement equipment, the forcing all plants to clean up to the average performance of the best plants had the practical effect of making them do nothing at all. The automobile industry had perfected this approach. In the late 1950s and early 1960s, auto makers in Detroit refused to try to develop ways to reduce automobile pollution. This collusion was later admitted and ended on September 11, 1969. On that date the Justice Department announced it had obtained a consent decree wherein the industry promised to refrain from further collusion to suppress cleaner technologies.

In selecting this technological approach to replace the discredited cost-benefit criteria, Congress rejected yet a third approach to pollution abatement favored by economists: pollution taxation. Alfred Marshall and A. C. Pigou, eminent British economists, developed at the turn of this century the concept of "externalities" to explain how the price system failed to debit producers the cost of the environmental damage of their effluents. If discharges from a paper mill close a commercial fishing area, the financial losses to the fishermen are an "external" effect of the paper mill's operations. However, by a quirk of our way of accounting the costs of production, they do not appear as a cost on the paper company's books. The actions of some firms yield positive externalities for which they do not get credit. For example, a firm that sets aside a portion of its land in downtown Manhattan as a park should receive a tax credit for the benefit it has provided to the community.

Economists urge that these externalities be "internalized" through the imposition of pollution taxes, or if benefits are involved, through credits. Presumably a tax per unit of pollutant—for example, per pound of sulfur oxide pollutant from a copper smelter—could be imposed at a level that would force industry to reform in one of three ways. The smelter could invest in a clean production technology. It could curtail production to the level necessary to protect the environment. Or, it could pay pollution taxes which the government would use to compensate those who suffer from the plant's pollution.

Nobel Prize-winning U.S. economist Paul A. Samuelson has suggested the pollution tax or credit solution. The Nixon Administration actually proposed a tax on lead in gasoline in 1970 and one on sulfur oxides pollution in 1972. In its 1972 and 1973 annual budget reports, the Brookings Institution offered pollution taxes as an alternative cleanup approach to that favored by the administrator and Congress. The Council of Economic Advisers has also repeatedly urged that charges be adopted.

But Congress has never given the environmental tax approach more than a few perfunctory hearings. Committee jealousies are one reason. Taxes are for revenues as far as the Ways and Means Committee, headed in 1970 by Wilbur Mills, was concerned. And in the Senate, Air and Water Pollution Subcommittee chairman Edmund Muskie had little hope of imposing taxes because Senator Russell Long's committee was in charge of any Senate action on tax measures. Besides, Muskie and his colleagues are lawyers; they do not think like economists. They are comfortable with regulations, fines, and incarceration. While there are many virtues to the tax approach, the subsequent experiences show that the lawyers are correct; the task of pushing technology on a reluctant industry is less suited to the finely tuned precision of an adjustable tax than it is to the brutal reality of a possible plant closure or a heavy civil or criminal fine and a possible jail sentence.

It is doubtful that pollution taxes will ever work. They suffer from the same flaw as Congress's pre-1969 environmental legislation: they are too logical. At what level should the tax be set? If industry is stubborn and colludes, it can choose to pollute and pass on the tax to its customers. The consumer pays the tax and bears the burden of pollution as well. The electric utilities would be the first to remind us in full-page advertisements of the share of higher rates due to "nonproductive" pollution taxes. The near-unanimous endorsement by economists of the pollution-tax approach is yet another example of the profession's growing isolation from the real world of economic behavior.

EPA now has almost four years' experience in implementing environmental laws mandating the technological approach. It has applied technology-based standards to the nation's largest industries. This experience serves to illustrate the complexity of the task of setting technological standards and making them stick. It also shows that Congress is finally on the right track.

THE TECHNOLOGY CONFRONTATION
WITH THE AUTOMOBILE INDUSTRY

There were two notable battles that vividly illustrate the character of the technological confrontation. They are landmark cases in environmental regulation. The first was the automobile decision of April 1972 which exhausted Detroit's last option for delay and forced the installation of the catalyst. The second was an uncertain guerrilla-type struggle. It involved EPA's efforts to force the nation's electric utilities to install "scrubbers" to remove sulfur oxide pollutants from power plant stacks.

In April 1972, EPA held public hearings on whether to grant requests by the automobile manufacturers for a one-year extension, from 1975 to 1976, of the date technology had to be installed on cars to achieve a 90 per cent reduction in car emissions of hydrocarbons and carbon monoxide. The Clean Air Act provided that these "Muskie standards" were to be achieved by the 1975 model year unless the EPA administrator determined (1) that the technology was not available, (2) that the industry applicant had made a "good faith" effort to develop such technology, and (3) that it was in the public's interest to suspend application of the standards for one year. To get a reprieve, the auto companies had to win all three determinations.

When EPA hearings on the matter began, Administrator Ruckelshaus was inclined to grant the extension. A National Academy of Sciences report had concluded no technology was available to meet the standard. Detroit's manufacturers convinced themselves nothing would do the job. Ruckelshaus appeared to have no choice.

Unknown and unannounced, a car run by a producer of emission-control devices had achieved the standard. From a chance visit to EPA by a representative of a British engineering firm, EPA discovered that a car had been driven 25,000 miles and achieved the standards. Two junior EPA members were sent to England to obtain a firsthand report. They confirmed the car's performance. As EPA's hearings opened, the car was still circulating on England's back roads, completing a twenty-four-hour-a-day 50,000-mile endurance test. Meanwhile, a United States catalyst maker quietly reported to EPA that Chrysler and Ford cars had also performed within the standard after lengthy U.S. test runs. One Chrysler car was successfully tested at 40,000 miles. But this manufacturer was fearful of announcing the results. If Detroit's auto men became unhappy, he could lose all hope of getting a big contract to supply his devices. At the hearings, informed by EPA's sleuthing and whispered information from catalyst makers, Ruckelshaus probed for the evidence he knew existed. It enabled him to put the auto makers on the defense. He demanded: "The public wants and deserves answers. If some companies can make it, why can't all of them?"

It was evident at the hearings that the automobile manufacturers, who alone had the capacity to conduct extensive tests of promising technologies, had not done so. The fact that only a few cars had met the standards was not a consequence of many having failed but a result of Detroit's refusal to put many of them on the road. No single manufacturer had a systematic approach to searching out the best technologies and testing them thoroughly and expeditiously. A catalyst supplier could achieve promising results, only to wait months before a manufacturer would be willing to test his product. Suppliers were short of funds for testing, but large manufacturers made no efforts to assist. A manufacturer might achieve successful results on one particular car and emission system but fail to follow up immediately with a "fleet" test of several cars equipped with such an "optimum" system.

Confronted with the pitiful effort by Detroit's manufacturers, EPA's technicians used a computerized predictive methodology to estimate, on the basis of the performance of a few successful test cars, how all of the manufacturers' model lines would perform if similarly equipped and tested. They concluded that the 1975 standards could be met. Ruckelshaus, irritated at Detroit's go-slow attitude, backed them up. He announced his decision to deny the extension request on May 12, 1972. It represents a milestone in technological standard-setting. By vigorous independent technological searches and creative technological forecasting, EPA resisted the auto industry's sluggish efforts.

Had EPA not taken a strong stand against the automobile industry, the fixed dates for compliance in the Clean Air Act would have been modified far more severely than the additional year's delay granted by Congress in early 1974 and the delay through 1979 granted in 1976. If the decision had gone in favor of the manufacturers, they would have continued their relaxed development efforts and built a strong case for changing the law permanently. Employing one out of every six industrial workers, the automobile industry could have forcefully argued to Congress in 1973 that shutdowns, costly to the unemployment rate, would be inevitable by mid-1974 if the standards were not changed. But Ruckelshaus's 1972 decision to stick to the 1975 model year for meeting the Clean Air Act standards forced the industry to accelerate its efforts dramatically.

From 1971 to 1973 the auto manufacturers more than doubled their expenditures for emission abatement as shown in the table.

AUTOMOBILE COMPANY EXPENDITURES ON POLLUTION CONTROL

	1971		1973	
	Total (Million $)	Per Car ($)	Total (Million $)	Per Car ($)
GM	181.6	33.63	350.7	62.63
Ford	131.9	45.52	349.6	100.00
Chrysler	14.4	9.29	30.6	15.81
American Motors Corp.*	2.4	9.48	4.6	13.17
TOTAL	**330.3**		**735.5**	

* American Motors by a special agreement had access to General Motors' technology.

While these developments were taking place, the manufacturers contested Ruckelshaus's decision in the courts. On February 10, 1973, Judge Harold Levanthal of the District of Columbia U. S. Court of Appeals remanded the 1972 decision for reconsideration by Ruckelshaus. He did not reverse Ruckelshaus's decision; he ordered another set of hearings. His remand was primarily based on his criticism of EPA's methodology. He was troubled by EPA's assumption that Ford's promising emissions test data could be assumed to be applicable to General Motors cars. Ford and the other manufacturers or catalyst suppliers who had successfully tested emission-control devices used a platinum-based or "noble" metal system. GM favored more plentiful and cheaper "base" metals, such as copper.

Judge Levanthal probably does not know to this day that GM later admitted to EPA that the catalyst it had described as base metal in its formal application in 1972 was in fact noble metal in composition. The world's largest company, carried away with its self-confidence that the others were making a mistake, had been duped by anxious potential catalyst system suppliers. GM had announced that it would utilize nonplatinum catalysts to save money and reduce its reliance on South African and Rhodesian sources of platinum. But suppliers were desperate not to lose the vast GM market. Since they did not manufacture base metal catalysts, they responded to GM's request by sending noble metal catalysts instead. The suppliers were protected from GM's scrutiny of their products by proprietary agreements. In other words, GM was not allowed to conduct chemical tests. Red-faced and apologetic, GM officials informed me of this discovery in early 1973.

Before the court ordered the rehearing, it became evident the situation was vastly different from a year earlier. During the year, Japanese automobile manufacturers announced that they had an alternative to the catalyst approach that would achieve the Muskie standards. They had successfully tested a "stratified-charge" engine, an approach that uses two combustion chambers per cylinder to improve fuel burning and reduce pollution. No add-on, catalystlike device is necessary; rather the engine itself is improved. The U.S. automobile companies neglected this technology. When Honda, the Japanese manufacturer, announced its success, GM had only three people working on the same approach.

Meanwhile the auto industry became convinced that the catalyst was the superior approach. On February 7, 1973, GM's president Edward Cole, with extensive technical data and charts and great enthusiasm, briefed high EPA officials. He wanted to say the 1975 standards could be met. But his lawyers, afraid of jeopardizing GM's position in future litigation, dissuaded him. A few days later, Lee Iacocca, president of Ford Motor Company, arrived in Administrator Ruckelshaus's office. Whereas GM's Cole is a brilliant engineer with a "can do" enthusiasm, Iacocca is a former car salesman.

Cole, with technical data, wanted to show that the problem could be solved. Iacocca wanted a "deal." He began by citing a speech I had given the previous fall in which Ruckelshaus's 1972 decision was characterized as holding Detroit's feet to the fire. Iacocca said his leg was burnt to the hip and he was ready to put on catalysts. He thought the approach of placing catalysts on cars in 1975 in California and nationwide in 1976 would be "politically unacceptable." He proposed to go to Capitol Hill for support, and to begin that effort with Senator Muskie. He said he needed Senator Muskie's "forgiveness for past sins." The senator had not forgotten Iacocca's refusal to attend a Muskie hearing on automobile pollution held in Detroit a decade earlier. In those days, the Ford Motor Company was still denying that the automobile caused pollution.

On April 11, 1973, after the second series of hearings, Ruckelshaus decided to opt for the course urged by Iacocca. He was pleased with Detroit's progress. The technology was proven. But his decision was based primarily on lengthy testimony that if catalysts were fitted on all new cars in their first year of use, rather than phased into use over several years, purchasers might experience high failure rates from hastily manufactured devices. Also of concern were reports that, as a by-product, catalysts might emit another pollutant. Because gasoline contains sulfur, catalytic action on exhaust streams can produce sulfates, which on contact with moisture in air become sulfuric acid. There was a heated debate within EPA on whether this problem would be significant. Ruckelshaus established a California standard that required the installation of catalysts on cars sold in California. Cars sold in the other forty-nine states had to meet a tougher standard than previously, but not sufficiently stringent to require the use of the catalyst. Ruckelshaus sought to allow two years for the construction and perfection of catalyst production facilities and permit a California-scale test of catalyst performance. As it turned out, once the fuel-economy benefits of the catalyst were appreciated by Detroit and in demand by car buyers, practically all 1975 model year cars were catalyst-equipped.

The infant EPA, backed by the most powerful environmental law in the world, succeeded in bringing the largest industry in the world into the age of the environment. Ruckelshaus had done to Detroit in the name of environment what Ralph Nader had done earlier in the name of safety. The U.S. manufacturers treated EPA, unlike the way GM treated Nader, with respect. They begrudgingly accepted the technology-based emission-standard approach pioneered by Senator Muskie. In the best of worlds, setting a standard requiring a technology that does not exist is a gamble. But it is probably not a bad bet for an industry that possesses the resources of the automobile industry, assuming they can be mobilized.

"DIRTY TRICKS" HELP THE ELECTRIC UTILITIES ESCAPE CLEAN AIR ACT REQUIREMENTS

EPA's second technological confrontation with big business was with the electric utility industry, like the automobile industry, one of America's largest. Coal-burning and sulfur-belching power plant smokestacks must be controlled by the application of a stack gas "scrubber" if the air is to be cleaned of industrial pollution. But, in its endeavor to require utilities to install scrubbers, EPA was not aided by an emission-control standard written directly into the law, as was the case with the automobile industry. Instead, the Clean Air Act called for the states to set standards for existing plants by mid-1972. By 1975, or under special conditions by 1977, the construction program for abatement compliance had to be completed. For all new power plants, EPA was to establish a separate standard requiring use of the best practicable abatement technology.

Many of the same problems encountered in regulating General Motors, Chrysler, and the Ford Motor Company plagued EPA's efforts to regulate the utilities. The largest U.S. utility is the Tennessee Valley Authority (TVA), a government agency. The largest privately owned generator of electricity is the American Electric Power Company. Its twenty plants, overwhelmingly fueled with coal, are located in seven states throughout the nation's industrial heartland. After these two companies, the three largest coal-burning utilities are the Southern Company in the southeast United States, Commonwealth Edison in Chicago, and Duke Power in the Piedmont region.

Together these companies burn 35 per cent of the coal consumed to produce electricity.

The combustion of this coal, about 2.5 per cent of which is sulfur, releases sulfur oxide gases to the atmosphere through power plant stacks, often hundreds of feet above the ground. One such gas, sulfur dioxide, has been identified by EPA as a health hazard. It causes serious respiratory problems such as emphysema, bronchitis, and pneumonia. Studies have shown that deaths increase during periods when sulfur dioxide concentrations in the ambient air (the air around us) are high. Until recently, EPA believed the threats to public health were to those in the vicinity of fossil-fuel-burning power plants. But more recent health information has led EPA health experts to believe that once the sulfur oxides leave the vicinity of power plants, they are converted to harmful sulfate compounds on contact with moisture in the air. The magnitude of these dual threats is best measured by the scale of sulfur oxide emissions from power plants: they more than doubled between 1960 and 1974. By 1980 another 40 per cent rise to 28.1 million tons is expected if utilities do not install cleanup devices. If, however, devices are installed, the 1980 emissions would drop to only 7.8 million tons. One estimate of what this difference could mean to the nation's health predicted that, without utility compliance, between 1975 and 1980 there will be 25,000 more deaths and multiple illnesses ranging from aggravated heart and lung disorders like bronchitis and pneumonia in otherwise healthy children.

There is only one technology available to reduce sulfur oxide emissions by the 75 per cent required to protect these people: the scrubber. The stack gas scrubber acts as a shower in the power plant stack. It rains an alkali chemical such as calcium hydroxide or lime which combines with sulfur oxides to cleanse the air. Two stack gas scrubbers operated in England before World War II: one began operation at the Battersea power station in 1932 and the other at the Swansea power station immediately before the war. The technology is not exotic by any means. But continuous large-scale operations were not demonstrated until the year following March 1972 at the large, coal-fired Mitsui power plant supplying electricity to a Japanese aluminum plant. As late as 1975 the two largest electric utilities in America, TVA and the American Electric Power Company, were still contending the technology did not exist.

The greatest scrubber problem involved existing, not new, power plants.[2] As mentioned, the Clean Air Act made it the responsibility of each state to regulate the use of scrubbers on existing power plants within its boundaries. The state regulations, established in early 1972, required that about seventy of these power plants put on scrubbers by 1975 and in a few cases by 1977. Thus, utilities had to make purchase decisions in 1973 in order to meet the national 1975 cleanup date mandated by the Clean Air Act to protect the public health. The utilities refused. As the subsequent story will show, they had EPA hostage.

Upon receipt of these plans in January of 1972, EPA's analysis showed that unless scrubbers were used, as many as 22,000 coal miners would be unemployed in 1975 because of power plant closures or conversions to low-sulfur oil. Conversion to oil would also have increased our oil imports and dependence on Arab supplies. Senator Randolph, chairman of the Senate Public Works Committee, whose subcommittee led by Senator Muskie fathered the Clean Air Act, was not about to see coal miners in his home state of West Virginia put out of work.

The utilities understood EPA's dilemma. If they could resist installing scrubbers until it was too late to do so and meet the 1975 deadlines, then they could claim their only option was to switch to oil, a much easier and quicker task than installing a scrubber. Senator Randolph would ease the Clean Air Act rather than have widespread coal unemployment. To date, the utilities have succeeded in procrastinating. In particular, the larger utilities mentioned earlier did very little toward proving and applying the scrubber.

In December 1971 only three plants in the U.S. had scrubbers installed. They were not working satisfactorily and were of a pilot

2 The Clean Air Act required EPA to set a technology-based emission requirement for new coal-fired power plants. In December 1971, EPA issued its regulation mandating that every new power plant burning medium- or high-sulfur coal had to use a scrubber. EPA reasoned that it takes four to five years to build a power plant but only two years to build a scrubber. Thus, by requiring a scrubber on all power plants constructed after the December 1971 regulation, EPA allowed up to two years of additional technological development before a scrubber selection had to be made. On September 19, 1973, after a legal battle with the utility industry, EPA's decision for new plants was upheld in court.

rather than full-scale size. The utilities rejoiced at their failures. The key government agencies with energy responsibility at the time, the Department of the Interior, the Office of Emergency Preparedness, and the Federal Power Commission, shared their skepticism. In June of 1972 these agencies joined EPA to form an executive-branch panel to review the status of scrubbing technology. As EPA's assistant administrator for air and water programs and convenor of the group, I told the panel, made up of technical representatives from the Department of Commerce, the Environmental Protection Agency, the Federal Power Commission, and the Office of Science and Technology, to talk to suppliers, utilities—anyone, anywhere, to determine the status of this technology.

Members of the panel traveled to Europe and Japan and throughout the United States. They asked about scrubber problems and the scrubber's potential. Agreement was difficult,[3] but the panel rendered its judgment on November 16, 1972: "We have examined the status of stack gas cleaning technology in the U.S. and Japan and have concluded that sulfur oxides removal from stack gases is technologically feasible in commercial-sized installations."

As was the case with the stratified-charge automobile engine, Japan's example played a key role in the application of scrubbing technology. In this instance, however, the technology applied to the Mitsui plant in Japan was built by a U.S. firm, the Chemical Construction Company.

EPA urged the utilities to accept the panel's conclusion. But they and the coal industry balked. In September 1972 the coal and utilities industries launched a counteroffensive. They persuaded Senator Randolph and the White House to call meetings at which they could confront EPA. At the Senate meeting, Senator Randolph stressed his concern for coal mine unemployment. He stated categorically that if coal mine layoffs were a consequence of the Clean Air Act, the act would be relaxed.

[3] The President's Office of Science and Technology (OST) could not wait for the panel's verdict. Chief presidential science advisor Dr. Edward David wrote Kentucky's Senator Marlow Cook on June 22, 1972, concluding, "To our knowledge no system has been demonstrated on a commercial scale which meets the performance and reliability requirements of the regulations and utilities." Thus, in another instance, OST was holding back technology rather than advancing it.

EPA rebutted that all the utilities had to do was what had already been done at the Mitsui plant. At the White House meeting a few hours later, the Mitsui plant was also cited by EPA officials as an example of the successful application of scrubbing technology. John Whitaker, of the White House Domestic Council, indirectly backed EPA's position. He replied to the Coal Association president Carl Baggie's prediction of despair as follows:

> I frequently have these meetings with EPA. EPA is saying the technology exists, and industry and the Department of Commerce are saying it does not. Ninety-five per cent of the time, EPA is right. I have concluded EPA talks to the engineers and the Department of Commerce talks to the board rooms. The problem is the board rooms do not talk to their engineers.

This outburst from the typically noncommittal Whitaker shocked both the industry and EPA representatives. But the former left the meeting unconvinced.

Whitaker's words neatly summarized an important aspect of the problem. The utilities had no commercial incentive to solve the sulfur oxides problem. Each company had every reason to wait until other firms had expended development and application funds and a clearly superior technology emerged from among the many candidates. In contrast, the Japanese polluters faced stiff penalties. They worked harder and committed more highly skilled technical personnel to perfect the scrubber than the U.S. utilities did. Not only had the Mitsui plant operated for over a year by 1973, but a scrubber on an oil-fired power plant owned by Japan Synthetic Rubber at Chiba had been operating since 1971.

The U.S. utilities adopted a "yes-but" posture: "Yes, it works on oil-fired plants, but not on coal-fired plants." "Yes, it works on small plants (the 156-megawatt plant at Mitsui), but it won't work on large (1,000-megawatt) plants." "Yes, it works on 2 per cent sulfur coal, but it won't work on 3 per cent coal." EPA's technicians refuted these arguments one by one.

The balance of the scrubbing story is more biography than it is engineering. Two men carried the debate to its conclusion. One was the chairman of the American Electric Power Company, Donald C.

Cook. He became the self-appointed champion of the antiscrubbing forces. Cook personally directed a public relations campaign against EPA's scrubber position. He spent about $4 million in 1974 on more than thirty full-page advertisements in all major U.S. newspapers and magazines as well as in papers in his company's seven-state service area. With humor, with total assurance of his correctness, and with a vengeance, Cook claimed loudly that EPA was run by a bunch of pompous, do-gooder, technically inept bureaucrats. CEQ chairman and former Delaware governor Russell Peterson and Federal Energy administrator John Sawhill took umbrage at one American Electric Power Company advertisement which suggested efforts to conserve energy would result in unemployment. Cook struck back at Peterson by writing President Nixon and asking that "you fully investigate both the official and clandestine activities of Mr. Peterson in the conduct of his office." Part of Cook's assurance surely came from his long experience in Washington, D.C. He was a former chairman of the Securities and Exchange Commission and long-time advisor and friend to former President Lyndon B. Johnson.

Few know the name of his antagonist, Robert P. VanNess, an environmental engineer employed at the Paddy's Run power plant in Louisville, Kentucky, on the boundary between American Electric Power Company and TVA territory. Paddy's Run power plant is owned by Louisville Gas and Electricity, a small, independent power company less than one-tenth American Electric Power's 15,000-megawatt size. The Paddy's Run scrubber was on 56 megawatts of the 330-megawatt installation. Whereas American Electric Power burned one tenth of the coal consumed in U.S. power plants, Louisville Gas and Electric used less than one hundredth.

VanNess is the closest thing to an authentic environmental hero America has. He proved the scrubber would work in the United States. From its start-up in April 1973, his scrubber operated without any significant difficulty. It removed well over 90 per cent of the emissions. He proved that United States engineers can perform as well as Japanese engineers. Not only did he solve the sulfur oxides pollution problem; he would not tolerate the self-serving utility propaganda against the scrubber.

Hired by the Louisville utility from a chemical company, Robert

VanNess was a straight talker. He had nothing but contempt for the limited technical skills of the utility companies. Uninhibited by the utilities' mechanical-engineering mentality, bred by years of building and operating boilers, he believed the chemical aspects of scrubber operation to be eminently solvable. He noted that a key chemical reaction in the process was used by the Romans to build roads more than two thousand years ago. He was scornful of the excuses offered by the giant utilities such as TVA and American Electric Power.

In the fall of 1973 TVA's then just-retired chief engineer, Archie Slack, wanted to visit the VanNess scrubber at the Paddy's Run plant. VanNess wondered why it had taken Slack so long to make the short trip to Louisville from TVA's nearby east Tennessee headquarters. VanNess thought TVA preferred to remain ignorant of his accomplishments, which were widely publicized, so it could continue to argue scrubbing technology did not exist. This TVA vigorously did in frequent letters from Chairman Aubrey Wagner to the White House. Called in late 1974 to brief a National Academy of Sciences panel debating whether scrubbers worked, VanNess was so convincing that, despite TVA's argument to the contrary, the panel concluded scrubbing was a proven technology.[4]

Meanwhile, Donald Cook waged his fight to overturn EPA's rules requiring the installation of scrubbers. His company contracted with the Battelle Memorial Institute for a rebuttal of the government's 1973 proscrubbing technology assessment. Battelle employed the Delphi method to reach its conclusion that scrubbing technology was not available. The Delphi approach boils down to a series of anonymous questionnaires circulated to a knowledgeable panel of technicians, seeking their judgment on a specific issue, in this case whether scrubbing technology was commercially available, would be available within two years, and so on. Needless to say, few of the respondents concluded it was available. Most thought it would be available in five to fourteen years. Technology has never been advanced by majority vote. Moreover, the report's conclusion ignored the performance of the Mitsui plant, saying in contented ignorance:

[4] See "Air Quality and Stationary Source Control," a report by the National Academy of Sciences and the National Academy of Engineers, Washington, D.C., 1975.

"It is difficult to believe the Japanese have done what no United States organization could achieve to date." This omission permitted the report to say the National Academy of Engineers' criteria for proven industrial-scale acceptability (one year of satisfactory operation on a unit of 100-megawatt or greater capacity) had not been met, whereas in actuality it had been achieved by Mitsui.

An American Electric Power Company subsidiary, the Ohio Power Company, was the instrument in another of Cook's "dirty tricks." It solicited scrubber bids for its plant in Captina, West Virginia, but the bid specifications were much stiffer than those for steam turbines or boilers. For example, the scrubber was to be warranted to operate 8,060 hours a year for fifteen years. An EPA survey of industry suppliers found that no steam boiler or turbine had ever been sold by them subject to such stringent contract provisions. Adding insult to injury, American Electric Power required the prospective bidder to agree to pay damages in the event of equipment failure. Yet the General Electric Company, a utility turbine supplier, limits its liability to the repair or replacement of its equipment. This industry tactic was clearly designed to permit American Electric Power to back its claim that the technology did not exist by citing the failure on the part of suppliers to respond. No suppliers put in bids.

In 1973 the American Electric Power Company (AEP) sold electricity valued at $967 million. Its profits were $183 million, a healthy 19 per cent. Yet AEP made Ohio Democratic congressman Charles Vanik's list of the ten major U.S. corporations that paid no federal corporation taxes. This performance put AEP into a good position to fund Cook's advertising campaign. One cannot help but wonder if the nation ever would have gotten the automobile exhaust cleaned up if General Motor's president Edward Cole had been replaced by Cook. Cole was more akin to VanNess. But he was in a better position to guide industry performance than VanNess. If VanNess had been chairman of AEP, the scrubber debate would have been over in 1973.

By 1975 the utility industry had persuaded President Ford to urge Congress to delay the requirement to install scrubbers on most power plants until 1985. Congress did not go along completely. But utility intransigence forced Congress to delay compliance until 1980. While the scrubber was rejected industry-wide, a few companies applied it on a small scale. By the end of 1974, over forty units were under construction, and there were at least five excellent plants in operation.

THE SEARCH FOR A BALANCED TECHNOLOGICAL APPROACH

EPA's advocacy of scrubbing technology for power plants and catalysts for automobiles was, by these accounts, difficult. The stakes were very high. Scrubbing costs are projected at $5 billion to $8 billion over the next five years, and automobile antipollution costs could reach more than $50 billion by 1985. If either technology fails, Americans could be subject to cuts in electrical power or in the mobility we all take for granted. If the technologies work, the cost of power will rise by as much as 10 to 15 per cent in high-sulfur coal burning areas and the purchase price of automobiles will rise by about $250 per year.

There are, of course, limits to the pace at which technology can be pushed. Congress, in its deliberations before the passage of the 1972 Water Pollution Control Act, almost lost sight of those limits, coming perilously close to adopting a technology standard that would have closed down a large portion of U.S. industry. The Senate wanted to adopt a standard which would have made *any* industrial effluent being discharged into the nation's waters illegal by 1983. EPA's analysis, shown in the accompanying figure, revealed that the standard would be difficult, if not impossible, to achieve. The nation would pay twice as much to remove the last 1 per cent of water pollutants as it did to remove the previous 99 per cent. It would cost almost five times as much to remove the last 15 per cent as it did to remove the first 85 per cent. The House balked at adopting the no-discharge standard, choosing the 85–95 per cent range instead. The House's actions forced the Senate to back away from a path to certain catastrophic economic dislocations.

Technology advances the cause of pollution control a step at a time. There is a premium on developing and finding the best technologies worldwide. Searches for new technologies in Japan and Europe have played key roles in making U.S. industry move rapidly to-

PROJECTED NATIONAL COSTS OF ACHIEVING "ZERO DISCHARGE" OF WATER POLLUTANTS

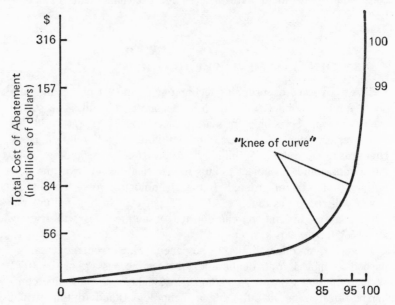

Per cent Reduction of Pollutants

ward cleanup goals. Environmental improvement can best be guaranteed by advancing technology by the following procedure: First, find the best technology by searching the world. Second, compare costs of the last few units or percentage points of pollutant removed by the technology with the costs of using the presently applied technologies per unit of pollutant removal. See if the costs are sharply higher. This can be done by plotting cost on a vertical axis and the per cent of removal on the horizontal axis, as is shown in the figure for water pollution-control technologies. A sudden rise in cost per percentage point of removal produces a diagram which looks like a half-bent leg. Third, choose the technology that places the outcome in the range of the "knee" of the curve. In the figure this is in the 85–95 per cent reduction range. Technology should be pushed to the point of the knee of the curve, but no further.

Soon exemplary firms, or firms located in highly polluted areas like Japan or parts of the United States that are forced by local standards either to close down or to exceed the national pollution standard will develop a new, cheaper technology for dealing with emissions. In effect, the new technology moves the above curve to the right. On the basis of this new technology, national standards can then be tightened another few notches or "ratcheted up" by a few per cent. The new technology may be an "end of pipe" technology or a new process of production. For example, a scrubber removes pollutants at the end of the process or "pipe." The abatement action takes place after the combustion process or at the point of final discharge into the environment. But a process change, such as coal gasification, may replace conventional coal boilers and, by converting coal to gas with dramatically reduced pollution, practically eliminate pollution. Sound technical and economic analysis is necessary if the ratchet-up principle is to be applied successfully. Firms must have adequate warning time before a new technological standard is imposed in lieu of an old one. New investments must be financially digested by industry over several years.

As technology is pushed foward, new problems will arise. These must be weighed carefully or a new technology will backfire. Some technologies consume great quantities of energy. By forcing industry to apply these, the net effect on the environment may be negative. There may be more pollution associated with producing the needed energy than is saved by applying the technology. Other technologies sometimes transfer pollution from one part of the environment to another. If sulfur oxides are removed from the air by mixing them with water, a sludge forms which, if it is not treated carefully, can pollute the water. Adding the catalyst to the tailpipe of our cars may have removed the carbon monoxide and hydrocarbons but it may at the same time cause the sulfur in gasoline to be converted into harmful sulfates. Today we are discovering that the chlorine used for decades to purify water for drinking may be combining with compounds in the water to form cancer-causing chemicals. Because of these possibilities, environmental officials suffer from an inevitable schizophrenia. The job of advancing the cause of a clean environment through regulations requiring industry to meet technological standards is not a job for the fainthearted.

APPLYING ENFORCEMENT MUSCLE

In regulating America's industry, it must be recalled again and again that the incentives are against environmental-technological progress. EPA, in pushing technology, acts in lieu of the profit motive which pushes technology where there are productivity payoffs. While over the long run the impetus of environmental requirements will probably spur new generations of technology that are profitable (for example, the stratified-charge engine for cars, or pollution-free flash smelters for copper smelting), in the short run environmental technologies are not profitable for industry to apply. Technology may be the brain of America's abatement effort, but enforcement is the brawn. Repeatedly EPA has applied its muscle. The first occasion on which industry saw the full force of EPA's legal power was in November 1971. EPA moved under the emergency powers of the Clean Air Act to force twenty-three industries in Birmingham, Alabama, to stop operations. Several days of stagnant air left the South's major industrial center engulfed in a yellow-black cloud. EPA received hourly reports on the level of health-threatening dirt in the air. When particulate pollution reached 771 micrograms per cubic meter, EPA acted. The "warning" level for this pollutant, 625 micrograms, is the level at which immediate health damage is probable. At the "emergency" level of 875, the number of deaths will increase. EPA acted under the Clean Air Act provision that triggers plant closures when there is an "imminent and substantial endangerment to the health of persons." EPA's vigorous action in this first emergency case provided a front-page message to industry throughout the country: the enforcement provision of the act would not be soft-pedaled.

The largest penalty incurred under the Clean Air Act was the $7 million penalty the Ford Motor Company paid for misrepresentation of emission test data on 1973 model year cars.[5] This was a knife-

[5] This sum is much less than the possible $60 million the Mitsubishi Oil Company will have to pay for an oil spill from its Mizushima refinery into Japan's Inland Sea. Already a $16.5 million downpayment has been made to the region's fishermen.

edge test of the act's provisions for gaining automobile industry compliance. In May 1972 EPA was notified by Ford executives that all cars in the process of certification for sale had been tinkered with to ensure that emission levels met EPA standards. Without EPA certification that emission standards have been met, cars cannot be sold or even shipped from the factory. Ford test cars had been illegally adjusted and modified as often as fifty times or more in the course of their hundred-day, 50,000-mile tests. Such tests establish emissions performance over the life of the car as it will actually be driven.

EPA referred Ford's case to the Justice Department. Ford entered into a consent decree agreeing to pay $7 million. EPA's chief automobile regulator still carries a copy of Ford's check of payment to the United States Treasury in his pocket. As part of the settlement, Ford also reformed its organization to ensure that in the future those who built the cars did not maintain them during EPA test runs.

In the early years of the vigorous EPA enforcement program, the agency had an important ally in economic prosperity. Scattered plant closures hardly made a ripple in a U.S. economy operating at or above full-employment levels. Workers laid off simply found jobs across the street. In 1974 the situation had dramatically worsened. Unemployment rates in most of the industrial cities of the North were above 10 per cent. When in September 1974, a month after taking office, President Ford sponsored throughout the country a series of conferences on the economy, corporation leaders saw an opportunity to seek relief from environmental requirements. The leading spokesmen against the environment were the chairmen of GM and DuPont. The true test came in Gary, Indiana, the day after Christmas 1974. U.S. district court judge Allen Sharp ordered the U. S. Steel Corporation to pay a daily $2,300 fine if it continued to operate ten open-hearth furnaces. In 1965 the company had agreed to shut down by the end of 1973 all fifty-three of these old, polluting furnaces, which discharge a noxious orange-colored smoke and dirt dangerous to human health. After repeated delays and two federal court orders, ten were still not shut down by the end of 1974.

The judge did not want to order the furnaces to close. He gave the company an option to operate them and pay the daily fine. But U. S. Steel issued a pious press release announcing the furnaces would be

shut down. Under U. S. Steel's union contract, closure of the furnaces would cost the company seven dollars per day per worker for
unemployment payments. Had the fine been paid instead, the company's cost would have been ninety-three cents per worker.

More was involved in the company's action than, as it alleged, a
reluctance to "accede to the principle" of operating its plant and
damaging the environment, which paying the fine implied. It appeared that U. S. Steel had picked the ideal time, place, and circumstances to successfully blackmail the environmentalists and perhaps
force Congress to weaken the Clean Air Act.

U. S. Steel is Gary's biggest employer, with a work force of
23,000. Local officials estimated Gary's unemployment rate was between 12 and 15 per cent. Closure of the units would make up to
2,500 U. S. Steel workers jobless, during a harsh recession Christmas. Further, the nation desperately needed the eighty thousand tons
of steel per month these furnaces produced to accelerate energy production. Gary's Mayor, Richard G. Hatcher, rose to the occasion. On
nationwide television he accused U. S. Steel of attempting to blackmail the city. He called the company's decision a "callous disregard
for Gary and the working people of northwestern Indiana." U. S.
Steel had tested and to its surprise found intact the commitment of
the city of Gary to healthy skies. Indeed, citizen outrage over steel
company air and water pollution in the Chicago-Gary area has been
a constant motivation for a variety of enforcement actions over the
past decade.

Unlike repeated cases of vigorous enforcement action against pollution of the air, enforcement against industrial water-pollution sources
proceeded sporadically from 1969 to 1973. Water enforcement was
hampered by the complex procedures of the 1965 Water Act. Efforts
began in 1969 to institute an industrial permit program using the authority of the 1899 Refuse Act. But these were quickly halted by a
court decision. Before the courts acted, 129 criminal actions had
been filed in 1970 and 191 in 1971, compared with only 143 such
actions over the entire 1967–69 period. The passage of the new
water law on October 18, 1972, gave EPA a clearer mandate to issue
permits to the nation's 45,000 industrial and 22,000 municipal water
polluters. The new law opened the door to a credible water-pollution
enforcement program.

One celebrated water-pollution case did reach a conclusion and it, like the Gary case, illuminated the basic dilemma environmental regulators face. The Reserve Mining Company, owned by the Armco and Republic Steel companies, operates a taconite iron ore processing plant at Silver Bay, Minnesota. For eighteen years this facility has dumped its wastes into Lake Superior, the largest body of fresh water on earth. Over the last decade the plant has had a daily discharge of 67,000 tons of "tailings," or fine residues of the ore-processing foundry. In 1969 evidence that these wastes contained a submicroscopic asbestoslike substance that could cause cancer was found. This discovery pitted 200,000 people down the shore of Lake Superior and dependent on tailing-infested water for their drinking supply against Silver Bay's 3,200 workers, practically all Reserve Mining Company employees. Citizens in cities like Duluth wondered if in twenty to thirty years they would be felled by painful stomach and intestinal cancers. They were alarmed by studies in Japan and among U.S. asbestos workers that showed cancer caused about 50 per cent of them to die, compared with a cancer rate of 15 to 20 per cent for the general population.

The states of Minnesota, Wisconsin, and Michigan, the federal EPA and Department of Justice, and half a dozen environmental groups asked the courts in the cities of Duluth and Superior to close down the taconite plant until it made provisions to dispose of its wastes on land. The case was tried by U.S. district court judge Miles W. Lord and he set numerous records in environmental litigation. The trial cost each side about $5 million. It took 139 days and is recorded on eighteen thousand pages of testimony. The judge concluded the 200,000 people on the western arm of Lake Superior were endangered by the asbestoslike tailings. In his opinion, Judge Lord accused Reserve Mining Company of using its Silver Bay work force as "hostages." He wrote: "In order to free the work force at Reserve, the court must permit the continued exposure of [Duluth and other Lake shore citizens] to known human carcinogens. The court will have no part in this form of economic blackmail."

Judge Lord's courageous April 1974 order was overturned by the U. S. Court of Appeals in St. Louis two days later. But the reversal still required Reserve Mining to end its pollution of Lake Superior after the two years necessary to construct a land disposal system had expired.

No law enforces itself. Battalions of federal and state enforcers can help. But in the final analysis, citizen interest and actions are the key to reducing industrial pollution. In the Reserve Mining case, a Duluth woman hairdresser, Arlene Lekto, had organized the Save Lake Superior Association. She had located in the scientific community the evidence of a possible cancer connection. Her decisive role provides, in this enforcement case, the common theme of citizen action.

INDUSTRY REFORMS

In the early 1970s across the United States, plant by plant, company by company, the industrial pollution was ending. In 1973 industry spent $4.9 billion on abatement equipment; in 1974 the sum jumped to $7.5 billion. Over the decade 1974–83 industry will probably spend an average of $11.3 billion per year to control pollution. Two thirds of these expenditures are taking place in five dirty industries: electric utilities, petroleum, nonferrous metals, chemicals, and paper. For every one of these industries except the electric utilities, the capital expenditures for pollution control are more than 10 per cent of all industry capital expenditures. A review of progress toward clean water performed for the National Commission on Water Quality in 1975[6] showed that about 90 per cent of all industries will meet the Water Act's 1977 target date of abatement. Unfortunately, the same study found only about half of all municipal waste-treatment plants would meet the same goal.

Of potentially more far-reaching significance is that environmental regulation has forced industries to investigate their basic production processes and techniques and search for better alternatives. Since the 1920s the copper industry and the automobile industry have mass-produced, respectively, the reverbatory furnace and the internal combustion engine. Now a new hydrometallurgical, pollution-free copper ore smelting process is being tried. Auto maker consideration of the

[6] A study of the National Pollution Discharge Elimination System, "The Permit Program," performed by Energy and Environmental Analysis, Inc., 1975.

innovative stratified-charge engine is also being motivated by environmental concerns.

We already have evidence that industry's efforts have paid off in terms of a cleaner environment, even though the major industrial cleanup programs will not be completed until 1977. Sulfur dioxide levels in urban areas have been cut in half, and particulate levels in most cities are down slightly. Health-threatening fecal coliform bacteria levels and oxygen-demanding industrial and municipal wastes in the twenty-two major river systems of the United States have decreased. Absent for a hundred years, the Atlantic salmon finally returned to the Connecticut River in 1975. It has also returned to the Penobscot and Union rivers in Maine. Even the Hudson River is cleaner, although polychlorinated biphenyls persist and contaminate some fish species. Pesticide levels are down sharply. All this has been achieved at a 1975 cost to the consumer of forty-seven dollars per citizen. When industry fully integrates environmental requirements in its technology-development and production-planning programs, the environmental awakening will have received its best hard-earned reward.

It is testimony to our political system that it can respond to and mobilize citizen support to force responsible corporate action. The outcome of this confrontation with big business will not make the Marxists, who believe industry runs this country, happy. Neither did it please Ford Motor Company or U. S. Steel. But it appears to be getting the cleanup job done.

4.

THE ENERGY-ENVIRONMENT CONNECTION: CONSERVATION

Almost all literate Americans know by now that while we make up a mere 6 per cent of the world's population, we consume one third of its energy. But few know what should be done about this apparently severe case of overindulgence. Just as confusing is the role of the environment in causing the energy crisis and its part in helping us sort our way out of it.

The single most important factor in the energy crisis is philosophical. Americans are committed to producing and consuming at fantastic rates. As our incomes rise, it is incumbent on us to spend more on such items as freezers, automobiles, and travel. All gulp energy. This consumption-production habit is an obsession, a more-than-three-hundred-year-old commitment dating from the time our ancestors set their eyes on the purple mountains' majesty and began to conquer that great frontier.

There are signs some of us have jumped off this treadmill. For one thing, we prefer leisure more; our weekly working hours have declined so that we can keep up the consumption side of our habit. Increasing productivity has given us so much more per hour of effort that we go home earlier and work harder at spending our income.

Then in the late 1960s a few intellectuals announced the "greening of America." Supposedly America's work ethic was on the way out, to be replaced by an inclination to idleness, a propensity to while away hours in green fields twirling daisies. However, there are no strong signs that we will opt for lethargy and sloth, or even plain idleness. This fad of America's greening probably survives only as a sociologist's relic dusted off for undergraduates by our wilder-eyed faculties.

For Americans, the curve of progress is the rising income curve— often chased, but occasionally led, by the energy consumption curve. Until recently, the energy production-consumption treadmill has been giving us a cheap ride. Relative prices have favored rising energy consumption. A barrel of crude oil cost $2.60 in 1948. If it had maintained its position relative to other prices, by the time of 1973's embargo it would have risen by 83 per cent to $4.75; instead it had increased only 30 per cent to $3.39.

All this has been changed by the Arabs and the Shah of Iran, who are pricing their product at about twelve dollars per barrel. This "Arab shock" is a direct affront to our energy-consumptive lifestyles. Many of us realized we could not unload our gas-guzzling monsters at the same time everyone else did, nor could we move out of our spacious, thin-walled homes. U.S. industries, long nourished by cheap energy, scrambled to cut energy wastage.

A bad habit and bad-habit forming prices are a formula for trouble; reinforced by inept planning, they are a prescription for disaster. The key energy decision-makers were living in the past. The planners for our largest automobile companies complacently asserted as late as January 1973 that car buyers were "not interested" in fuel economy. I was told this by Ford, General Motors, and Chrysler vice-presidents at a Society of Automotive Engineers panel discussion in Detroit in January 1973 when I asked them why they were unconcerned about fuel economy.

The automobile companies failed to note the small car's steadily rising popularity. The small car's share of the market rose from 31 per cent in 1971, to 37 per cent in 1972, to 41 per cent in 1973. Such poor planning was rewarded with production cutbacks of one-third in the first quarter of 1974. In that period, before the nation skidded into a deep recession, over 100,000 automobile industry employees were laid off, and General Motors profits were down 87 per cent. A year later, hit by the recession their executives helped bring about, 250,000 automobile workers, or more than one third, were idle. At the same time, fuel-economy-conscious foreign car manufacturers increased their market penetration in the United States by one third, taking over 20 per cent of the market. For their part, the oil companies prepared for the energy crisis by maximizing profits in the finest corporate tradition. Oil company planners, the chairman of Exxon later admitted, made key investment decisions in 1968–69, expecting that national energy consumption in 1973 would be 5 per cent less than it proved to be, and that oil consumption would be 10 per cent less. These mistakes helped contribute to the shortage of U.S.-produced energy supplies in the mid-1970s.

No one was keeping the energy books, or keeping books on the energy industry. The oil companies were mesmerized by the low twenty-cents-per-barrel cost of producing Middle East oil. Average U.S. cost was about two dollars. Of the growth in U.S. oil consumption between 1971 and 1972, 17 per cent of the additional supplies came from the Middle East and North Africa. This figure of growth dependence on Middle East oil doubled to 34 per cent from 1972 through mid-1973. At the same time, Middle East imports rose from 500,000 barrels a day in 1971 to two million in late 1973.

Another signal should have been noted by electric utility and government energy accountants: fully 16 per cent of the total increase in electrical power consumption in the United States in 1971 was for the operation of air conditioners. It was like going from marijuana to heroin. Once we built our society and lifestyles on cheap energy, withdrawal became impossible. The ineptitude of corporate planners in missing the signs of excess was at least matched by their government counterparts. Most of our public officials did not recognize the signs of impending crisis. But a few did sound warnings. Secretary of Commerce Rudolph Peterson prophetically said in a September 1972 speech:

The national security implications of permanent and substantial reliance on fuel imports would be unpalatable. The largest clean fuel reserves are located in areas of low political stability or areas where political interests have traditionally been at odds with our own. The danger of supply interruptions at the source and risk of adverse price manipulation are simply too great under these circumstances to warrant wholesale dependence on foreign energy sources.

But no policies were designed to link the key considerations, from the Arabs to the air conditioners. Events were allowed to propel us into crisis.

BLAMING
THE ENVIRONMENTALISTS

When the crisis struck, the environmentalists were blamed. The accusers smugly handed out bumper stickers with the message, "Let the Bastards Freeze to Death in the Dark." Five principal charges were made.

First, the oil companies accused the environmentalists of holding up oil refinery construction. Mobil Oil made such a charge in advertisements in April 1973 when the first shortages were appearing. The facts have since proven the charge unfounded. But they are not easy to unravel. It is true U.S. refinery capacity fell far short of U.S. needs. In 1972 the United States consumed 16.0 million barrels of crude every day, but it had refinery capacity to process only 13.4 million barrels. Yet after years of lagging U.S. refinery construction, a complete turnabout occurred in 1973, when refinery capacity grew by 4.3 per cent while oil demand actually fell by 2.3 per cent. Moreover, industry announced plans to add another 3.5 million barrels per day in capacity by 1977. This turnabout cannot be attributed to the environmentalists who, before 1973, had opposed some refinery sites and have even today not ceased their opposition. For example, in 1974 New Hampshire, Mayland, and Florida refused proposals to site refineries on their coastlines.

The principal reason for the sudden surge in refinery construction was President Nixon's April 1973 decision to abolish the oil import quota system. President Eisenhower initiated the system in 1959. The quota limited crude oil imports, while refined products like residual oil for East Coast power plants entered the United States without quantitative import restrictions. To assure supplies of crude, a

THE NEW AMERICAN DREAM MACHINE

company building a $200-million oil refinery would have constructed it in an offshore area such as the Caribbean. The role of this ill-advised government policy was acknowledged by an American Petroleum Institute vice-president in a letter appearing in the August 14, 1973, *Washington Star:* "Last April's revisions in the oil import program have helped to somewhat clarify this situation and now provide an incentive for new U.S. refinery construction." This view was supported with a tone of incredulity by a July 1973 Federal Trade Commission staff study: "Spokesmen for several major oil companies argue that the lack of refinery expansion can be attributed to environmental problems. However now that import controls have been removed, and governmental intervention into the industry has become a strong threat, these companies have suddenly overcome their environmental problems." Naturally, the industry's underestimate of the demand growth rate, cited above, also caused it to underplan for domestic refinery capacity.[1]

The second charge leveled against environmentalists is that they opposed increased coal production, placing U.S. consumers in the hands of the Arabs. Two actions are alleged to have caused this to happen: opposition to strip mining and environmentally motivated bans on coal burning in eastern power plant boilers. U.S. coal production in 1973 was 591 million tons, up only 5.5 per cent from the 1969 level, a puny 1.3 per cent per annum compounded rate. Production from underground mines dropped from 364 million tons in 1969 to 316 million tons in 1973, a 13.2 per cent drop. Over the same period, strip-mined output rose 40 per cent, from 197 million tons to 275 million tons; its share of total coal output rose from 35 to 46 per cent.

Such dramatic growth in strip mining hardly supports the argument that the environmentalists held back coal production by opposition to strip mining. Nor did they have the tools for opposition; no federal legislation was on the books. And states with strong strip mining control programs have enjoyed more than their share of the

[1] The Arab cutoff and the subsequent drop in oil demand ended the debate over refinery capacity. Crude availability during the embargo was sufficient to utilize only 82 per cent of U.S. capacity, and in 1974 and 1975 U.S. refineries operated far short of full capacity. Several companies canceled plans for new refineries, reducing the 1974–77 planned augmentation of 3.5 million barrels to 2.3 million barrels per day.

increased output. However, federal safety legislation, if not environmental legislation, played a role in the decline in underground mining. The Federal Coal Mine Health and Safety Act of 1969 helped cause coal output per man-hour to drop steadily from that year forward. Over the 1969–73 period, underground coal miner productivity fell an astonishing 35 per cent.

Part of the coal case against the environmentalists is the allegation that they forced East Coast power plants to convert from dirty coal to cleaner oil. It is true, as the table illustrates, that increased dependence on foreign oil was a result of these conversions. The

U.S. OIL CONSUMPTION ANNUAL GROWTH RATES

	Total Oil Consumption	Vehicle Gasoline	East Coast Utilities (mostly imported)	
			Distillate	Residual
1967-72	5.4%	4.5%	5.2%	·7.2%
1971-72	7.3%	6.0%	8.5%	10.1%

highest oil consumption growth rates fed East Coast boilers. Meanwhile, oil's share of total U.S. energy supplied rose between 1950 and 1973 from 39 per cent to 46 per cent. Did environmentalists cause this to occur by forcing eastern electric power-generating plants to convert?

Conversion to oil took place for primarily economic reasons. In the 1960s the price of imported oil for East Coast utilities was $0.25 per million BTU[2] compared with a price of $0.30 per million BTU for coal delivered to the East after a costly railroad trip from Appalachia. Now that cartel-dictated oil prices have made coal more attractive, the utilities on the East Coast are not anxious to concede the role of profits in increasing our dependence on oil imports.

Environmentalists must accept responsibility for the third accusa-

[2] A BTU is the amount of heat needed to raise the temperature of one pound of water by one degree Fahrenheit. The BTU is the universal energy accounting unit, allowing coal, nuclear, oil, and gas energy to be viewed in common terms.

tion: their actions delayed oil production from fields on the North Slope of Alaska and offshore. To some, this alone is sufficient to place full blame for the 1973–74 crisis on the environmental movement. The 10-billion-barrel North Slope field was discovered in February 1968. Permit applications to install the 789-mile pipeline from Prudhoe Bay to Valdez was made on June 6, 1969. Significant amounts of oil could have been delivered by early 1974.

In 1969 the environmentalists were fresh from their early successes in the three-year battle to shoot down government funding for the SST. They sought another victory and thought they had achieved it in 1970 when the courts ordered the Department of the Interior to withhold its permit for the Alaska pipeline pending the completion of an environmental impact study. And defeat for the oil companies and the federal government at that stage was necessary. Oil company plans for exploiting the North Slope were poorly conceived, with few safeguards on construction and production to protect wildlife and the sensitive Alaskan tundra. The pipeline plans were in fact transferred to the Arctic circle from the hot, desert-dry Arab world. The incompetence of the federal government matched that of the oil companies. The Department of the Interior forgot its management responsibilities as guardian of much of Alaska's territory.

These deficiencies were soon corrected. By May 1972 the government had responded and much improved construction plans were on the table. Yet the environmentalists persisted. What had been a victory became a costly defeat: in 1974 Congress waived application of the National Environmental Policy Act to the Alaskan pipeline.

A more conciliatory environmental strategy could have resulted in at least another million barrels per day for U.S. markets in 1974, some from the North Slope and the rest from greater offshore oil production. While this amount would not have covered the 2.7-million-barrel-a-day shortfall and eclipsed the 1973–74 crisis entirely, it would have replaced the difference between our 15 per cent shortage and our 10 per cent savings from conservation efforts. More importantly, it would have vastly improved the movement's image, causing environmentalists to be seen as constructive opponents rather than obstructionists.

The fourth accusation against the environmentalists blames them for increasing the demand for energy to fuel cleanup efforts. For example, reduced automotive miles per gallon performance resulted from emission controls on cars. In 1973 the automobile consumed 4.3 million barrels of petroleum products per day, or about 26 per cent of total U.S. oil consumption. Of this amount, 300,000 barrels per day, or 7 per cent of automotive consumption, was due to the fuel penalties associated with emission-control devices. Indisputably, environmental controls contributed to the 1973–74 crisis.

The story of automobile emission controls and fuel consumption is not a simple one of environmental zealotry. The 1973 cars with emission-control devices experienced a 10 per cent fuel penalty compared with uncontrolled pre-1968 cars. But small cars under 3,500 pounds experienced a 2 to 3 per cent benefit, while large cars suffered a 14 to 18 per cent penalty. Furthermore, car air conditioners caused a 9 to 20 per cent fuel penalty, car weight up to a 50 per cent penalty, and the use of an automatic transmission a 2 to 15 per cent penalty. Over the 1968–73 period, average car weight went up about 150 pounds, the proportion of cars with air conditioning increased from 46 per cent to over 70 per cent and the proportion of cars with automatic transmission went from 8 per cent to 93 per cent.

These developments had an impact on fuel economy and gasoline consumption in 1973 comparable to the 300,000 barrels caused by emission-control penalties. Such a comparison adds a necessary perspective when it is recognized that the public health is being protected by emission reductions, a claim difficult to make for the increasingly luxurious automobile. But it does not deny the fact that emission controls played a major role in boosting U.S. oil requirements.

The other major energy cost attributable to the environmental movement is the 20,000-barrel-per-day energy equivalent needed to operate municipal and industrial facilities removing air and water pollutants. While this energy cost is small, it can be expected to increase sharply over the next few years and must be addressed by environmental policymakers.

The fifth and last charge against the environmentalists relates to the failure of nuclear power to meet expectations that it would be providing a major share of U.S. power in the 1970s. About 5 per cent of electrical energy, or 1 per cent of all energy, was supplied by nuclear plants in 1973. Environmentalists sought and obtained the landmark Calvert Cliffs court ruling that environmental impact statements must be filed before the Atomic Energy Commission (now the Nuclear Regulatory Commission) grants interim operating licenses to nuclear power plants. Critics have blamed this decision and related environmental actions for nuclear power's disappointing performance.

By mid-1973, thirty-two nuclear power units were in operation with a net electrical capacity of 17,212 megawatts, more than a threefold increase from 1970's 5,000 megawatts. Over the years the AEC made repeated projections of the future availability of nuclear power. Almost invariably these were optimistic. Of the eight forecasts over the 1955–67 period predicting 1970 capacity, seven were high, one by more than fivefold, none was lower, and one (1962's) was correct. Environmental concerns cannot be blamed for delays in reaching the 1970 goals, because at that early date environmentalists were not actively opposing nuclear plants. Neither were 1975's estimates proved correct—they averaged 50,000 megawatts, but 1975 capacity was only 35,000 megawatts.

A variety of studies have been made of the licensing delays caused by environmental reviews. One cited by Council on Environmental Quality chairman Russell Train found only nine of seventy-five plants delayed by environmental interventions. The other plants were delayed by low labor productivity, strikes, poor equipment, and similar problems alone, or by some of these factors together with environmental opposition. For example, thirty-five plants were delayed by fuel densification and possible steam line breakage problems.

In 1973 the Federal Power Commission studied delays in the twenty-eight plants slated to be operating that year. The study found 229 plant-months of delay attributable to labor problems, production shortages, late deliveries, breakdowns, and other production and engineering failures. The delays due to public lawsuits and regulatory requirements were only thirty-two plant-months, or 14 per cent of those caused by developments unrelated to the environment. Clearly the failures of nuclear power cannot be laid at the doorstep of the ecologists.

In considering the full range of energy costs associated with the environmental program and their contribution to the sharply rising demand that placed the United States at the mercy of the Middle East kingdoms in 1973, it is fair to say that the environmentalists were no more prescient of the problem than others and no more capable of acting to prevent it. A visionary policy would have permitted more rapid development of U.S. offshore and Alaskan oil supplies and sought more vigorous actions to improve automobile fuel economy. More compelling is that the environmentalists have been unfairly blamed for holding up oil refinery and nuclear power plant construction and coal mining. Nor did the environmentalists spur East Coast power plant conversions to the consumption of cheap oil. Industry made the switch, motivated by profits, not purity.

Nothing the environmentalists could have done would have prevented the 1973–74 crisis, short of yielding on cleanup altogether, and even this would not have saved an energy industry and government so poorly equipped to plan a few years ahead. The public seems to agree. A December 1973 Gallup Poll found the public apportioning blame as follows: oil companies, 25 per cent; the federal government, 23 per cent (including 3 per cent who said Congress); the Nixon Administration, including President Nixon, 19 per cent; U.S. consumers, 16 per cent; Arab nations, 7 per cent; and ecologists, 2 per cent. While the environmentalists must accept a small share of the blame, they look good by comparison with government and oil industry ineptitude. But next time things could be different. A wise policy does not assume others will be negligent—again.

Environmentalists must shape a positive energy strategy for the next decade. Such a strategy cannot be the "no-no" strategy of the past and present which finds environmentalists opposed to energy production from every major source. It is not enough to be futile opponents; environmentalists must have a positive plan. This is the lesson of the energy crisis.

ENERGY, A DOMINANT COMMODITY

The point of departure for an environmentally responsible energy strategy is a full assessment of the ways energy production and consumption affect the environment. The short answer is: every way. For energy is a "dominant commodity" (see Chapter 1), so pervasive in its environmental impacts and its role in our lives that it needs special public policy attention. No foreseeable technology will permits us to have a clean environment and energy in the amounts to which we have become accustomed. The only course is conserve it. And conserving energy means purging America's lifestyle of its energy excesses.

A catalogue of energy abuses of the environment would fill several shelves. In the extraction of raw energy sources like strip-mined coal or offshore oil, the ecologies of land and sea are threatened. In transport, oil spills are a risk. In the processing of energy for eventual combustion, radiation is emitted from nuclear fuel processing plants, and oil refineries pockmark the East Coast. When combustion takes place, practically every known air pollutant is emitted, and heated effluents threaten our rivers. Our commercial airlines could navigate from coast to coast by following the smoke plumes from our power plants. And airplanes mark their own paths with pollution.

A perversity complicates the task of cleaning up these sources of pollution. If we reclaim land, more energy is consumed in grading to prepare the earth. The application of scrubbers and cooling towers to remove sulfur oxides and heat will consume the equivalent of thousands of barrels of oil per day. We face a law of diminishing technological returns to clean up. The more we clean up, the more the energy required. Meeting these new environmentally related energy demands will in turn result in environmental damage.

The scale of our energy activities all but exceeds man's grasp and his ability to comprehend their environmental impacts. We presently have more than a thousand steam-electric power plants. To this we must add, if our energy habits do not change, one new U.S. power plant unit per week for the next twenty-five years, requiring one new site per month if we assume four 1,000-megawatt units per site. To meet U.S. oil demand, at least seventeen 975,000-barrel supertankers would have to dock in the United States every day. And energy investments may require $750 billion, which is up to 35 per cent of all U.S. investment over the next decade. This compares with only 21 per cent during the 1960s. It is fair to say that increasing energy output and environmental quality are linked as two sides of the same coin: if one goes up, the other goes down.

Water Pollution   Energy is the source of three of the major causes of water pollution; acid mine drainage and suspended solids runoff from coal mines; thermal discharges from power plants; and oil spills from oil transport, storage, and waste disposal.

Fish populations in major U.S. rivers, including the Delaware and Hudson, have changed toward less desirable "rough" fish such as carp and shad because heavy thermal loads have raised river temperatures. The low efficiency of fossil-fueled power results in about 65 per cent of the heat being wasted through discharge to the air and water. Nuclear power plants are even less efficient, losing 70 per cent of the heat generated. Today's nuclear and fossil-fuel electric power plants discharge about 50 trillion gallons of heated waste water annually, roughly 15 per cent of the total flow of U.S. rivers and streams.

EPA's new standards will require all new power plants and many of the larger existing ones to utilize cooling towers to reduce thermal discharges to a level that does not alter the fish population of our natural waters. Presently only 20 per cent of the existing U.S. power plants are so fitted, but by 1980 another 20 per cent of present plants and all new ones will have constructed the capacity to reduce thermal discharges to zero. The cost of meeting this requirement is about $10 billion over ten years.

Damage from surface mining is caused by suspended solids or silt runoff and acid mine drainage. In 1975 the dirt load on our rivers and streams was about 84 million tons. By way of comparison, the 1973 sediment discharge from the mouth of the Mississippi River, which drains most of the country, was 245 million tons. Coal-mine-related siltation and acid mine drainage pollute nearly 13,000 miles of streams. Because fish cannot live in acid, these streams are sterile of life. Another 145,000 acres of lakes and reservoirs have been similarly polluted. One study estimated that in 1966, four million tons of sulfuric acid were leached into 5,700 miles of our waters. These wastes kill fish, ruin water supplies, and deny the public recreational opportunities in lakes, rivers, and streams. The Department of the Interior has fixed the cleanup bill of this difficult pollution problem at about $7 billion.

Oil spills are another major category of energy-related water pollution. EPA is reasonably sure that about 18.8 million gallons of oil were spilled into navigable U.S. waters in 1972 by approximately eight thousand incidents. About half that again was spilled on U.S. soil. EPA is still trying to account for the fate of 700 million gallons of waste oil removed from automobile crankcases and similar activities. A large portion of this is poured down city sewers.

Worldwide annual oil spillage has been estimated to be 1.4 billion gallons, half of which goes into the oceans. A 1972 National Oceanic and Atmospheric Administration survey of 700,000 square miles of ocean from Cape Cod to the Caribbean found globs of floating oil in up to 90 per cent of the area. It is true, as some have argued, that supertankers, not now used in the U.S., can reduce the number of collision opportunities over what might occur if smaller tankers are deployed. Yet there is a price. The largest of these tankers carry 300,000 tons, or about two million barrels (one eighth of one day's U.S. consumption). Complete spillage of such an amount in one accident would increase oil pollution by 15 per cent.

The advent of the supertanker illustrates the futility of reliance on technological solutions alone to reduce the ecological threats from energy. In 1967 the *Torrey Canyon,* a 100,000-ton-class supertanker, broke up off England's holiday coasts. Hardly a corner of the world has been spared since. A 200,000-ton-class tanker, the *Metula,* ran aground in the Strait of Magellan in September 1974, spreading one fourth of its cargo on seventy-five miles of Chile's coastline. This accident was quickly followed by the grounding of the 237,600-ton supertanker *Showa Maru* halfway around the world in the Straits of Malacca. The supertankers struck again in Europe in early 1975 when the 88,000-ton *Jacob Maersk* hit a sandbar off Portugal's shoreline and exploded.

Thus far America has been spared. There is no U.S. superport. We, fortunately, can only estimate, as a Corps of Engineers study concluded, that the loss of a 300,000-ton supertanker off the Atlantic coast would saturate every foot of two hundred miles of our cherished and most used beaches and coastlines.

It takes twenty-two miles to bring today's 300,000-ton supertankers to a stop. Shipbuilders are not yet satisfied. They continue to escalate the risks. At least four 500,000-ton supertankers are under construction. Controlling supertankers is likely to prove as difficult as any ecological endeavor. Five years after the Santa Barbara oil spill, the responsible U.S. oil companies agreed in an out-of-court settlement to pay $9.7 million for damages. This occurred in the United States, where strong laws are in effect and the public outcry was unprecedented. World Court litigation takes decades. Its effectiveness in controlling supertankers operating under many country flags, often having passed through several hands in the used-supertanker market, is not likely to constitute a credible threat to supertanker operators.

Air Pollution   Energy-producing and energy-consuming activities are by far the principal cause of air pollution. Try to name a source of air pollution that is not caused by fuel burning. Power plants, oil refineries, automobiles, even oil-burning home heaters, all contribute millions of tons of air pollutants to the atmosphere each year. Over 80 per cent of all sulfur oxides and nitrogen oxides emissions and over 60 per cent of all carbon monoxide and hydrocarbon emissions are from energy sources.

Several assumptions are necessary to get a more precise estimate of the *damages* caused by energy-related emissions. First, carbon monoxide measured in tons is the major pollutant. Energy sources emit over 70 million tons of carbon monoxide per year. But carbon monoxide is not on a per-ton basis as threatening to human health as are sulfur oxides and derivative sulfates or particulates (fine dirt particles). These have been present in the major air-pollution disasters: the Meuse Valley, Belgium, in 1930, when in five days more than six thousand people became ill and about sixty died; Donora, Pennsylvania, in October 1948, when six thousand became ill and twenty died; and the biggest recorded air pollution disaster, London in 1952, when four thousand died in two weeks.

Adjusting the tonnages of each pollutant by its severity results in a single indicator of the energy air-pollution problem. The accompanying graph shows energy-related pollutants to be responsible for 63 per cent of the air-pollution problem.

Without controls to reduce emissions, total air-pollution damage (including damage to health, property, and vegetation) to the U.S. citizens in 1976 would have been $23.5 billion. As indicated by the graph, energy would have been responsible for 63 per cent, or $14 billion of the damage from air pollution.

Every day in our major cities people get sick and people die be-

SHARE OF AIR-POLLUTION PROBLEMS AS MEASURED BY TONS EMITTED TIMES SEVERITY FACTORS*

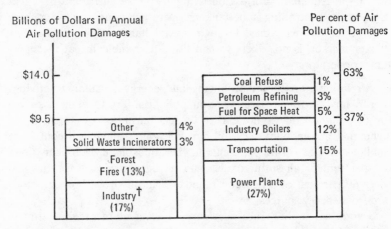

Billions of Dollars in Annual Air Pollution Damages

Per cent of Air Pollution Damages

* As developed by Lyndon R. Babcock and Niren L. Nagda, the severity factors are: particulate matter 52, sulfur oxides 29, nitrogen oxides 24, hydrocarbons 10, and carbon monoxide 1. "Cost-Effectiveness of Emissions Control," *The Journal of the Air Pollution Control Association,* Vol. 23, No. 3.

† Except for petroleum refining.

cause of energy-caused air pollution. A recent study of south central Los Angeles found long-time residents to be up to 40 per cent more likely to have lung cancer than those residing in less smog-prone areas, a finding attributed tentatively and in part to refinery emissions. Not only is the increased incidence of cancer related to air pollution in various studies, so are cardiovascular and respiratory diseases. Infants and aged adults are the most frequent victims of air pollution. One study of 117 metropolitan areas found that if sulfur dioxide levels were cut in half, the mortality rate would drop by 4.5 per cent. A study of New York City found that over a six-year period, 12 per cent of the over one-half million deaths would not have occurred when they did except for air pollution. This is an "excess death" rate of twenty-nine per day, or ten thousand per year.

Land Pollution   Our land is greatly abused by energy production. As of 1972, four million acres had been strip-mined, an area about the size of Hawaii. Strip mining affects 241,800 acres per year, an area six times the size of Washington, D.C. If coal production is doubled (a low 1985 estimate in the eyes of energy planners) and strip mining continues to be favored over underground mining, the land area affected will likely increase threefold. Moreover, for every ten tons of coal utilized, another ton of solid wastes is produced. At the mine there is spoilage. At the power plant a place must be found to dispose of ash by-products and sludge from the sulfur dioxide removal processes.

But the land-pollution problems of coal production are small in comparison with those expected from shale oil production. From the recently leased lands in Colorado, Wyoming, and Utah, the government hopes to demonstrate the feasibility of producing one million barrels per day by the early 1980s. Were this done by surface mining, the process would require the movement of land tonnages about equal to the entire coal output of the United States in 1973, almost 600 million tons—six hundred tons of shale and overburden for every barrel of oil. The solid waste problems of coal production would be multiplied twenty-two times to get the same amount of energy.

Not just mining but energy combustion requires land. Anyone who has seen a 2,000-megawatt steam-electric power plant realizes only so many can be sited in the United States. With associated transmission lines and support facilities, the plant scars the landscape like a gigantic moon crater. Assuming the energy demand growth rate continues at the rates of the last decade, the Federal Power Commission has estimated that by the year 2000 these new plants will pre-empt eight million acres of land plus another three million acres for transmission lines. The ability of power plants to pre-empt land was vividly illustrated by a Rand Corporation study that foresaw by the year 2000 a nuclear power plant every twenty miles along California's coast.

Radiation Perhaps the most difficult energy-environmental dilemma is posed by nuclear power. Electricity from nuclear power plants is cheap. In day-to-day operation these plants are almost devoid of activity. Constant materials movement is not required and in place of the belching smokestacks of fossil-fueled power plants is a gleaming white dome. Appearance notwithstanding, the threats of nuclear power constitute a scary list: increased frequency of cancer and genetic mutations caused by radiation emissions from power plants and fuel processing and disposal; catastrophes, killing up to thousands and injuring up to tens of thousands; and terror, with consequences impossible to estimate, at the hands of those diverting enriched materials or wastes to weapons or explosive use.

If nuclear risks are estimated, assuming only a 5.2 per cent per year nuclear energy growth rate, the prospects are frightening. Yearly nuclear fuel shipments at the end of this century could number ten thousand by rail or sixty thousand by truck. If past accident experience is a guide and the material is shipped by rail, we should expect a minor rail accident involving nuclear fuel at least every three years and a severe accident every twelve years. If shipments are by truck, a severe accident would be expected every other year.

The emergency core cooling risks of nuclear power generators are even more troublesome. AEC estimates suggest a pipe rupture will occur by 1983. By the end of the century we can expect one a year if a thousand reactors are operating. How many of these failures will require the operation of the emergency core cooling system? How often will this system fail, causing large amounts of radioactivity to escape, cutting a swath of lethal effects for miles? These issues are still being debated, while we build feverishly.

An AEC-sponsored study by MIT professor Norman C. Rasmussen concluded the worst-case accident would kill or injure 48,300 people. Critics of the study set this number at 120,000 people. On the issue of the likelihood of such an accident, the AEC study suggests that an accident causing ten or more fatalities would occur once every 2,500 years if one hundred plants are operating or once every 250 years if the one thousand plants expected are built. The report's critics note that the methodology used to predict the probability of such occurrences has already proved wrong. The National Aeronautics and Space Administration used the same approach to predict there would be a rocket motor failure once in every ten thousand starts. Actual experience was much worse: four failures for every hundred starts.

Who should be believed? One sign the public utilities do not believe the AEC studies is their vigorous lobbying for the Price-Anderson Act, which would use federal funds to indemnify victims of nuclear accidents causing more than $160 million in losses. Another disconcerting recent development was the failure in March 1975 of the emergency core cooling system in the U.S.'s largest operating nuclear power plant. An electrical fire was started at TVA's Browns Ferry plant in Alabama when a worker's candle ignited wiring insulation. Because of the fire, the plant's operators attempted to activate the emergency core cooling system. It failed. Fortunately, an improvised approach cooled the reactor.

Strontium 90, cesium 137, and plutonium 239 sound like rock groups. But they are far more potent. They are the by-products of nuclear fission. These radioactive wastes will most likely outlast the U. S. Constitution. Strontium and cesium decay over a period of six hundred years and plutonium, among the most toxic materials known to man, will be around for 250,000 years. Presently neither the government nor the utilities know where to dispose of these wastes. By 2000, roughly 60 million gallons will have been produced. Already 430,000 gallons of wastes from weapons production operations in Hanford, Washington, have leaked from underground tanks, endangering the water table.

A recent EPA study has assessed the health consequences that can be linked to just the low-level continuous emissions of radiation over the next fifty years. An additional 1,500 illnesses and between 3,070 and 5,890 deaths will occur as a result of normal, day-to-day radiation emissions from nuclear plants and associated facility operations. Leukemia, or cancer of the bone, and lung and thyroid cancer are among the effects. This additional health damage accompanying nuclear power production compares with the three thousand to four thousand cancer deaths per year attributable to background or natural sources of radiation like the sun.

For a time some believed nuclear power represented a lesser environmental threat than fossil-fueled energy generation. Now nuclear power is beset by its own environmental problems. Most likely nuclear power will demonstrate again the central theme of ecology: there is no such thing as a free lunch.

This recitation of the environmental risks of energy use is not intended to indict energy production; energy has given society incalculable benefits and opportunities. It is not intended to condemn all forms of energy production; some, like natural gas, are inherently clean, and others can be controlled to practically minimize pollution.

Wishful thinking about solar, geothermal, or wind-powered energy production, however, is not a credible contribution to a serious effort to reduce external energy dependence by 1985. Wind power, for example, even at its peak use in 1850, provided only 11.8 million tons of coal equivalent in energy. Today this would represent about 2 per cent of national coal production, and today coal is far behind oil and gas as the third largest current source of energy in the United States. Geothermal energy, which has been lavishly praised by the environmentalists, does not prove so clean on close scrutiny. A recent review in the publication *Science* (March 7, 1975) of the world's largest geothermal power project in New Zealand found it in many respects more of a threat to the environment than a fossil-fueled plant. It discharges more waste heat, more arsenic and mercury. It even emits hydrogen sulfide, the gas that smells like rotten eggs. Solar energy is also much touted. But there is a major economic deterrent to the widespread application of solar power. To install a solar unit for heating a home would cost $4,000 to $6,000. This investment in most U.S. climates will not pay for itself in energy savings for almost two decades. By contrast, better insulation and storm windows cost about one- to two-tenths as much and can save up to half as much energy as a solar collector provides. Few Americans will be willing to invest in solar energy until entirely new systems are devised, and this will take decades.

The quantities of energy demanded, the alternatives available, and the pollution abatement technologies that can be employed yield an inescapable conclusion: there is no way to eliminate energy-caused pollution. The most efficient steam-electric plant in the engineer's dreams will still put half its raw energy input into the environment. While radiation risks can be reduced, they cannot be eliminated. Every power plant occupies scarce land. Every additional tanker raises the probability of a major oil spill. And every ton of coal produced yields a solid waste residue. Even efforts to reduce the pollution problems to a minimum incur substantial energy costs: 5 per cent of total power plant energy output is required to operate a sulfur dioxide scrubber and cooling tower on a coal-fired power plant.

True to form as a dominant commodity, energy must be controlled and managed by policies that have conservation or reducing the growth rate in consumption as their first objective.

THE GREAT ENERGY DEMAND GROWTH RATE DEBATE

The years 1973 and 1974 witnessed a continuous stream of suggestions from energy and environmental spokesmen on the desired energy demand growth rate. EPA's administrator Russell Train urged the annual demand growth rate be cut in half, to 2.5 per cent, and CEQ's Russell Peterson argued for 1.8 per cent. Later, government energy spokesmen William Simon and John Sawhill suggested 3 per cent. Oil industry executives sought more. Mobil Oil's president argued for 4.5 per cent as the best basis for a projection, since it represented an extrapolation of the growth rate of recent years. But Exxon's chairman thought 3 per cent would be enough. In March 1974 the Ford Foundation Energy Project issued a report intended to encompass the full range of possibilities. It had three scenarios: a "historical growth" projection at 3.4 per cent, a "technical fix" estimate at 1.7 per cent, and a "zero energy growth" option.

With so many spokesmen advocating growth rates from 1.7 per cent to 4.5 per cent, the public is understandably confused. Historical performance offers no clear guidance. Past energy consumption per annum growth rates have ranged as follows:

1900–1950	2.0%
1950–1960	2.8%
1960–1965	3.6%
1965–1973	4.8%

The clear upward trend is not encouraging. The statistics suggest, however, that in the first part of this century, when industrial growth surged, energy demand at 2 per cent was not excessive. This experience indicates that high employment levels (employment is most directly related to industrial output) and a lower energy demand growth rate may be compatible.

The debate on the energy growth rate is important to the United States not just for the preservation of the environment. A lower demand growth rate would simplify the task of reducing our dependence on foreign and possibly unstable sources of oil. There would in addition be an economic dividend. We would save at least $2 billion each month in payments to foreign oil suppliers. And the domestic investment required to increase U.S. energy production to levels adequate to free us from external oil dependence will be about one-third less if we can achieve a 2 per cent rather than a 4 per cent demand growth rate.

THE COAL IMPERATIVE

An energy policy can be constructed on a few key facts and assumptions. Three items are important: what is believed about the demand growth rate, what is believed about the availability of new U.S. supplies of natural gas and oil, and what is desired in terms of U.S. energy independence. All of these determinations converge to produce two possible 1985 situations, described in the accompanying table. One outcome (see the right column) assumes an energy demand growth rate between 1973 and 1985 of 2 per cent per year. This projection yields a total U.S. energy demand in 1985 from all sources (coal, oil, gas, imports, hydroelectric, nuclear, and oil shale) of 46.5 million barrels per day energy equivalent. The alternative 4 per cent per year demand growth rate projection pushes U.S. energy demand to the 58.9-million-barrel-per-day level in 1985, compared with 36.6 million barrels per day in 1973.

Sources of Supply   If these demand levels are to be met as fully as possible from domestic supplies, oil and gas production and nuclear output must be pushed to the maximum. From a practical standpoint neither oil nor gas production can be pushed very far. In 1975 U.S. oil production was two million barrels per day below the 10.9-million-barrel-per-day level shown in the table for 1973, just two years earlier. To increase U.S. production by five million barrels per day will more than consume what higher oil prices and new Alaskan and outer continental shelf oil fields can add to U.S. capacity. At most, another two million barrels per day from the outer shelf are

1985 PRODUCTION NECESSARY TO ACHIEVE ENERGY
INDEPENDENCE AT 4 PER CENT AND 2 PER CENT
ENERGY DEMAND GROWTH RATES (IN MILLIONS OF
BARRELS PER DAY)

U.S. Production	1973	1985	
		4%	2%
Oil	10.9	◄——— 13.8 ———►	
Natural Gas	11.2	◄——— 11.0 ———►	
Coal	6.9	26.9	14.5
Hydro	1.4	◄——— 1.6 ———►	
Nuclear	.1	◄——— 2.6 ———►	
Shale	—	◄——— 0.5 ———►	
Geothermal-Solar	—	◄——— 1.0 ———►	
TOTAL U.S. SUPPLY	30.5	57.4	45.0
TOTAL DEMAND	36.6	58.9	46.5
NET OIL IMPORTS	6.1	1.5	1.5

expected. The natural gas outlook is far bleaker. Already U.S.
supplies dropped 10 per cent between 1973 and 1975. Covering
these losses—and other losses as more fields expire—with offsetting
new gas production will be about the best that can be hoped for.

Nuclear power will assume a larger share of the growth burden.
The 1975 level shown in the table is thirteen times 1974 capacity.
Finally, the geothermal, solar, and shale-oil projections are probably
optimistic.

Oil Imports One solution would be to turn to oil imports. Indeed, before the October 1973 Arab embargo, that was U.S. policy.
The Department of the Interior's official forecast assumed that a
total of 25 million barrels of oil would be consumed in 1985. Of this
it was predicted that 14.8 million barrels per day of oil would be imported. Such a sum would have represented more imports than all
the oil consumed in the United States in 1970. The table assumes

only 15.3 million barrels per day of oil consumption in 1985, about a million barrels less than 1975's experience. Now it is widely accepted that the U.S. national security cannot tolerate the "dependence" implied by this obsolete government forecast.

Implicit in the table's projections for 1985 is a policy of reduced reliance on imported oil. Both the 2 per cent and 4 per cent forecasts assume that in 1985 the United States is dependent on external energy sources for no more than 10 per cent of total petroleum needs. At the bottom of the first column, the table describes where we stood in 1973, a useful point of reference. In that year the United States needed 17.0 million barrels per day of oil, of which 6.1 million barrels, or about 36 per cent, was imported. Imports from the Organization of Petroleum Exporting Countries (OPEC) accounted for half of all oil imports. Thus the 10 per cent oil dependency assumption for 1985 would leave the United States less than a third as vulnerable to foreign cutoffs as it was in 1973. In reality we would be much better off because Venezuelan, Nigerian, and other non-Arab imports could easily supply the 10 per cent oil import requirement (1.5 million barrels per day) for 1985.

Some environmentalists may be tempted to argue against efforts to reduce oil imports on the grounds that if domestic supplies are not exploited our environment will be spared. But there is an important environmental justification for avoiding dependence on overseas energy sources. If the United States were to devour a large share of the Arab world's energy supply—and that is essentially what our energy planners assumed before the embargo—risking primarily ocean pollution in the process, the rest of the nations of the world would be forced to bear heavy environmental as well as economic expenditures to increase their economic output and levels of income. The United States would be pre-empting more than its fair share of the ecologically and economically cheap Middle East oil. It is an ecological benefit that because of Arab action, the United States now must face directly the environmental cost and consequences of its profligate energy habits. We waste more, we should save more.

Coal: The New "Swing" Fuel   The outcome in 1985, if we experience a 4 per cent per annum growth rate while reducing oil dependence to less than 10 per cent, is inevitable environmental havoc. Coal is the problem. Even if a 2 per cent rate is assumed, we must cope with serious environmental problems from dramatically increased coal production. Referring to the preceding table, 50 million tons of coal per year is roughly equivalent to 492,000 barrels of oil per day. Thus, in the 2 per cent case for 1985, coal production would rise from today's 600 million tons to 1.3 billion tons. To meet a 4 per cent growth rate, assuming coal is the only source for which a *further* acceleration is possible, 2.3 billion tons of coal would need to be produced in 1985.

This difference of one billion tons of coal can be measured in a variety of ways: 12.4 million barrels of oil, or, if nuclear power plants could be built to carry the load, 360 of them with a generating capacity of 1,500 megawatts per site. We do not have these options. Increased coal production is the only choice. And coal output would have to increase at about 10 per cent per year to meet the requirements of the 4 per cent per year energy consumption growth case.

In 1972 and 1973, when domestic supplies fell short or demand rose more than expected, imported oil picked up the shortfall. For this reason, before the embargo, experts called imported oil the "swing" fuel. In the future, coal is the swing fuel, filling unexpected gaps between energy consumption and supply.

The environmental consequences of a fourfold increase in coal production required in the 4 per cent demand growth rate scenario are so large they are impossible to grasp. Sulfur oxide emissions would increase sharply, yielding sulfur dioxide and sulfate levels more than double present levels. The production of clean coal technologies such as stack gas scrubbers or coal gasification plants could not keep pace with the demand. Available production capacity and engineering skills are now estimated as just adequate to clean up emissions from existing plants. Strip mining difficulties will mount, in the West in particular. Meeting the supply side requirements of the 4 per cent option will simply mean the environment will be ignored; controls will have to be eased to achieve such an increase. In 1974 the National Academy of Engineers concluded that even if *all* environmental requirements were waived, coal output in 1985 could not exceed 1.8 billion tons.

In summary, the fight for a 2 per cent demand growth rate is a fight for survival of the environmental movement. If the country chooses a 4 per cent demand growth rate, massive environmental degradation will be the inevitable consequence.

To achieve a 2 per cent rate, all major sectors would need to alter fundamentally the way they use energy. For the two years 1972 and 1973, the average annual energy demand growth rate was a hefty 4.8 per cent. Conservation has a long way to go.

To reduce the energy demand growth rate to 2 per cent, we must get more national economic output per unit of energy input. The nation must build homes with reduced energy requirements to heat and cool them, design automobiles with much improved fuel economy, and devise manufacturing processes to produce everything from paper to steel with a reduced rate of energy consumed in the production process.

5.

SETTING ENERGY GOALS

In the early 1960s President John F. Kennedy set the goal of landing a man on the moon by the end of the decade. Without that goal the extraordinary success of the space program would not have been achieved. Major, once-in-a-decade national efforts need a focus for motivation and direction. For these reasons, goals must be set to reach the 2 per cent energy demand growth rate target established in the previous chapter. Such goals must have meaning for the public in terms of the day-to-day choices and opportunities people face. And the goals should be set with full knowledge of their monetary costs. Perhaps of most importance, Americans need to be told how their lifestyles will be changed by a reduced energy consumption growth rate, from more than 4 per cent to 2 per cent.

National goals are meaningless unless backed by public policies to facilitate their achievement. These policies could range from a laissez-faire belief that higher energy prices will inevitably reduce energy demand, to direct government regulation. Government policy can be flexible; it may start with guidelines or information and move on to regulation only after it is evident that higher prices have failed to yield a result consistent with a 2 per cent strategy. Higher prices alone will not achieve the 2 per cent goal. Economic studies predict that higher prices will reduce the demand growth rate to about 2.9 per cent. It is probably not a bad rule of thumb to expect the United States can get just over halfway from 4 per cent to 2 per cent with the aid of market forces. To travel the last part of the full distance, from about 3 per cent to 2 per cent, will require government intervention. Such intervention might include a gasoline tax, regulations on car size and air conditioning efficiency, and tax incentives to industry for the installation of new energy-saving equipment.

Devising an energy conservation strategy must proceed on a sector-by-sector basis. In round numbers, the largest U.S. energy-consuming sector is the industrial sector. Industry consumes about 41 per cent of energy used in the United States. However, since 1960 this sector has experienced the lowest growth rate in energy consumption, between 3.5 and 4 per cent. Next in size is the transportation sector, which consumes about 25 per cent. Consumption growth rates in transportation have been pushed to higher than 4.5 per cent by the sharp rise in gasoline energy consumption. Home or residential use is the third largest consuming sector, absorbing about 20 per cent of all energy used. Consumption rates in this sector, pushed upward by the surge in home-building and air-conditioning use in the 1960s, have far exceeded 4.5 per cent in the last fifteen years. Next, about 14 per cent of energy used in the United States in recent years has gone to the commercial sector to heat and cool large shopping centers and new glass-enclosed office buildings. The growth rate in energy use in this sector has also exceeded 4.5 per cent. In every sector, therefore, major cutbacks in energy use are necessary if a national 2 per cent per year rate of growth in energy use is to be attained.

TRANSPORTATION
PUTTING THE AUTOMOBILE
ON A DIET

The transportation sector is the most promising target for energy-saving reforms. Gasoline demand grew by 6 per cent in 1973. The share of energy wasted in conversion to useful work is greater in the transportation sector than in any other. Our cars waste about 78 per cent of the energy we feed them. Moreover, the lifestyle value of much of the work we ask our cars to perform with the remaining 22 per cent is about nil. For example, it takes about twice as much energy to move a 5,000-pound car as it does to power a 2,500-pound car. The former gets about ten miles per gallon, the latter, twenty miles per gallon. How much would our lifestyles suffer if the over half of all Americans who drive gas guzzlers would shift to smaller, more efficient cars?

We have over 107 million cars in the United States. Recently about 10 million (10 per cent) have been added and fewer (7 per cent) retired or junked every year. The average car is driven ten thousand miles yearly and consumes seven hundred gallons of gas. It will travel about a fourth further in 1985. More cars and more driving will combine to increase miles traveled by cars about by 34 per cent by 1985.

Automobiles currently consume about 14 per cent of the energy used in this country. But they require 31 per cent of the petroleum consumed. Because oil imports are the key U.S. energy problem, automobiles must bear the brunt of a conservation program. Automobiles, while they are inefficient now—the average gets about 13 miles per gallon—are traded in and retired so quickly that vastly more efficient cars can be put into use in a few years. Many families realized this potential overnight in the 1973–74 crisis by leaving their gas-guzzling heavyweight in the garage and driving their small car. Others bought new small cars. Compact and subcompact sales jumped from 37 per cent of total car sales in 1972 to 41 per cent in 1973 to almost 54 per cent in January 1974. Unfortunately, as shortages eased, the economy car share fell back to 48 per cent in March 1974. Drivers also helped by reducing highway speeds, saving about 100,000 barrels per day. U.S. gasoline consumption in February 1974 was 13.1 per cent below levels projected without the embargo, but after the embargo ended these conservation savings almost vanished, to about 7 per cent for the year of 1974.

The appropriate target for automobile energy savings between now and 1985 is a 3.3-million-barrel-per-day saving, in comparison with the unrestrained 4 per cent demand growth rate forecast. Fully one fourth of the reduction for all sectors from 4 per cent to 2 per cent demand per year could be attained by this achievement alone. A zero demand growth rate for automotive gasoline use is the equivalent of a 0.5 per cent per year reduction in the overall energy demand growth rate, from 4 per cent to 3.5 per cent. This result can be achieved by improving the fuel economy of all automobiles on the road from 1973's thirteen miles per gallon to twenty-two miles per gallon in 1985 and by reducing average vehicle weight by five hundred pounds.

Improved Fuel Economy   New Car fuel economy must improve dramatically from 1975's average performance of 15.8 miles per gallon. In 1980 it must reach 22.9 miles per gallon, and in 1985, 25 miles per gallon. In 1975 President Ford got a commitment from the automobile industry to improve fuel economy to 19.5 miles per gallon by 1980. Detroit can do more, although it is doubtful that it can reach the 27.5 miles per gallon target established by the Energy Policy and Conservation Act in December 1975.

A potential improvement to 28 miles per gallon for some cars has been identified by EPA. Diesel cars get 70 per cent better fuel economy than gasoline engines. A four-cylinder Volkswagen diesel has been tested at EPA's laboratory in Michigan that achieved 50 miles per gallon for highway driving and 40 miles per gallon in the city. Two entirely new technologies show promise—the stratified-charge engine and the Stirling engine. Shell has demonstrated a "hot-spot" stratified-charge system that employs heat from the exhaust manifold to vaporize fuel entering the combustion chamber, which achieved fuel economy gains of up to 50 per cent. The more revolutionary Stirling engine is an external combustion engine that could be coming off production lines by 1985 with at least 25 per cent better fuel economy.

A more mundane improvement would be to equip all cars with radial tires, which improve fuel economy by about 3 per cent. In 1972 only 7 per cent of U.S. cars had radials; in 1973, 20 per cent; and in 1975, 50 per cent. Closer inspection of our cars to keep them in tune could save another 6 per cent.

Smaller Cars   If, in addition to better fuel economy, there is a dramatic shift to small cars so that by 1985 80 per cent of all cars sold are either compacts or subcompacts, the full 3.3 million barrels per day can be saved. As a consequence, average car weight would be reduced by 500 pounds, from 4,000 pounds today to 3,500 pounds in 1985. This is equivalent to increasing the share of compacts and subcompacts of the new car market to 80 per cent by 1985. In 1985 62 per cent of all cars on the road would be small cars.

In the process of achieving automobile fuel economy improvements, there may be additional energy savings. Twenty-five per cent of the economy's energy demand is utilized to support the automobile industry. While only 14 per cent is consumed in our gas tanks, the rest is consumed in the production of steel, aluminum, and other materials for vehicles, road building, and servicing and repair. Smaller cars will facilitate gains in these areas.

Hard policy choices must be made to achieve the automobile fuel economy gains just described. Obviously reliance on the market will help; higher prices and shortages have spurred a shift to small cars and an interest in Detroit in improving fuel economy. Yet additional incentives and regulations will be necessary to supplement market forces. For one thing, the consumer is unlikely to get the full story. Detroit's Big Three—Ford, General Motors, and Chrysler—are determined to resuscitate big-car sales. Big-car advertising campaigns have not abated. Television personalities are making claims that big-car fuel economy is high, citing tests of warmed-up cars driving long distances (usually downhill) at optimum fuel-economy speeds. Most of our driving is done under less efficient suburban conditions. As long as profit margins are higher on large cars, and they inevitably will be if Detroit's advertising continues to mislead many to believe that big is best, automotive fuel economy will escape us.

In 1973, while at EPA, I instituted a fuel-economy labeling program to place on each new car a label describing its energy performance relative to other alternatives, particularly smaller cars. While the Detroit manufacturers put the labels on, many of their dealers, witnessing the devastating effect they had on purchasing choices, scraped them off. In 1975 Congress made mile-per-gallon labeling mandatory and set a 1980 fuel-economy standard for new cars of 20.5 miles per gallon. It is likely that achievement of the automobile fuel-economy goal will also require controls over industry advertising to ensure the small-car case is made, and an increased per-gallon gas tax.

Gasoline taxes have proven a difficult policy measure for either the President or Congress to adopt. This performance is lucid testimony to the difficulty of implementing lifestyle reforms. Our political system is not prepared. In 1973 on five occasions, Treasury deputy secretary William Simon urged President Nixon to propose a ten-cent-per-gallon tax on top of the then four-cent federal tax. By 1975, per-gallon prices had risen by about twenty-five cents, to sixty cents. Weakened by Watergate, President Nixon was reluctant to propose a tax that Congress would probably not have passed before the November 1974 election. In December 1975, as Federal Energy Administration staff members began to see the much-ballyhooed Project Independence goals slipping away, the idea of a gas tax was revived. But when the White House heard about the studies, they were summarily quashed.

Yet a tax would help ensure against a return to the heavy-car era and put windfall energy profits in the public till rather than in oil industry pockets. A ninety-cent-per-gallon price would ensure that 79 per cent of cars sold would have high fuel economy. In Japan, where gasoline sells for $1.50 per gallon, cars are small. In Europe, where the price is near $1.25 per gallon, average car weight is 3,080 pounds, having increased from 2,680 since 1960. A gas tax is regressive, taxing the poor proportionally more than the rich. But it is not as regressive as is generally believed; the poor own smaller and fewer cars, which together yield better fuel economy than the heavyweights driven by the rich. The poor drive less and use mass transit more. Of course, the regressive effects of a gas tax can be offset by other tax concessions for lower income groups.

A literally fatal disadvantage of policies to encourage small cars is the potentially deleterious consequences for automobile safety. Conventional wisdom holds that large cars are safer. If one is engaged in a two-car collision with a heavier car, the conventional wisdom is correct. The small-car occupant is 38 per cent more likely to be injured and 75 per cent more likely to be killed than the large-car occupant. But in a single car collision the small car is safer. A car absorbs the energy represented by its own mass and the square of its velocity. Thus, if one hits a fixed object, whether a car or a bridge, the larger car holds a disadvantage because the so-called "crush distance" between the front bumper and the passenger must absorb the higher momentum. The "crush distance" in a small car is proportionally greater in comparison to its weight than the large car. Finally, because large cars are more difficult to control, they have more accidents than small ones.

In short, the small-car driver is endangered not because he drives a small car, but because others drive large cars. The answer is to reduce the number of large cars on the road. A weight tax would be a good approach to achieving this goal, and it would help fuel-economy performance. But Congress has been oblivious to the threat to small cars on America's highways. In 1974 Congress passed a law permitting maximum truck weights to increase from 73,280 pounds to 80,000 pounds. In this action Congress ignored a National Highway Traffic Safety Administration finding that the number of non-truck fatalities per hundred car-truck accidents increases at a rate of 1.1 for each 10,000-pound truck weight increase. Also ignored was advice that the increase in truck weight approved would reduce highway life by between 25 and 40 per cent.

An additional fuel saving of up to 185,000 barrels per day is possible if the country adheres to a fifty-five-mile-per-hour speed limit. More probable is a lesser gain of around 125,000 barrels from the base-line projection because, legally or illegally, higher speeds will probably prevail on sparsely traveled open roads, particularly those between the Mississippi and the Rocky Mountains.

Public Transit Another provision of a 2 per cent strategy is an incentive to use mass transportation. The next chapter details the necessary reforms to reduce automobile traffic in urban areas and/or highly traveled interurban routes by shifting trips to mass transit, rail, and bus. The bus is 2.5 times as energy-efficient as the automobile: assuming an average load factor of 1.5 for the car and only 30 per cent for the bus, the car consumes 6,400 BTUs per passenger mile, compared with a bus's 2,380. Urban electrical rail traffic is about two times as efficient as urban automobile travel, whereas intercity rail is only 20 per cent more energy-saving than intercity automobile, primarily because many interurban trains have low load factors.

A reliable estimate of the energy savings achievable by shifts to mass transit and car pooling is highly dependent on important local circumstances, such as the extent to which transit fares are subsidized, the disincentives to parking and operating a car such as tolls and limited parking spaces, and the aggressiveness and skill with which mass transit operators make public transit available at times and locations attractive to potential riders.

EPA considered some of these problems in devising plans that seek to reduce traffic in twenty-two major U.S. cities by 10 to 20 per cent. These plans are illustrative of the nature of traffic reductions that might be achieved with a national commitment to shift from the private car to mass transit. Assuming 25 per cent of the reduction called for in the plans is achieved by car pooling and the other 75 per cent of trips are picked up by mass transit, by 1977 a fuel saving of 154,000 barrels per day is possible. If in our major cities by 1985 a 10 per cent reduction is achieved, the energy savings would be 347,000 barrels per day. These are conservative estimates. Any substantial effort to implement a thoroughgoing transit reform in this country will achieve these results.

Freight   An additional opportunity for transportation energy savings is in the transport of freight. The range of efficiencies of the alternative modes of freight transport is apparent in the accompanying table.

COMPARATIVE FREIGHT TRANSPORTATION ENERGY
EFFICIENCIES AND SHARES OF FREIGHT MOVED*

	Energy Efficiency ('000 BTUs per Ton Mile)	1970 Share of Freight Moved
Pipeline	450 ⎱	46.0%
Waterway	680 ⎰	
Railroad	670	35.0%
Truck	2,800	19.0%
Airplane	42,000	0.2%

* Source: Eric Hirst, *Science and Public Affairs,* Nov. 1973, p. 38.

Recent experience has witnessed a dramatic improvement in energy efficiency in the movement of intercity freight. In fact, comparing 1970 with 1950, total energy consumption for intercity freight *decreased* by 12 per cent, even though the tonnage moved increased by 74 per cent. This is explained by the conversion of trains from coal-burning steam locomotives to diesel engines. Diesels require one-fifth the energy used by their chugging predecessors.

However, over this same period, trains lost 12 per cent of the freight market, 5 per cent to the comparably energy-efficient waterways and more efficient pipelines, and 6 per cent to the much more energy-wasteful truck. Trucks have been favored by vast subsidies to the interstate highway system and their advantages for short, timely, and flexible hauls.

We are not likely to achieve substantial energy savings in freight transportation. We have already reaped the gains of diesel-powered locomotives. It will be difficult to reverse the freight shares in favor of railroads because of the truck's many convenience advantages. But the 1985 projection, which anticipates an even further eclipse of rail freight's role by truck and air freight use, can be reduced.

Some reforms are already under way. Whereas before the embargo piggyback train freight (trucks on flatcars) was expected to grow by 5 per cent in 1974, after the embargo there was a 20 per cent jump. Piggybacking provides many of the advantages of truck traffic with the energy advantage of one-fourth as much energy use between cities. Another development is the renewed interest in waterborne transport.

If by 1985 rail freight holds its own at 35 per cent of all freight moved and pipelines and waterways hold at 46 per cent, then the energy savings will be the equivalent of 220,000 barrels per day. Diminished subsidies for road and airways use and aggressive rail management will be needed to achieve this result.

Thus the four points of a 2 per cent plan for transportation savings —smaller and more fuel-efficient cars, fifty-five-mile-per-hour speed limit for most traffic, automobile traffic reductions in our major cities accompanied by better mass transit, and more energy-efficient freight movement—yield a total 1985 energy savings of four million barrels per day, the equivalent of reducing the per annum growth rate by 0.7 per cent.

The environment will benefit from these savings in many ways. Smaller cars require fewer resources. Traffic reductions in our cities will help reduce air and noise pollution. And reduced truck use will reduce air pollution and the need for highway construction. Presently

28 per cent of our highway capacity is needed to accommodate trucks. Barry Commoner has estimated that the land-use needs per billion ton miles for rail transport are 4.7 square miles, compared with 34 square miles for truck transport.

Residential Use: Cooling It   The energy consumed in our homes constitutes 20 per cent of total U.S. energy use. As has been the experience across the full range of energy-consumptive activities in our society, energy consumption in the home has suffered from increased reliance on energy-wasting activities. Foremost among these are the construction of poorly insulated and increasingly larger homes, which are more difficult to heat and cool; the use of air conditioning in 41 per cent of our homes in 1970 as opposed to 13 per cent ten years earlier; the electrification of our homes, wherein instead of direct fuel-burning for heating and refrigeration we rely on electrically supplied energy, which consumes two to three times as much raw energy to do the same job; and the proliferation of other energy-consumptive appliances such as clothes dryers and frost-free refrigerators.

The average American home utilizes seven thousand kilowatt hours per year, which if provided in the form of electricity would consume 5,400 pounds of coal at a steam-electric power plant. We correctly welcome such consumption as the provider of a dramatically improved lifestyle, primarily for America's women. The increase in utilization for the following appliances between 1960 and 1970 illustrates the lifestyle gains: freezers from 22 per cent to 32 per cent, clothes washers from 83 per cent to 92 per cent, clothes dryers from 18 per cent to 45 per cent, and dishwashers from 6 per cent to 26 per cent. The clothes dryer is a true energy guzzler. For one drying cycle it consumes the equivalent of 0.25 gallons of gasoline or 2.5 pounds of coal.

Efforts to conserve energy in these activities should avoid returning the wife to her toilsome past. Of course, we could save 35,000 barrels of oil a day by washing dishes by hand and 130,000 by hanging out clothes in the summer. But the objective is to conserve energy where it is wasted or makes only a marginal and doubtful contribution to improving our standard of living and lifestyle. The objective is not to forego energy use simply to prove we can return to the practices of our ancestors.

Reduced Energy Requirements for Heating and Cooling Fortunately there is plenty of wastage to do away with. In most cases phasing out inefficient practices will reduce the family budget. For example, improved insulation and conservation practices can reduce home energy consumption by at least 20 per cent for existing homes and by up to 50 per cent for new homes. And half the energy consumed in homes is used for space heating.

Unlike cars, homes stay with us a long time. We add to our present 70 million homes about 3 per cent each year and tear down 1 per cent. Thus a policy to save energy must achieve improvements in heating and cooling efficiency for present as well as new homes. We have already experimented with one such measure. Turning down the thermostat to 68 per cent degrees Fahrenheit during the day and to 60 degrees at night in the winter, and turning it up to 78 degrees in the summer will save 676,000 barrels of oil per day.

The Federal Housing Administration has established minimum insulation guidelines for newly constructed homes. If achieved they would represent a 19 to 29 per cent savings over earlier criteria. Some test homes recently built to conserve energy actually achieve a 50 per cent reduction. If the government required that home builders install insulation in amounts that would pay for themselves in three years, new homes would use 47 to 49 per cent less energy than those built before 1971. But we can expect few gains unless home builders are regulated. Too often there are reports of builders, anxious to cut costs, who leave new homeowners with inadequate insulation. It is this motivation that leaves our homes on average with less insulation than necessary to reap reductions in our annual heating bills.

As already noted, increasing electrification is costly in energy terms. Whereas in 1970 only 8 per cent of our homes were electrically heated, nearly 45 per cent of those built in 1973 had electric heat. Gas, which heated 55 per cent of homes in 1970, is generally no longer available for new homes. And now oil must be conserved for the transportation sector. This leaves electricity as the only option as the nation increases its reliance on nuclear and coal power for the generation of electricity. Nuclear power is expected to provide 24 per cent of our electricity in 1985, up from 5 per cent in 1973. Perhaps solar facilities can pick up some of the energy burden, but not until after 1990 at the earliest.

A possible offset to this shift from direct fuel burning (and its two-fold greater efficiency) is a new device called the heat pump. It delivers two units of heat energy for each unit of electric energy it consumes. Heat pumps, employing a compressor and heating and coolant coils, reject hot household air in the summer by pumping the heat to the air outside. Operating in reverse, heat pumps bring the heat from outside air inside during the winter. Now used in the South, the heat pump performs well unless winter temperatures drop below 30 degrees Fahrenheit. If it gets colder, the pump operates, supplemented by electrically heated coils, to warm the air.

Vigorous policies, not now being implemented, are a prerequisite to reaping energy savings in home heating. Increased energy prices will help, but the public has been educated for years by utilities to think carelessly about electricity. Home builders will not insulate homes adequately or build in heat pumps without regulation and supervision by informed consumer and financing agencies. Overcoming the obstacles to retrofitting homes with improved insulation will require guidance by government and industry, and incentives to the homeowner. One company is showing the way. The Michigan Consolidated Gas Company lends money to its users to finance loans for insulation, storm windows, and other energy-conserving improvements. Even minor improvements can save large amounts of energy. For example, plugging a quarter-inch crack along a three-foot length can save twenty gallons of fuel oil per year in a moderate climate.

The California Assembly on May 16, 1974, passed a landmark piece of legislation empowering the state to set strict standards for insulation of new buildings. Another dozen states have the authority to require all new homes, whether Farmers Home Administration–financed or not, to meet FHA or similar insulation standards. In 1975 Congress acted to require all states to set up similar programs. Still needed is a federal policy establishing national insulation requirements that can be delegated to and implemented by state and local governments if they accept the responsibility.

Another easily remedied obstacle to reduced home energy consumption is the calibration of home thermostats. Most cannot be turned below 55 or 60 degrees Fahrenheit. For second homes or even for long vacations from first homes, calibration to as low as 35 to 40 degrees is a requirement to save energy. Another possibility, too remote no doubt for Congress, is to eliminate the mortgage interest deduction from taxable income for mortgage payments on second and third homes. Two or more homes are a luxury and should be taxed like any other purchase.

The contribution of such policies to reducing the demand growth rate to 2 per cent could be substantial. If we assume that in 1973 10 per cent of new homes had a 50 per cent better energy efficiency in heating than existing ones, in 1974 20 per cent, and so on, and that we insulate and improve the heating for 2 per cent of our existing homes each year, achieving a 25 per cent reduction for each retrofitted home, the nation's energy demand growth rate would be reduced by 0.2 per cent per year. The 1985 savings would be 1.32 million barrels per day energy equivalent.

Saving on Appliances   The other major area of potential household energy savings is in appliance use. The table lists the chief household appliance consumers of energy. These appliances consume about 80 per cent of the home energy consumed aside from energy used for space heating. Lighting, electric toothbrushes, can openers, and other devices consume the rest. The rate of turnover of appliances is again a limiting consideration on the rate at which energy conservation savings can be realized, although appliances are replaced more frequently than homes. The Energy Policy and Conservation Act of 1975 calls for a 20 per cent overall reduction in energy usage by major appliances by 1980 compared to the base year of 1972. The air conditioner tops the appliance list of big energy consumers.

The least efficient air conditioner needs 2.6 times as much energy to do the same cooling job as the most efficient. Performance is measured by the ratio of the BTUs of cooling output to the watt-hours of electricity input. Even at credit-card interest rates of up to 18 per cent per year, one is justified in spending the sixty dollars, or 15 per cent more, for the more efficient model. The additional investment cost and interest will often be saved by the end of the first summer of operation and inevitably by the end of the second. Afterward the wise buyer will save twenty to a hundred dollars per year. Air conditioning energy consumption will be further reduced by insulation installed to help save winter heating costs. If such insulation

CHIEF HOUSEHOLD APPLIANCE ENERGY CONSUMERS

	Kilowatt-hours Per Year	Potential Conservation Savings
1. Air conditioning		
—central cooling system for 1,500 sq. ft.	4,000	20-30%
—room air conditioner	860	20-30%
2. Water heater	4,219-4,811	10-36%
3. Freezer	1,195-1,761	16-30%
4. Range	1,205-1,175	20-30%
5. Refrigerator (12 cu. ft.) self-defrosting	728-1,212	25-40%
6. Clothes dryer	993	30-50%
7. Color TV	660	10-20%

is installed to the point of optimum financial savings, electricity consumed for air conditioning will drop by between 18 and 26 per cent. Another air conditioner saver is the attic fan. A fan uses about three hundred kilowatt-hours per year, compared with four thousand kilowatt-hours for an air conditioner. If the conservative estimates of possible efficiency improvements indicated in the table are accomplished as old appliances are retired in favor of new ones, the savings in 1985 would be 540,000 barrels per day energy equivalent.

REDUCING COMMERCIAL ENERGY CONSUMPTION

Commercial activities consume 14 per cent of the energy we use, primarily to heat and cool shopping centers and office areas and to provide light for sales and workplace activities. Some major high-rise office building have already demonstrated 10 to 30 per cent savings in energy use. This has been achieved by improved air circulation and thermostat adjustments. Exxon's New York office building saved 30 per cent. Such savings are important because large office buildings are mammoth consumers of energy. One of the largest, New York City's World Trade Center, uses more energy than Schenectady, New York, a city of 100,000 people. If we can obtain a 20 per cent average reduction in energy use for existing commercial buildings, we can save 200,000 barrels a day by 1985. In addition, if newly completed buildings beginning in 1975 are 30 per cent more efficient, an additional savings of 125,000 barrels is possible by 1985. To achieve such gains, office building codes at the state and local levels should incorporate more efficient insulation and lighting provisions for new buildings, and existing buildings should be subject to an energy audit.

IMPROVING THE EFFICIENCY
OF ELECTRIC POWER GENERATION

The way energy raw materials like coal are converted to the energy we consume has a great influence on our total energy needs. For example, the energy required for one shower can range from 10,000 BTUs to 4,500 BTUs, depending on whether the water is heated by electricity or natural gas. In the process of electricity generation about two thirds of the energy content of the raw energy material (coal, oil, or gas) goes up the smokestack or as heated water into a stream. There are losses in the home combustion of natural gas, but they are about half those lost at the power plant. Increased electrification is inevitable as we rely on nuclear power for which there is no home-use option other than electricity. But we can strive to reduce energy losses in the conversion process.

The measure of the efficiency of electricity production is the heat rate, or the number of BTUs per kilowatt-hour of electricity output. Until recently the heat rate was improving. In fact, at the turn of the century it required seven pounds of coal to produce one kilowatt-hour of electricity. Now less than a pound is required. After a long decline, the heat rate leveled off at about 10,500 BTUs per kilowatt-hour in 1966. Yet by the early 1970s the heat rate increased by about 5 per cent, meaning 500 additional BTUs of raw energy were needed to produce each kilowatt hour of electricity. Delays in bringing new and more efficient plants into use were one reason for the drop. Utilities underestimated demand, had engineering problems with new nuclear plants, and used underpriced and precious natural gas in inefficient gas turbines.

The official Department of the Interior forecast expects efficiency to improve at least through 1985. The rate of improvement is 0.7 per cent per year, dropping the heat rate to 9,760 BTUs per kilowatt hour in 1985. An additional improvement of 0.4 per cent per year to a total rate of 1.1 per cent per year is a worthwhile target in the new era of higher energy prices. If achieved, this improved rate would contribute in 1985 1,170,000 barrels per day in energy savings, a major contribution to the attainment of a 2 per cent energy consumption growth rate.

Policies toward electric power generation and sales must have a special place in a 2 per cent strategy. Electricity demand is the fastest growing energy consumer. In 1975 it grew at over 5 per cent even though industry electricity consumption dropped sharply because of the recession.

Advertising to promote the use of electricity should be terminated. Industries often can burn fuels directly rather than use electricity and should be given incentives to do so. Past practices have done the opposite. Heavy industry users have been receiving power at cheap bulk rates. Some can today purchase power, often from the TVA or other government-run power administrations in the West, for as little as five mills per kilowatt-hour (a mill is a tenth of a cent). Yet the costs of producing power at a new plant are as high as fifteen to twenty mills per kilowatt-hour. A 1972 Federal Power Commission study revealed that industry paid an average of only 1.02 cents per kilowatt-hour for electricity, while the residential user paid 2.22 cents. Even large residential users are favored over smaller customers. The poor of inner-city Detroit, who use a small amount of energy, pay one-third more for a unit of electricity than occupants of suburban homes. More realistic electricity pricing is a key to the attainment of a 2 per cent demand growth rate. It is essential to spur energy-saving actions in industry, commercial, and residential energy use.

INDUSTRIAL CONSUMPTION

Conventional wisdom holds that energy use is the sine qua non of industrialization. Most believe that from the outset of the Industrial Revolution in the nineteenth century, labor productivity has been on a steady upward trend because man has invented energy-consuming machines to work for him. But just as technological change and the resulting capital investment save labor, itself a form of energy, they can save energy resources. Take the example of the oxygen hearth furnace used in steel-making. It is a relatively recent steel-making process that uses half as much energy per ton of steel production as its predecessor, the open hearth furnace.

The premier reason more energy has been associated with industrialization is that energy has been cheap. Now that it is expensive, we should expect things to change. But it is difficult to predict how much energy can be saved as production continues to increase, and how much industrial energy savings can contribute to the attainment of 1985's 2 per cent strategy goal. There is no record of industry responding to such unprecedented energy price hikes. There is even some question whether industry will feel the full brunt of the increases. In 1971 46 per cent of the energy consumed by industry came from natural gas. Industry used more of this expiring and precious clean fuel than households, transportation, or commercial consumers. Natural gas prices are controlled. They will not rise with other energy prices unless gas is deregulated. Such a step is important if industry is to have the incentive to save energy.

Industrial energy consumption, itself about 41 per cent of all U.S. energy consumption, encompasses manufacturing, agriculture, construction, and resource extraction activities. Almost 60 per cent of the consumption is in manufacturing. The leading energy-consumptive industries are displayed in the accompanying table. Today's papers are full of stories of energy-saving breakthroughs in the production of the commodities manufactured by these industries. The DuPont Company, our largest chemical producer, has achieved a 15 per cent savings. Its competitor, the Dow Chemical Company, saved, on a per-unit product basis, 10 per cent successively in 1972 and 1973, and 7 per cent in 1974.

ENERGY CONSUMPTION IN MANUFACTURING*

	Manufacturing Consumption		U.S. Consumption	
	% of Total Manufacturing Consumption	Cumulative Total (%)	% of Total U.S. Consumption	Cumulative Total (%)
1. Industrial chemicals	15.0		3.7	
2. Petroleum refining	11.6	26.6	2.8	6.5
3. Steel	11.6	38.2	2.9	9.4
4. Paper	8.7	46.9	2.1	11.5
5. Nonferrous metals (primarily aluminum and copper)	4.6	51.5	1.1	12.6
6. Hydraulic-cement	3.5	55.0	0.9	13.5

* Source: "Energy Management in Manufacturing 1967–1990." Prepared for the Federal Energy Administration by Energy and Environmental Analysis, Inc.

DuPont also provides a consulting service to help major industries implement energy-saving improvements. These experts have found that industry can save 7 to 15 per cent in one year. In other words, without major investments, simply by shutting off valves and otherwise being smart plant operators, industries can reap substantial savings. Assuming 10 per cent as an industry-wide gain, this achievement alone will reduce 1985 national energy demand by the equivalent of 1,110,000 barrels of oil per day. Another way of viewing these savings is that they will permit between two and three years of energy-free industrial growth.

But more important is the contribution that can be made by investing in new ways to manufacture goods. The scope for improvement can be illustrated by two industry examples. In 1971 the average rolled-aluminum plant consumed the energy equivalent of 17,331 pounds of coal to produce one ton of aluminum. Yet the best plant used only 9,878 pounds of coal. Likewise, to produce a ton of cement the average plant used 592 pounds of coal in 1971, whereas the best plant used only 354 pounds. These examples illustrate that the potential for energy savings is almost 50 per cent. In the paper industry, where the use of pulp wastes as a source of energy offers the prospect of energy-free production, even greater gains are possible. In steel and copper we can expect less. In some cases the efficiencies contemplated for the best plants in the 1980s are already in operation in Japan and Europe, where energy prices have been higher.

The key determinant of the industrial energy savings by 1985 will be the rate at which old energy-inefficient plants are phased out in favor of new energy-saving processes. An industry-by-industry assessment to provide the definitive answer has been completed. The results for a single industry, cement, illustrate how the studies were done. About 15 to 18 per cent of the price of a bag of cement you buy at the hardware store is for energy. Cement is limestone heated to a high temperature in combination with materials like clay and sand. The "cooking" takes place in a kiln, an oversized and rotating barrellike device. The fuel burns inside the kiln, like a backyard charcoal burner. There are two types of kilns: one in which the raw materials are fed in wet, and another where they enter dry. Not surprisingly, the dry process, because energy is not required to boil the water away, uses a lot less energy, up to 45 per cent less. Roughly 60 per cent of U.S. kilns are wet process; the rest are dry. Where higher energy prices have prevailed, in Japan for instance, practically all kilns are of the dry type. How much energy is saved by 1985 will primarily depend on how fast the wet kilns are replaced by dry ones. We can estimate this by assuming that all new capacity will be dry. Vendors of kilns report no interest in wet-process kilns but a surge of interest in dry ones. Output is expected to grow by 2.75 per cent per year—meaning that by 1985 the added plants constituting 35 per cent of capacity will be of the more efficient type. Also, worn-out plants will need to be replaced. If the industry is interested in maximizing its profits, and the cement industry is quite competitive, it will want to retire wet-process plants faster than usual. Together these considerations can be expected to result in dry kilns' constituting about 67 per cent of 1985's capacity, compared with today's 40 per cent.

This process of upgrading the energy efficiency of production is under way in all industries. For cement it will result in vast energy savings by 1985: instead of energy demand growing at a rate slightly

below the 2.75 per cent rate of increase in output, it will increase
each year at less than half that, or 1.125 per cent. This means that by
1985 energy requirements for this industry will be 15 per cent less
than they would have been otherwise.

The pace of this industry-wide conversion will vary depending on
the share of energy in the ultimate price of the product (which tends
to push cement faster because the share is high), the availability and
cost of the new energy-saving process (steel's oxygen furnace and
paper's wood wastes as a source of fuel are readily available alternatives, whereas the most promising energy-saving aluminum process is
still being tested), how energy-saving the new process is compared
with the old (highest for paper; lowest for copper), the rate at which
plants become obsolete in the industry, and how competitive the
industry is (paper, cement, and chemicals will be propelled more by
competition than steel, copper, and aluminum). Energy savings for
the entire industrial sector in 1985 will be the equivalent of 2.9 million barrels per day. This achievement would reduce industry's energy demand growth rate from 3.9 per cent to 2.6 per cent per
annum.

RESOURCE RECOVERY AND RECYCLING

As a society we create a gigantic pile of waste, adding hills to the
landscape every day. Consumers and industries dispose of tons of
valuable metals such as iron, steel, and aluminum, paper, and food
wastes. If we can capture the energy content of these wastes, the
mining of millions of tons of coal will become unnecessary.

Energy can be saved by burning these wastes directly in a power
plant, thus "recovering a resource." Or energy savings can result
from recycling processed raw materials like paper and aluminum
back to the marketplace.

The energy content of the economy's wastes if they were to be
combusted in power plants is equal to about 2.4 per cent of the energy we use, or about 831,000 barrels per day. Because of high garbage and industrial waste collection costs, economics would justify
actual recovery operations only in our densely populated areas. The
quadrupling of the price of oil also quadrupled the price of the energy content of garbage. In fact, the Arabs have done more to solve

our garbage problem than all the solid-waste acts ever passed by Congress and the states.

St. Louis and Rochester are among the eighteen cities with firm plans to meet 10 to 15 per cent of their electric energy needs and solve up to 40 per cent of their solid-waste problems by burning garbage in their power plants. Many northeastern states, such as Connecticut and Massachusetts, have launched comprehensive programs to turn garbage into power. By 1985 these programs will save the country the equivalent of 350,000 barrels per day.

Much has been said about the energy-saving potential of the returnable bottle. Oregon has implemented a program that bans the nonreturnable bottle, mandates a refund of five cents for returned bottles, and requires standardized containers, exchangeable among brands. The American steel, glass, and aluminum industries—management, stockholders, and workers united—oppose similar national legislation. A national bill to ban nonreturnables has been introduced into the U. S. Senate, but its fate is certainly not promising. Whereas studies in Oregon and for the nation have shown the net employment effects of a ban are positive, this is small comfort to workers who disdain becoming bottle carriers, washers, and collectors in a returnable economy.

The potential energy savings of a ban would be a major contribution to the attainment of the 1985 2 per cent goal: 246,000 barrels per day of energy could be saved. On a human scale, it might be remembered that the energy saved per soft drink or beer drunk from a returnable bottle will light a hundred-watt light bulb for twelve hours. A returnable-bottle six-pack of Coca-Cola saves a hot bath's worth of energy.

Naturally, without a ban some of the energy that has gone into aluminum cans and other nonreturnable containers can be salvaged by recycling. The steel, aluminum, glass, and paper wastes not eliminated by bans on nonreturnable containers can be separated from our combustible wastes and recycled for reuse. By reusing aluminum we could save up to 20,000 pounds of coal per ton of aluminum available to the economy. For steel, the coal savings would be 920 pounds per ton of recycled steel. And for glass, 100 pounds of coal per ton could be saved.

Again, only in our major cities would it be economical to pick up

SUMMARY OF MEASURES TO REDUCE ENERGY
DEMAND GROWTH TO 2 PER CENT PER YEAR

	Amount Saved by 1985 in Barrel-per-day Energy Units	Policies
1. TRANSPORTATION (25% of total energy demand)		
a. reduce vehicle weight to 2900 pounds and impose fuel economy performance in each weight class to best-in-class performance levels	3,300,000	—mandatory labeling —excise tax on heavy vehicles —a fuel economy standard
b. adhere to 55 mph speed limit on heavily traveled highways	125,000	—reduce speed limits
c. 10% traffic reduction by 1985 with increased transit use	347,000	—reduce city traffic in accordance with EPA transportation plans —vastly augment mass transit
d. emphasize more energy-efficient intercity freight transport modes	220,000	—eliminate highway construction subsidy for trucks —give preferential rates to rail and water freight
Total Transportation	3,992,000	
2. RESIDENTIAL (20%)		
a. adjust thermostat by 4°	676,000	—citizen action
b. add insulation	1,320,000	—utility financing of insulation investments with monthly repayment —eliminate pro-energy and electricity consumption advertising —impose state regulations on insulation —end mortgage deduction on other than first home
c. household appliances	540,000	—mandatory air conditioner energy standards —mandatory labeling on top seven energy-consuming appliances
Total Residential	2,536,000	
3. COMMERCIAL CONSUMPTION (14%)		
a. Improved heating and cooling practices and added insulation	325,000	—state and local building codes for new buildings —energy audits of largest commercial consumers
b. installation of energy-efficient lighting and elimination of over-lighting	25,000	—lighting audits
Total Commercial	350,000	

SUMMARY OF MEASURES TO REDUCE ENERGY
DEMAND GROWTH TO 2 PER CENT PER YEAR

	Amount Saved by 1985 in Barrel-per-day Energy Units	Policies
4. INDUSTRIAL (41%)		
a. energy-efficient practices	1,110,000	—deregulate natural gas prices to industry —promote "energy conscious" plant operation
b. installation of energy-efficient plant and equipment	1,308,988	—rapid write-off
c. shift to direct energy burning from electricity	516,900	—allocation program to deny electricity to convertible plants
Total Industry	2,935,888	
5. ELECTRICAL POWER GENERATION	1,170,000	—improve heat rate to 1.1% per year
6. RECYCLING-REUSE		
a. combination of consumer and industry wastes in power plants	350,000	—government assistance to state and local programs
b. ban on nonreturnable bottles	246,000	—nonreturnable bottle ban
c. recycling of copper, aluminum, paper, glass and steel from wastes	47,000	
Total Recycling-Reuse	643,000	
GRAND TOTAL	11,626,888	
NEEDED FOR 2%	12,400,000	
SHORTFALL	773,112	

and separate steel, copper, glass, and paper from our wastes. But such programs are easy to couple with preparation of wastes for power plants. The 1985 energy savings if our major cities undertake such programs would be 47,000 barrels per day.

A NEW ENERGY OUTLOOK

Summed up, the savings achieved in each sector yield a total energy saving just short of the 12.4 million barrels per day needed to reduce the national energy demand growth rate from 4 per cent to 2 per cent (see table). Specific policy measures have been proposed to secure these savings, not because they represent the last word in how it can be done but because it is important to demonstrate that there are real options available.

Some studies estimate more potential savings than are assumed in the foregoing analysis—for example, from the reuse and recycling of materials or by reducing intercity truck freight transport. There may be better choices. Other studies will show smaller savings for some measures. The purpose here is to demonstrate it can be done, not to contend there is a single, exact solution.

Some will argue achievement of a 2 per cent demand growth rate will deny us an essential part of Americana. They will marshal curves that with apparent rigor will "prove" that higher incomes are correlated with higher levels of energy consumption. Such curves are easy to plot. How then can it be argued in the face of such strong relationships that, by cutting our demand growth rate in half, we will not be sacrificing something of vital importance?

Achieving a 2 per cent demand growth rate does entail giving up something. For the individual it entails driving a 3,000-pound car rather than a 4,500-pound car, riding mass transit if it is available, living in a cooler home in winter and a warmer one in summer, studying the energy efficiency of appliances before purchase and insisting on the most efficient, insulating his home, and using returnable bottles.

The broader economic significance of investing in energy-saving means of production is probably neutral in its net effect on prices, employment, and gross national product. What is invested in energy-saving plants and equipment or mass transit need not be invested in additional coal mines, oil drilling, and shale oil production. The West Germans are as well off as we are economically from a personal-income standpoint, but they consume less energy. In transportation West Germans consume one-fourth less than we do; in their homes they use half as much energy; and their industries use one-eighth less per dollar of production.

The net impact on the consumer is best measured by how his transportation and home energy use lifestyles are altered and the impact of energy-saving measures on his pocketbook. Any inconvenience or losses on these accounts must be weighed against the gains in environmental quality that will result from lower levels of pollution. In terms of costs, a smaller car will save the average driver from $300 to $500 per year at today's gasoline prices if he trades his 5,000-pound car for a 3,000-pound model. New bus riders will do as well or better. The typical homeowner will save another $150 to $250 in electricity and fuel costs for heating and appliances. By any accounting, money will be saved.

In is difficult to put a price on inconvenience, whether it is the inconvenience of squeezing into a smaller car or riding mass transit. One estimate of the value of a car ride is the amount of daily tax the car commuter must be forced to pay before he will ride a bus passing within three blocks of his home. Of course, some people ride now. And the die-hard commuter would not give up driving until charged two dollars per day for the privilege. For most, one dollar a day would be enough persuasion.

Thus, if we reduce energy consumption, the average driver can switch to a small car or ride mass transit. The "price" of inconvenience for the mass transit shift, a dollar per work day or $264 per year, represents an outside estimate of the "inconvenience cost" of transportation energy conservation. He will save this much by driving a small car, purchasing energy-efficient appliances, and turning the thermostat down in winter and up in summer. On balance, as a very rough approximation, the 2 per cent strategy will save the American who does not object to riding in a small car or sleeping under blankets in winter, a hundred dollars or more each year. And the American who prizes these aspects of our luxurious way of living will come out about even after balancing increased inconvenience with dollar savings. If the reduced death and illness associated with lower levels of energy output and pollution levels are added in along with the reduced abuse to our physical environment resulting from a reduction in required coal production of about one billion tons, the balance is clearly on the side of the 2 per cent strategy.

The policies to achieve reduced energy demand are summarized in the preceding table. All the ingenuity of our political process must be mobilized to pass the necessary legislation, inform the public of its choices, and remove the multitude of subsidies that promote energy wastage. Natural gas prices, particularly for industry, must be increased, housing insulation standards established, automobile fuel economy boosted by taxes and regulation, and industry granted tax benefits for newly installed energy-saving plants and equipment.

As part of an energy-conservation strategy, environmentalists must modify regulations that consume large amounts of energy. These should be eased where the abuses of the increased energy production necessary to operate pollution abatement equipment exceed the benefits of reduced pollution. Environmental policy should strive for a net zero energy account balance. Current projections for 1980 show a 916,000-barrel-per-day energy equivalent cost of meeting automobile emission-control requirements, removing lead from gasoline, and meeting air emission and water effluent requirements. This energy cost can be reduced by the following energy savings credited to the environment: 201,000 barrels per day from solid waste combustion in power plants, 204,300 from traffic reductions in cities to meet air standards, and 246,000 from banning nonreturnable bottles. This 651,000-barrel-per-day energy equivalent saving leaves environmentalists with a net energy "overdraft" of 265,000 barrels per day. Environmentalists should accept the burden of reducing their energy demands by this amount. They must also refrain from imposing such heavy reclamation requirements on coal mining that the net energy output per ton mined is reduced to near zero.

In return, the environmentalists and all Americans can welcome the multiple improvements in our society that implementation of a conservation strategy will bring. We have already had a preview of those benefits since the Arab embargo. The oil companies have closed 20,000 filling stations which no one will miss. We still have 300,000. In 1974 the demand for electricity flattened, whereas it had been growing at 7 per cent per year. Utilities took their expansion plans back to the drawing boards and scaled them down. Planned power plant expansions dropped from a pre-embargo 360,000 megawatts on top of our present 450,000 megawatts to a more prudent 170,000 megawatts. Conversation was the key reason, despite utility hand-wringing about capital financing shortages. The utility system experiencing the largest drop in demand in 1974 was the Potomac Electric Power Company (Pepco). Demand for its electricity fell almost 9 per cent. Accordingly, the utility cut its three-year construction budget in half. The utility's chairman said the cutback "was a result of reduced projections of energy use in Potomac's service area."

The same story was repeated throughout the country. Nuclear plants which were projected to produce 130,000 megawatts of electricity in 1980 are now projected to produce 86,000 megawatts. Because of conservation, the environment will be threatened by one hundred fewer nuclear power plants. Another conservation casualty is the supertanker. With the drop in world oil demand, shipyards from Göteborg to Tokyo have received cancellations.

Conservation, assisted by high production costs, has also taken its toll of a variety of ambitious large-scale energy projects that threaten to damage fragile environments. Production plans at the Colony Oil Company's shale oil project in Colorado were suspended when the estimated break-even per barrel costs reached twelve dollars. In Canada, Alberta's Athabasca tar sands have been yielding sixty thousand barrels per day for the Sun Oil Company. But after a short period of euphoria over this vast reserve's potential, projects have been canceled, partners have dropped out, and the oil companies have sought U.S. and Canadian government support. Another conservation casualty was a proposal to float nuclear power plants off New Jersey. Finally, the cancellation of the $3.5 billion Kaiparowits coal-fired plant in Utah, which at three thousand megawatts would have been the world's largest, while due primarily to environmental objections, was in some measure a conservation casualty.

These unfolding events illustrate how profoundly the world has changed. When the embargo hit, a chorus of commentators announced the environment would be put aside in favor of all-out energy production. Instead, there is abundant evidence that our energy habit rather than our environmental habit can be "kicked." A year after the embargo, a public opinion survey (by the Valados Company) showed that only 3 per cent were less in favor of fighting polluters than they were the year before, and 71 per cent favored driving small cars.

Achieving a 2 per cent strategy is within everyone's grasp, if everyone reaches for it. A conscious national effort to reduce the energy demand growth rate by half is essential to saving the environment and to reducing energy dependence. At worst, the citizen will come out even; at best, he will benefit in terms of improved health, dollars saved, and the assurance that his physical environment is being protected.

6.

ENDING AUTOMOBILE DOMINANCE

If one were to describe our lifestyles to a visitor from another planet, to our ancestors of two centuries ago, or even to the secretary-general of the Communist party of the Soviet Union, as former President Nixon did, a description of the automobile as our most-consumed commodity would not be a bad place to start. It is the consumer good par excellence. Food and housing are big budget items, too, but when we indulge ourselves, the automobile is most often the object of our indulgence. Khrushchev was interested in how we produce so much corn per acre. But Brezhnev, rising above essential concerns, received from our President a Cadillac, a Lincoln Continental, and a silver-and-white Chevrolet Monte Carlo Landau. He really appreciates us.

RIDING HIGH

New cars purchased annually in this country outnumber new babies by three to one. Of course, cars don't last as long as babies. Nonetheless, currently there is more than one car on the road for every two Americans. Europeans have half as many cars per person as we do—one for every four people—partly because they have more efficient mass transit systems. About one third of our households have two or more cars; only 20 per cent have no car at all. Two-car families have increased 50 per cent in the last decade. Denver is our most automobile-dominated city. Cars in Denver number 1.9 per family, well above the national average of 1.2.

The car occupancy rate has been falling because the car population is growing faster than the human population. On the average, each car carries 1.9 persons per trip. But the occupancy rate is only 1.2 for the most common trip type, the work commute. If the car population growth pace does not abate, by the 1980s some cars will be tooling along without drivers.

Of all the lifestyle reforms necessary to secure a clean environment in America, the likelihood of success is lowest in transportation. Probably the land-use and energy changes will occur more readily and with less opposition than changes in our transportation lifestyle. Land and energy are in large part simply commodities, whereas the automobile's role as a cultural and social symbol probably outweighs its role as a commodity.

However compelling the rhetoric of the perpetrators of the automobile lifestyle has been, something new is happening. If it is not a rejection of auto dominance, there is at least a cooling of the affection that has accompanied it throughout this century. Two startling developments have occurred. Mass transit ridership has increased, reversing a continuous downward spiral that has lasted just short of a quarter century. And car sales for model year 1974 were the lowest in eleven years. In 1974 the energy crisis pushed sales down to 8.8 million new cars, 7.4 million American-made. U.S. production in 1975, depressed below 1974 levels by the recession, fell to 6.7 million. Foreign producers, geared to the fuel-economy, small-car era, usurped 21 per cent of the U.S. market in 1975 compared to 16 per cent in 1974. Nothing in the Constitution says America ever again needs to produce 9.7 million cars a year, the peak level reached in 1973. Including imports, that year witnessed the manufacture of 11.4 million new cars. Even with a recovery in 1976, let's hope the 1973 record will continue as the high point of our automania.

To change our transportation lifestyle, we need to do three things:

reduce reliance on the automobile in our major cities; switch from cars to high-speed trains on our frequently traveled intercity transportation routes; and, when we must resort to the automobile, moderate the speed and heavyweight gimmickry attendant to our travel.

The average household in the United States makes 1,400 trips each year, putting 12,400 miles on its car(s). This represents a daily pace of 3.8 trips covering thirty-four miles. Such utilization is a reflection first and foremost of the benefits that the automobile has brought to Americans. Increased mobility for jobs and pleasure has given us better work opportunities, as well as the ability to commute to more spacious homes and a variety of social and recreational activities. The interstate highway system, from its beginning in 1956, has multiplied these benefits severalfold. Any strategy to reduce automobile dominance must recognize the real strengths of automobile speed, convenience, luxury, and privacy. We cannot and should not hope to supplant these. A successful strategy must emerge from a solid assessment of the weaknesses of the automobile. For in some environments, particularly downtown in our major cities, the car is truly an endangered species.

Already in cities of over a million population, we use automobiles less than we do elsewhere: we take 1.9 trips per day and travel twenty-two miles. But the bulk of our trips are in such cities; over half of the automobile miles traveled in the United States—or 1.2 trillion miles—are in urban areas which occupy less than 1 per cent of our land.

Pollution in these cities is caused primarily by the automobile. Of the five major air pollutants that are public health problems, three come out of the automobile tailpipe. These are carbon monoxide, nitrogen oxides, and hydrocarbons. Nitrogen oxides and hydrocarbons react in sunlight to form smog. The exact share of these pollutant emissions in urban areas due to automobiles varies from 50 per cent to 90 per cent, depending on the presence of industries and trucks. Automobiles cause practically all of the pollution in Los Angeles, San Francisco, Denver, and Washington, D.C. In Baltimore, Chicago, Houston, and Pittsburgh, industry makes a large contribution as well.

The automobile air-pollution problems overshadow all others. The first is smog. Smog receives the most attention because we can see it. It lingers, a yellow-brown fog, over Atlanta, New York, Tokyo, Chicago, Denver, and of course, Los Angeles. Mexico City, Djakarta, Madrid, and Rome suffer too. Unburned gasoline, or hydrocarbons, is the chief cause of smog, called photochemical oxidants by technicians. Emerging from automobile tailpipes, hydrocarbons rise as a gas to interact with nitrogen oxides, also emitted by cars, and oxygen, already present in the air. Sunlight cooks these chemicals, propelling the reaction to its conclusion: smog.

In 1542 Juan Rodríguez Cabrillo, the Spanish discoverer of the Los Angeles area, named what is now San Pedro Bay the "Bay of Smokes" because of the overhanging haze he encountered. Historians and chemists ponder whether Cabrillo's smog was caused by natural hydrocarbons from vegetation or by Indian fires. Tiny drops of water as well as naturally emitted hydrocarbons are the reason the Great Smoky Mountains of Tennessee and North Carolina are so named. What is unique about the oxidants over Los Angeles and most of our major cities today is that their concentration is much greater than the naturally occurring phenomenon. Los Angeles commonly experiences oxidant readings in the 0.4–0.6-parts-per-million range, more than five times the 0.08-ppm standard established by EPA to protect human health. An oxidant concentration of 0.5 ppm is equivalent to the strength of the world's driest martini, with one ounce of vermouth to 14,800 gallons of gin. At this concentration, oxidants harm man's lungs, causing increased infection and reduced pulmonary capacity. Asthmatics are particularly vulnerable. But reduced lung performance can affect us all. This explains why the outdoor play period activities of schoolchildren are canceled during smog "pollution alerts."

Controlling oxidants is exceedingly difficult because the exhaust emissions that cause the problem can linger in a large urban area for hours. Often the highest pollutant readings occur far from the central city along major highways and beltways, in the suburbs, or even over relatively unpopulated land near urban centers, shopping complexes, and highway interchanges.

Carbon monoxide is also a widespread problem. Heavily traveled streets or "street canyons" with poor air-current movement experience the highest carbon monoxide readings. Traffic policemen, garage attendants, pedestrians, drivers, and occupants of homes and offices above heavily traveled roads are exposed. A recent study of 29,000 nonsmoking persons in urban areas across the United States found 45 per cent of them had excessive carbon monoxide levels in their blood. The health of about 1 to 3 per cent of these people is in jeopardy. Carbon monoxide inhibits the blood's oxygen-carrying capacity. For example, sufferers of coronary artery diseases are extremely susceptible to carbon monoxide. The general population experiences slowed mental reactions caused by carbon monoxide pollution. This is a cause of higher accident rates on heavily traveled roads. An uncounted number of the headaches experienced by Americans are due to carbon monoxide.

The prevalence of photochemical oxidants and carbon monoxide is easy to demonstrate. Of the 247 air regions in the United States, 54 had oxidant readings exceeding health standards in 1970, the year the Clean Air Act was passed, and 29 exceeded the carbon monoxide standard. A third automobile pollutant, nitrogen dioxide, is present in only four air regions. It is a cause of bronchitis and reduced lung activity.

The prospects for cleaning the air in these regions through better controls on new cars were summarized in Chapter 1. From the 55 per cent of the U.S. population exposed to unhealthy air in 1971, the portion exposed in 1975 will be reduced to 42 per cent and in 1985 to 11 per cent. This assumes automobile emissions are reduced by 95 per cent by 1979. After 1985 the percentage of the population exposed will rise again, because by 1985 there will be enough additional cars and additional travel per car to offset the greatly reduced emissions per car.

Therefore, even if the new emission-control technologies work as planned, 24 million people will still be exposed to polluted air in the mid-1980s. Unfortunately, new developments suggest that even more people will be affected. There is increasing evidence that the automobile cleanup program is not working as well as planned. Recent emission tests in several locations in the country have found that about half the cars built since emission controls began to be installed in 1968 are exceeding the standard they were designed to meet. One study in the Washington, D.C., area at the height of the 1973–74 energy crisis, found that the emission-control devices had been disconnected on 13 per cent of the cars tested. Another 35 per cent had been tampered with but emissions were not measured to determine how much they exceeded the standard. In May 1974 EPA began to exercise its authority to require automobile makers to recall for correction those models found to exceed standards. EPA ordered 1.4 million 1972-model cars recalled. While these corrections would be free to the consumer, experience with safety recalls does not argue that a high share of owners will return their cars for correction. Safety corrections are more directly self-protecting than emission corrections, and those who have disconnected or tinkered with their controls believing they could save fuel are not likely to bear the inconvenience of a dealer repair for what they expect will be reduced fuel economy. EPA studies suggest that tinkering with emission devices by nonexperts (including garage mechanics) will as likely worsen fuel economy as it will improve it. Oddly, the Clean Air Act imposes penalties for dealer tinkering with emission devices but not for the garage that advertises such tinkering as a line of business, as many did during the 1974 energy crisis.

Thus, not only is the technological solution to clean up the automobile not sufficient to clean the air, it is not working as perfectly as planned. The casual observer has seen the evidence. Smog pollution should be decreasing. But many cities—including Los Angeles, Chicago, and Washington, D.C.—in either 1974 or 1975 experienced the highest pollutant concentrations on record. This is striking evidence that technological solutions or fixes alone are failing to get the cleanup job done. Far-reaching transportation reforms to reduce traffic in our major cities are an additional prerequisite for the attainment of air standards.

Reducing automobile traffic will ameliorate appalling conditions on many other environmental fronts as well. Automobile dominance is a disease that afflicts not just the human lungs, eyes, and heart, but it is harmful to our hearing in the form of noise pollution. And the lead emissions from pre-1975-model-year cars contribute to excessive blood lead levels for a sizable number of urban dwellers. The most extreme manifestation of this affliction is mental retardation and even death, particularly among the infant population. Even this toll is small against the more than 55,000 lives lost in traffic accidents each year before the energy crisis. This problem was brought into focus recently by the 20 per cent reduction in deaths experienced, a savings of over 10,000 lives in 1974, because of speed reductions to save energy. While most drivers are ignoring the fifty-five-mile-per-hour speed limit, average speeds have dropped by about eight miles per hour.[1]

Our psyches are burdened by the din of highway-dominated neighborhoods where human-scale living is impossible. The impact of such distortions on family and community is no less important because it is immeasurable. Local economies are destroyed as well as nourished by the asphalt corridors of our automobile-dominated lives.

More than 30 per cent of the land in major urban areas is devoted to the automobile. A study of Providence, Rhode Island, put the automobile's share of that city at 40 per cent. Roads, parking facilities, rights-of-way, and cloverleafs are stuffed into the urban landscape where 75 per cent of us attempt to concentrate our activities on 1.5 per cent of the nation's land. Too often the automobile has triumphed in the land grab, particularly when the poor's land was at stake.

Of course the automobile is not an inanimate pre-emptor of our urban lifestyle. Its manifestations are an extension of our preferences. The tragedy is that our political and economic accounting systems fail to impose on the car owner and driver the full cost to society of his activities. First, the full implications of automobile use are difficult to measure, much less translate into an environmental charge per car or per mile. Second and of far greater importance, our political leadership has been timid both in informing the public of the full scope of automobile abuses and in securing reform. Affecting up to 18 per cent of economic activity and 13 per cent of energy consumption, and employing one in every seven workers, the automobile industry can easily demonstrate its self-importance. Its failure to over-

---

[1] One country, France, lost its nerve during the energy crisis; France sacrificed lives for automobile industry profits. When the French government reduced highway speed limits to save energy, the French automobile industry, its profits hurt by declining medium- and large-car sales, persuaded the government to reverse its policy and raise highway speed limits to eighty-seven miles per hour.

throw the tough automobile emission standards of the Clean Air Act was the exception, not the rule. The rule is best demonstrated by the repeated triumphs of the highway lobby in its campaign to prevent gasoline taxes from being used to finance mass transit.

Ownership of a car has been the talisman of manhood. Recent movies reflecting the sociology of the post-World War II period, *The Last Picture Show* and *American Graffiti,* for example, have featured the automobile in a lead role. Automobile eroticism is most pronounced in the West and South. The latest craze is the van. "Trucked out" with playboy-pad gadgetry, including ceiling mirrors, the boxy paneled van is a throwback to the rumble seat. One survey has found that over half of the premarital sex experiences of the Harvard student population took place in cars. "They drive Cadillacs" tells us more about a group's status than a shelf of sociological studies. Either Richard Petty or A. J. Foyt, among the South's legendary stock car drivers, alone has more followers than Bill Ruckelshaus and Barry Commoner together. Voter registration would be more easily denied many Americans than automobile registration.

The automotive lifestyle issue boils down to this: we must be willing to forego the automobile and try transit. Even Ruckelshaus, a frequent preacher of the ills of the automobile, slips into the routine of ignoring readily available bus service in favor of the car. Recently arriving at New York's La Guardia Airport, he instinctively turned to the taxi line. When reminded by his colleague that he was not practicing what he preached, he tried the bus. Ruckelshaus's bus zipped down a fast bus lane, passing hundreds of creeping commuters. He disembarked at 42nd Street in midtown, paper read, nerves intact, a block from his destination and a few dollars richer.

In short, reducing automobile use is a social experiment of major proportions. While the issues are not as confounding as the web of complexities that crippled the welfare and housing reforms of the Great Society, they are no less momentous. Whatever hard fact tells us about the potential for reduced automobile use must be tempered with an equal measure of automobile lore and prejudice.

Actually much more is known about our automobile driving habits than has ever been put to use. If we want to reduce automobile use we need to provide a substitute. Bus or rapid rail mass transit are the likely alternatives. They become economically feasible where ridership is high, and high transit occupancy is achievable on trip routes with high traffic flows or a high "trip density."

Urban areas with a population of one million or more are the best places to start an examination of feasible traffic reduction approaches. In 1970 there were thirty-three such areas. A survey of car-driving habits in cities of 1 million or larger reveals trip characteristics as shown in the accompanying table.

AUTOMOBILE TRIP CHARACTERISTICS IN
METROPOLITAN AREAS OF ONE MILLION AND LARGER

Trip Purpose	Daily Trip Rate	Miles Traveled
Work	0.9	11.4
Family business	0.5	2.8
Social and recreational	0.3	7.1
Education, civic, religious	0.2	1.1
Other	Less than .05	0.1
TOTAL	**1.9**	**22.5**

The work trip tops the list in frequency and distance. Social and recreational trips are second in miles traveled but they are first in efficient utilization of the automobile; on average there are 2.5 occupants per car for such trips, compared with an average occupancy of 1.2 for work trips. Besides, long distances outside urban areas make up a large share of recreational trips. Even some of these trips could be captured by efficient intercity transit or by more "auto-trains." Many have used auto-trains to travel to Florida. They depart from Lorton, Virginia, and Louisville, Kentucky.

Shopping is an important type of family business trip, contributing 5 to 10 per cent of all trips. It happens to be the only trip type that is more efficient than it was in the past. We use fewer rips per real shopping dollar spent today because shopping centers allow us to make large dollar purchases of a variety of goods for one stop. In the past, more trips were necessary to make stops at several stores.

Any strategy to reduce automobile use must focus on the largest trip catagory, the business trip. It represents about half of all vehicle miles traveled. Eighty-two per cent of the Americans who commute to work travel by car. This share has been rising. In the Washington, D.C., area, for example, 60 per cent of commuting was by car in 1960. In 1970 it was 70 per cent.

Commuting is slow. Average commuting speeds in Boston, St. Louis, Seattle, and Louisville are between fifteen and eighteen miles per hour. Many people go slower. Few stop to add up their time investment in commuting. About 225 hours per year are spent driving to and from work. If the commuter were paid for this time on the road, he would receive a salary increase equal to his earnings for a month and a half.

Automobile commuting is also a financial burden. The cost of operating a standard size car is nine cents per mile at gasoline prices of fifty-two cents per gallon. For every seven cents per gallon increase in the price of gasoline, the average car's operating cost increases half a cent per mile. Owning a car requires financing it and paying for depreciation and insurance. These requirements run the total cost of car ownership to about seventeen cents per mile.

On a daily basis the total cost of vehicle ownership and operation is about equal to the price of a good bottle of wine. To own and operate a car costs five to six dollars per day. Over the 100,000-mile, ten-year lifetime of a standard-size car, an owner can expect to pay out the following amounts: depreciation, $4,201; gasoline, $4,032; maintenance and repair, $2,940; insurance, $1,618; and parking and tolls, $1,960. All told, a car represents a commitment of about $15,000 over ten years.

Together, the time invested in commuting and the cost of car ownership make commuter automobile use vulnerable to competition from mass transit. Mass transit's prospects would be even further enhanced if the automobile operator were required to pay the cost of air pollution, police salaries, taxes forgone from the highway-occupied landscape, and the court costs for automobile-related litigation. These costs have never been tabulated, an oversight that speaks volumes about the unwillingness of the Department of Transportation to support an evenhanded transportation policy. A thorough cost accounting of automobile "externalities" is essential to an informed U.S. transportation policy.

WHAT REALISTICALLY
CAN TRANSIT ACCOMPLISH?

The overriding imperative of reducing automobile traffic in our major cities cannot and need not await further proof that the transportation incentive structure is unresponsive to environmental needs. Properly conceived, a program to reduce automobile use in our major cities has explosive political potential. Such a program will help alleviate serious air pollution and other environmental problems; it can provide service to the elderly, who number 25 per cent of our population and often cannot drive, and it can save Americans millions of dollars and, for many, extraordinary inconvenience. For our largest cities we can estimate what such a program could hope to achieve. Already models exist to make the necessary calculations for a strategy to reduce automobile use by commuters. Such models are based on data from major cities reflecting real commuter choices.

Computer models tell us that if mass transit were perfectly competitive with the car in terms of travel time and cost, we would expect about 65 per cent of work trips to take place on transit. Such a "modal split," as the transit planners call it, represents the dream of every transit manager. Few will come close to achieving this goal. With today's poor-quality bus service—the typical transit trip takes thirty-eight minutes longer than by car—transit carries only 14 per cent. By contrast, excellent bus service is exemplified by the Shirley Highway bus lane from northern Virginia to Washington, D.C. Buses on exclusive lanes equal or better travel car times by beating automobile congestion. Ridership on this corridor is about 40 per cent of all potential riders.

Inevitably, however, city-wide bus or transit travel time will exceed automobile commuting performance. On some travel corridors with fast bus lanes that bypass slow-moving cars, the bus commuter can beat automobile performance. But on other routes, because of frequent stops and walking-time to the transit stop, time on the bus will exceed time by car. Of course, car drivers cannot read the paper, and bus or train travelers can. Nevertheless, a realistic estimate of the possible traffic reductions, based on the assumption that the transit trip takes twenty minutes longer (fifteen minutes on the bus and five minutes to walk to and a half blocks to the stop), reduces transit ridership from 65 per cent to 45 per cent. The overall traffic and air pollution reduction can then be calculated to be 7 per cent.[2]

We should at this point acknowledge mass transit's cost advantage over the automobile. While home-to-office travel time is more important than cost in determining the choice between the private car and mass transit, cost can also persuade drivers to switch. Rising automobile costs are putting transit in a new economy role. Gasoline prices alone are up 60 per cent over 1973 levels. Two-car families can trade in one car and save ten cents per mile, or over a dollar a day, even after paying transit costs of seven cents per mile. One-car families, by riding transit on the work trip, can save twenty-three cents per work day and keep their car for vacations, family business, and social and recreational purposes. While these savings are important, they were already reflected in the preceding calculation because they are already being enjoyed by bus riders. Thus no additional potential traffic reduction above 7 per cent can be claimed because of these savings.

To devise an optimum strategy, however, the external social cost to society of automobile use should be added as a tax on automobile commuters. Drivers, rather than the general taxpayer, should pay for air-pollution damages, court costs for traffic cases, the property tax losses on parking lots, the cost of road construction and maintenance, and traffic policing. Such an "internalization" of these external costs to society of automobile use in our cities is theoretically desirable. It is not likely, however, because economists cannot calculate the cost precisely, and even if they could, politicians would vote for

[2] The calculation follows: first the increase in transit ridership is 31 per cent (from 14 per cent to 45 per cent). This increase applies only where transit is an option, or for about half the commuting population in a well-served city. Therefore, automobile work trips will decline by half of 31 per cent, or 15.5 per cent. Overall automobile trips will drop by 45 per cent of this amount because work trips are 45 per cent of all trips. Thus automobile pollution will drop by 7 per cent.

it at their peril. Some estimates of the cost of automobile externalities
are recorded. For example, a still-unpublished 1970 Department of
Transportation study estimated that for every dollar the automobile
owner spends, another thirty cents in general revenues are expended
for police, air pollution, and to mitigate or bear other automobile externalities. In 1959 a Philadelphia official estimated that the city was
subsidizing the automobile driver by fifty dollars per car per year.
And a 1972 New York City study estimated the cost to the community of congestion at over a billion dollars annually.

While politicians will not vote for an explicit tax on the automobile owner or driver to reduce travel, politicians will vote to subsidize
mass transit.[3] This is happening in our major cities today. If we use
the mysterious Department of Transportation study's 30 per cent external cost estimate as the public burden of private driving, up to
thirty cents per day represents the external cost per automobile if
calculated on the basis of the automobile cost for commuting. This
sum represents the transit fare subsidy necessary to put transit on a
comparable "cost to society" basis with the commuting automobile.
If transit fares were so subsidized, more people would forego the automobile commute. As a practical matter, transit would cost about
twenty-five cents each way. Recent experiments with reduced bus
fares have caused transit ridership to increase by 5 per cent. Such a
development would, in our example calculation, cause traffic to drop
by another 1 per cent on top of the 7 per cent reduction achieved by
implementing good transit alone.

Increased car pooling can also reduce traffic. If commuting trip occupancy rose from 1.2 passengers per car to 1.4 passengers, traffic
would drop by about 6 per cent.[4] However, about half this increase
would be competitive with mass transit; therefore, only 3 per cent
would represent real savings in a city improving its transit system.

[3] A disadvantage of this approach is that travel becomes too cheap. If the automobile were taxed directly, driving would be reduced and reasonable transit
fares would not "encourage" excessive travel.
[4] Seventy-four per cent of work trips are in single-occupancy cars. Car pools
have proven themselves for commuters beyond the reach of transit. But where
transit is available, the disadvantage of car pooling resulting from its one-time
pickup and return character makes it less attractive than mass transit. Thus,
while environmental, energy, and transportation officials have touted the car
pool as a solution, it can at best play only a secondary role to mass transit in
reducing automobile use.

Together, improved transit, subsidized transit fares, and increased car pooling can cut commuting travel to the point that all traffic is cut by 11 per cent.[5]

A comprehensive effort to reduce traffic would also reduce non-commuting travel, the other 55 per cent of travel in our major metropolitan areas. Models have not been devised and tested to estimate feasible reductions in trips to the store, to see friends, or simply to "drive around." Some of these could be shifted to mass transit. But mass transit will surely be relatively inefficient in attracting the non-commuting trips which are not along common trip corridors and at predictable times. Other trips are "wasted" in that better planning or trip consciousness such as we learned during the energy crisis can help reduce travel. A survey by the Department of Transportation showed that during the energy crisis about a 13 per cent drop in recreational and social trips occurred, whereas overall travel fell by only 4 per cent. By conservative estimate, perhaps 5 per cent of all non-work trips could be saved. Such an achievement would reduce total traffic by almost 3 per cent.

In total, therefore, improvements in bus and rail transit service, such as special rush-hour lanes on heavily traveled routes and subsidized mass transit fares, if coupled with car pooling and a reduction of wasted noncommuting trips, can reduce traffic by about 14 per cent. There is no magic in this number. Every city is different, each with its own potential for mass transit and suitable routes for "fast bus lanes." But generally all cities can, within about three years, reduce traffic by at least 10 per cent.

With this knowledge of how traffic can be reduced and money saved, it would appear feasible, even attractive, to vote-seeking politicians to argue for and lead the country in implementing the reforms to free our cities from the scourge of excessive traffic and all that goes with it, from air pollution to the type of community alienation

[5] There are vocal advocates of a variety of innovative transportation solutions that go beyond transit and car pooling. But dial-a-ride systems, people movers, and similar technological gimmicks hold little promise at all. They are too costly. The failure of the Morgantown, West Virginia, people mover is a case in point. It contemplated passenger capsules traveling along overhead guide-ways between the downtown area and the University of West Virginia. But a tenfold cost escalation and technology failures moved university officials to threaten to invoke a clause in their contract with the Department of Transportation requiring the system's demolition if it does not work satisfactorily.

that occurs when highways dissect local communities and cultures. After all, in 45 B.C. Julius Caesar saw fit to order that no car or chariot, except those carrying the vestal virgins, could enter the city of Rome between sunrise and sunset. The crusty chairman of the U. S. House Administration Committee, the Honorable Wayne A. Hays, heard 2,018 years later that the Environmental Protection Agency was planning to charge a daily parking fee to the more than two thousand people who park free in congressional garages and parking lots at the taxpayers' expense. Hays's verdict: "I can only say that it will be a cold day in hell when they get away with that." Refusing to emulate Caesar's efforts to reduce congestion, the congressman demanded instead the treatment Caesar accorded vestal virgins.

HOW NOT TO IMPLEMENT
TRAFFIC REDUCTION REFORMS

Hays was responding to one of thirty EPA plans for reducing traffic in major U.S. cities. The saga of EPA's effort to implement traffic reduction measures is a lesson in the ways not to implement lifestyle changes for environmental improvement.

In many respects already noted in this book, the Clean Air Act of 1970 is a marvelous piece of legislation. In remarkably few words it instructed industrial and automotive sources to clean up. Then, almost as an afterthought, it recognized that applying the best technology to such sources may not be enough. The law concluded in those cases that "land use and transportation controls" were to be implemented as necessary to clean up the air to national health standards by 1975, or at the latest 1977. The record of congressional deliberation on the 1970 act contains references by Senators Muskie, John Sherman Cooper, and others to the substantial traffic reductions necessary to reach clean-air goals in the stipulated time period. Yet only five words in the act itself addressed the issue. A single phrase, therefore, became the origin of EPA regulations requiring an 85 per cent reduction in Los Angeles automobile traffic in four years, and between 45 and 84 per cent reductions in Baltimore, San Francisco, San Diego, Sacramento, and Newark.

Whatever chances such scantily clad provisions had of sneaking through a social revolution were quickly dashed by EPA's inept implementation. EPA's first approach was to delay. The states devised their implementation plans, or complete list of controls on every pollution source, and sent them to EPA in January 1972. But EPA's guidance excused the states from the requirement to develop measures to reduce traffic. The environmental litigator, the Natural Resources Defense Council (NRDC), argued before the U. S. Court of Appeals for the District of Columbia circuit that the court order EPA to initiate and expedite the submission of traffic-control plans to achieve clean air by 1977. In his January 1973 ruling, Judge John H. Pratt ordered EPA to act as requested by NRDC. He informally and sympathetically pled with EPA and Justice Department lawyers, suggesting that the only method of avoiding a calamitous shutdown of major U.S. cities was to seek congressional relief in the form of an amendment to the Clean Air Act. Meanwhile, another judge in California acted in a case brought by Riverside, California, citizens fed up with the failure of anyone to curb Los Angeles traffic. He issued an order in November 1972 directing EPA to propose within sixty days a transportation plan for meeting air standards in Los Angeles.

At this point EPA administrator Ruckelshaus was cornered. He could not hope to obtain a congressional amendment in two months. He had available to him neither the expertise to devise such a far-reaching plan to free Los Angeles of air pollution, if indeed there is such expertise, nor the time to employ it. He struck back in uncharacteristic fashion.

Ruckelshaus had perfected an extraordinary decision-making process at EPA. On major decisions he held large meetings, open to all EPA employees knowledgeable on the subject. He absorbed diverse views and facts. He tested the participants' views on all the options. For this decision, however, he failed to follow his usual practice. Instead, he entered the room convinced of one solution and explored only that solution: gas rationing. He had seized on a plan developed in EPA's California office to reduce gasoline sales by 85 per cent to force the reduction in traffic to meet air-quality standards. Despite staff objections that such a proposal would be a folly, that it could not be implemented, that it would be laughed at, and that it might arm the enemies of clean air with a powerful club, Ruckelshaus proposed the plan.

Some have accused Ruckelshaus of deliberately proposing gas rationing as a ploy to force Congress to weaken the Clean Air Act. This was not his motivation. Instructed repeatedly by Congress to do the impossible, sued at every turn by industry and the environmentalists for doing it—at one count seventy-six separate suits were pending—Ruckelshaus responded in kind. He was not helped by his staff. No more attractive alternatives were offered.

He dropped his bombshell on January 22, 1973, at a press conference in Los Angeles: 85 per cent gas rationing. Today he recalls his dilemma with a remembrance of an exchange with a front-row reporter at the conference. The reporter asked plaintively why the administrator was proposing such a Draconian measure. Ruckelshaus replied with his foxhole sense of humor. Reminding his audience of the judge's order and the substantial fines and possible jail sentence behind it, he said, "Faced with a choice between my freedom and your mobility, my freedom wins."

By June–July 1973, after Ruckelshaus left EPA to become acting director of the FBI, similar traffic reduction plans had been put together by EPA for another thirty cities in eighteen states. Only a few benefited from substantial local input. After a summer of public debate, they were to be promulgated in the fall.

These plans, though hastily devised, constituted technically responsible approaches to reducing traffic and pollution by substantial amounts. After the public consternation that followed the gas rationing plan for Los Angeles, these plans incorporated a new EPA strategy. The new plans, including a revised one for Los Angeles, contained reasonable but stringent measures to control traffic, to reduce emissions from cars on the street by the addition of "hardware retrofits" to older car engines, and to reduce industrial pollution beyond already-imposed controls. These EPA plans did not promise traffic reductions adequate to meet air standards. Only "practical" measures were included.

Of the twenty-nine plans eventually completed, twenty-seven had inspection systems to check emissions from on-the-road vehicles, fourteen required installation of pollution control devices on some pre-1974 cars, over twenty included augmentation of mass transit (including thirteen cities to add express bus lanes), eighteen had special car pool programs, and nineteen contemplated restrictions on the number of on-street and off-street parking spaces including, for some, controls over the construction of new parking capacity.

The traffic reductions called for by the plans ranged broadly. New York City was to reduce traffic by 40 per cent. Most cities were to achieve a 10 to 20 per cent reduction. Because of the very high levels of transit usage in New York, major automobile traffic reductions were feasible without overburdening the transit system. In New York City, 27 per cent of all trips and 83 per cent of downtown trips take place by transit. A 40 per cent reduction in downtown auto traffic for Manhattan would mean only a 5 per cent increase in transit ridership. But in a city like Los Angeles, where only 3 per cent of trips are by transit, much less was possible. Even if Los Angeles could achieve the transit ridership levels of New York, its auto use would be reduced by only 25 per cent. Of course, Los Angeles's bus system would have to be expanded seven- or eightfold over its present size in order to achieve a 25 per cent traffic reduction goal, itself far short of that required to meet air standards.

As a result of calculations like these, EPA concluded that only a 10 to 20 per cent reduction in traffic was probably feasible for most cities by 1977. Had EPA realized this distinction at the time of Ruckelshaus's January 1973 announcement in Los Angeles, it could have spared the environmental movement considerable grief and a substantial loss in credibility. People thought EPA was cleaning out America's cities rather than cleaning them up. As it turned out, by the time EPA had forged a reasonable strategy for its plans, no one was listening.

State and local political figures and members of the U. S. Congress either denounced transportation controls or ignored them. San Francisco's Mayor Joseph Alioto said that the EPA plan to obtain an 84 per cent traffic reduction "would cause severe economic problems in the Bay Area." On the East Coast, Newark's Mayor Kenneth A. Gibson, faced with the prospect of a 68 per cent reduction, identified a key weakness of the plan. "This is a commuter-oriented city," he said. "Until adequate transportation alternatives are developed and funded we are not in a position to ban automobiles from our cities."

Governor Jack Williams of Arizona wondered aloud: "I don't know how they [EPA] will enforce anything. How many troops do

they have?" Even Governor Francis Sargent of Massachusetts attacked the Boston transportation control plan. In early 1970 Sargent
had halted work on all major planned expressways within the area
encompassed by state route 128, a beltway around greater Boston.
He described his plan as an effort to "decisively reverse the trend toward ever-increasing dependence on the automobile." Yet he feared
EPA's measures would "weaken the economic life of the core city."
It was clear to Sargent that his city would "choke and die on the automobile." It was equally clear that without the automobile the core
city would starve unless major improvements in mass transit were
implemented. Mayor Pete Wilson of San Diego judged achievement
of EPA's planned 45 per cent travel reduction impossible without a
"massive increase" in federal funding to add 1,250 buses to a city
fleet of 250.

Beyond almost uniform opposition to EPA's efforts, each part of
the country added a local flavor to its reactions. In the East, the editorials grumbled but as often as not concluded on a note of hope and
resignation. Perhaps Easterners have suffered congestion and federal
government intervention and assistance more than others. Midwest-
erners rejected the concept of federal intervention, but not the need
to curb their automobiles. In the West, except for California, there
was outrage. The *Salt Lake City Tribune*'s editorial response, quot-
ing Governor Calvin Rampton, was labeled "Damn Fool Thing Indeed." And the *Arizona Republic* led with "Stop EPA Dictatorship."
The attitude of Texas officials clarified the reasons for Western opposition: the EPA might just as well have sought to take away the cowboy's horse. No Westerner was going to be told by a "Fed" to dis-
mount his car.

Only California, long exposed to rolling clouds of automobile pollution, recognized the need to reduce automobile use. Governor
Reagan's closest associates, when urged by White House aide
Richard Fairbanks to testify before Congress in favor of amending
the Clean Air Act to relieve it of the transportation control mandate,
would not touch it. Outright anti-Clean Air Act posturing was not a
winning position, even for a conservative California governor.

Throughout the nation, the groups with access to power in Washington, D.C., recorded their strong opposition to traffic reduction
measures. Within hours of the unveiling of EPA's plans, the House

had made up its mind to amend the Clean Air Act. To a man, Arizona's six-member congressional delegation pledged to seek amendments to the act rather than reduce traffic by 35 per cent. The response of New Jersey's delegation was, at least superficially, no different, despite the positions of Senators Harrison A. Williams, Jr., and Clifford Case on the opposite end of the political spectrum from Senators Paul Fannin and Barry Goldwater. But the New Jersey verdict, no reductions without adequate mass transit, did not exclude an eventual curtailment in traffic. The Arizona politicians, with the exception of Congressman Morris K. Udall, denounced *any* federal plans to reduce automobile traffic.

For two cities there was a brief interlude of confidence and hope before they, too, backed away from the challenge. In both of these cities, New York and Washington, D.C., newspaper editorials supported plan implementation, and a substantial group of political leaders reacted favorably. These plans were unique. Both called for traffic reductions that could realistically be achieved. Both were developed by local governments. In New York, capable environmental officials developed a plan to reduce city traffic by 40 per cent. In Washington, D.C., a skilled Council of Governments staff fashioned a plan amid crosscutting interests expressed by Virginia, Maryland, and District of Columbia officials. In both cities mass transit was a credible alternative. In Washington, D.C., a $4 billion mass transit system was under construction; its completion was scheduled in 1977, the identical date of accomplishment of the proposed traffic reductions. Washington had also witnessed the most successful U.S. fast bus lane, mentioned earlier. New York's transit system is in shambles, but many, having no choice, ride it anyway. *The New York Times* put the city's dilemma succinctly: "In a logical world such drastic curtailment in the use of the private auto would be expected to follow sweeping improvement in the public transit systems rather than to precede it. But the condition of the air now makes it impossible to wait for such a development."

Ultimately the Washington area and New York City plans were so watered down that they no longer promise clean air in 1977. Important provisions were sustained, such as inspection and maintenance of emission-control systems on cars and mass transit improvement including dedicated bus lanes on expressways. But in New York,

Governor Malcolm Wilson, replacing Governor Rockefeller and facing a close election contest in November 1974, joined Mayor Beame, who had replaced Mayor Lindsay, in junking the proposed tolls on the toll-free Harlem and East River bridges and in retreating from the planned ban on taxi cruising. It turned out that one of Mayor Lindsay's last defeats before his term expired, the failure of his proposal to create a vehicle-free fifteen-block mall on Madison Avenue, was a portent of the policies of his successor. Mayor-to-be Beame voted with the taxi lobby against Lindsay.

The Washington, D.C., plan faltered too because local politicians like northern Virginia congressman Joel T. Broyhill (later defeated) and Maryland governor Marvin Mandel objected to the plan. The most controversial provision was a hike in the cost of commuting by increasing all-day parking costs. First, Washington's federal work force was to pay commercial rates for parking. (A survey of automobile commuters on the Shirley Highway route into Washington, D.C., found that 56 per cent parked free and over 80 per cent paid a dollar per day or less.) It seemed incontestable that federal employees who demand every pay break the private sector gets should pay the same rates for parking. But Congressman Wayne Hays and others refused to admit to the possibility that employees of Congress and the congressmen themselves could be treated like the tax-paying masses they serve.

The key element of the District plan was an additional commuter parking tax of fifty cents per day beginning in mid-1975 and rising to two dollars by 1977 for commuters to seven selected areas within the District and in Virginia and Maryland with adequate mass transit service. This charge was designed to coincide with vastly improved bus service (nine new fast bus lanes and 750 new buses for an area total of 2,530 buses) and the advent of the new Metro train system. As a practical matter, all-day commuters to these areas would be banned by the forty-dollar-per-month charge on top of twenty to thirty dollars commercial parking costs. Three-man car pools would save the commuter forty to fifty dollars over single-car commuting costs. Single-occupancy car commuters would save forty-five dollars by switching to the bus or Metro. EPA argued strongly that the revenues from this system, to be collected and used by local governments to fund mass transit, could range upward from $1 million per month.

This sum would have covered a large part of the mass transit operating deficit at that time.

EPA's withdrawal of this proposal in January 1974 is probably the epitaph to financial measures designed to reduce automobile traffic by taxing driving directly. Congress protested the approach and quickly passed legislation prohibiting EPA from imposing such charges. Congressional action was sparked not only by the District plan. Rather Congress was protesting similar EPA measures proposed for California, where no credible mass transit alternative was even on the drawing boards and no local jurisdiction had even suggested the idea of a surcharge.

REFORMING
URBAN TRANSPORTATION

The lessons of the Environmental Protection Agency's abortive venture into the field of transportation controls are fundamental. Necessary reforms by EPA and the environmental movement are suggested by the failures. Inescapable as well is the additional evidence on how difficult it will be to free our cities of the punishment they suffer daily because of excessive automobile use. Many torturing political decisions lie ahead on the road to clean air. On a pragmatic level, EPA's plans were not professional. The proposals for traffic reductions of 45 per cent or more were a travesty. Legal thinking, untempered by sound technical advice, caused EPA initially to propose ridiculous measures. By the time, six months later, when EPA had professionally judged that a 10 to 20 per cent reduction was practicable, the damage was done. Political and popular support for the plans was sparse at best. Environmental groups, although experienced in litigation, lacked influence among the people. Real estate and parking interests acted against the transportation plans, but they did not defeat them. The people did. In actuality, the plans were like a single hand clapping. The other hand, a credible and substantial effort to aid cities in constructing mass transit systems, was Richard Nixon's, and it never moved.

Frequently, EPA administrators Ruckelshaus, Fri, and Train visited the White House, the Office of Management and Budget, and the Department of Transportation to secure support for mass transit. No one wanted to help. At one particular White House meeting EPA officials forcefully pressed Secretary Brinegar for a Department of Transportation funding initiative in support of mass transit in the EPA-impacted cities. Brinegar responded, "I don't see any need for additional mass transit funding." On no occasion did Brinegar or Nixon voice any support for EPA's efforts, nor were Department of Transportation personnel in the field ordered by Brinegar to do so.

Despite EPA's failure, the promise of successful efforts to reduce traffic in our major air-polluted cities is still great. A variety of developments point toward ultimate success in saving at least some of our cities from automobile strangulation. Oddly, one of these is the energy crisis. When EPA proposed in early 1973 to reduce traffic to reduce air pollution, energy savings were not an issue. Moreover, the concept of reducing traffic to achieve air-pollution improvements had never been tested on a city-wide scale. The energy crisis, spanning the December 1973 to May 1974 period, was a test case of the ability of mass transit systems to increase ridership, of reduced traffic to lower air-pollution readings, and of the ability of the economy to thrive despite reduced traffic. Traffic reductions were recorded in every major American city. In New York City, traffic was down 5 to 10 per cent on weekdays and 25 per cent on weekends. In Washington, D.C., early 1974 traffic was 20 to 30 per cent below levels a year earlier.

Two inevitable occurrences accompanied these traffic reductions: pollution declined and mass transit ridership rose sharply. Carbon monoxide levels in New York fell 10 to 20 per cent on weekdays and 31 per cent on Sundays. Mass transit ridership rose by about 4 per cent in New York, Dallas, Baltimore, and New Orleans, 8 per cent in Los Angeles, 16 per cent in Atlanta, 22 per cent in Denver, 26 per cent in San Diego, and 7 per cent in Miami. These ridership gains helped boost 1973 mass transit ridership by 1.4 per cent over 1972. And in January 1974 nationwide ridership was up more than 4 per cent. But as the energy crisis eased, air pollution rose and transit ridership fell back to 1973 levels. The economic impact on cities of traffic reductions of this magnitude was apparently slight. No systematic study has been performed, but core city areas like New York reported higher retail sales. Had EPA had such evidence to point to in early 1973, its advocacy of modest traffic reductions of less than 20 per cent would have been more credible.

The energy crisis forced people to reconsider their attitudes toward mass transit and the automobile. They witnessed, for the first time since Henry Ford, an automobile performance failure. They wondered how much they could rely on this endangered species, its food supply jeopardized by gasoline shortages. Some people thought twice about buying homes miles from their places of work; families considered locating near mass transit routes and debated the cost of operating a car in a high-gas-price era.

A number of "experiments" with reduced automobile use have been under way in Europe for several years. Most involve vehicle bans in small areas or along specified streets to create shopping malls. One of the earliest, in 1960 in Bremen, Germany, is, after a decade and a half, evidence that economic activity can continue without the automobile. More recently, an experimental ban on parking in Marseilles lowered pollution 40 per cent. Banning the private car from London's Oxford Street has pleased merchants. A twenty-five-acre vehicle-free zone near the Trevi Fountain in Rome has created a new atmosphere of small-town neighborliness. All told, more than one hundred European cities from Athens to Göteborg have tried partial or complete traffic bans in their cities with no adverse economic effects, air-pollution reductions of about 50 per cent, and significantly reduced noise levels.

Why have the Americans, so long the leaders in the automobile age, been tardy in experimenting with reduced automobile use? One view is that the Europeans are appalled at the damage the automobile is inflicting on their cherished city life. The urge to protect the traditional centers of European civilization, cities like Florence, Paris, Rome, and Athens, has motivated Europeans to act where America's politicians have hesitated. It is also important, of course, that gasoline costs $1.25 per gallon in Europe.

Unlike their leaders, not all Americans have hesitated. Not all are reluctant to spend tax dollars for mass transit, to halt highway construction, or to ban automobiles from central city areas. A variety of polls and citizen actions reveal a powerful antiautomobile, pro-mass transit constituency in America. The construction of major new highways in our large cities has virtually ended. Powerful citizen lobbies have persuaded politicians in Boston, Philadelphia, Washington, D.C., and practically every other major city to treat each new highway proposal with a presumption of guilt, rather than to accept the discredited arguments that more concrete will somehow relieve congestion and restore the city economy. The urban highway is the best argument against itself. Even Congress, long the handmaiden of the highway lobby, acknowledged in the 1973 Highway Act this strong public aversion to further city highway construction by permitting for the first time the use of revenues from the Highway Trust Fund for rail and bus transit capital improvements. Previously, failure to construct an urban highway resulted in a loss of federal funding.

One of the most important highway decisions ever made, because it is symbolic of the relative power of highway versus antihighway forces in the nation's capital, was the decision on whether interstate route 66 was to be built over the ten miles from the Capital Beltway to downtown Washington. Backed by its consultant's report, the Virginia Highway Department and the governor of Virginia proposed to the Secretary of the U. S. Department of Transportation that the road be constructed. The road was opposed in a series of decisive votes, generally with an eight-to-two margin, by the Transportation Planning Board of the Washington area Council of Governments. These votes reflected opposition in all of the affected northern Virginia counties and towns and the District of Columbia. Likewise, the road was opposed by the EPA, the President's Council on Environmental Quality, the Department of Housing and Urban Development, the Department of the Interior, and the Federal Energy Administration.

Under the 1973 Highway Act, construction of this proposed route had to be judged by the Secretary of Transportation to be consistent with the Clean Air Act-mandated transportation control plan for the Washington, D.C., area. This provision subjects proposed new urban highways in Washington and the other twenty-eight cities with transportation controls to an overriding air-pollution test that few, if any, can pass. Unlike the impact statements required by the National Environmental Policy Act and assessments by the EPA administrator called for by section 109-j of the Clean Air Act, which are advisory assessments only, this requirement applies a rigorous test to highway projects. Citizen suits could be brought against any Secretary of Transportation whose highway approval decision is not consistent with cleaning the air.

These new and imposing authorities were a factor in Secretary of Transportation William T. Coleman's decision to reject the proposal to build I-66. Two recent citizen actions in the New York City area further attest to the strength of community preservation as a newly emergent antihighway force. A score of West Side Manhattan community groups angrily voiced their eternal opposition to plans for transforming the West Side Highway and the Henry Hudson Parkway into a multilane interstate highway. A New York State-City plan for a further expansion of the Long Island Expressway was shelved by the state in the face of strong environmental and community preservation opposition.

The other side of the antihighway campaign must encompass a willingness to support large-scale public funding for mass transit if increasing citizen mobility is to continue to be a factor in U.S. economic growth and lifestyle diversity. A variety of polls have found the public anxious to increase funding for mass transit. A California poll revealed that 62 per cent of the population of the most motorized state favored construction of rail rapid transit, even at an increased tax cost of a hundred dollars per year per family. On the same willingness-to-pay scale, perhaps bulging transit deficits could be covered by a local gas tax of one to two cents per gallon on top of or in lieu of the four cents per gallon that finances the Highway Trust Fund. According to other polls, however, these same Californians were reluctant to give up freeway construction. A small minority wanted either to ban or to reduce freeway construction, while most wanted highway projects to continue subject to environmental criteria.

A Gallup survey of a sample of the 14 million adults in the Connecticut-New Jersey-New York region found one in eight advocated free mass transit and a majority favored subsidies for mass transit. A 1973 poll of 1,209 in the Washington, D.C., area found increased funding for mass transit the number-two priority for increased local government spending, behind increased spending for schools. Another survey on public attitudes toward highways and mass transit in the Washington area found what is probably a typical view in large metropolitan areas. Of northern Virginians questioned about the desirability of additional highway construction (I-66), about 65 per cent favored it, whereas of the District of Columbia residents on the receiving end of the road's traffic, only 38 per cent were in favor. However, residents of both areas agreed mass transit improvements were more important: the ratio of those favoring mass transit improvements over road improvements was thirty-six to one in the District and four to one in Virginia.

Congress is responding to these citizen preferences, but slowly. The new Urban Mass Transit Act, recently passed by Congress, calls for $11.8 billion to be expended for mass transit over six years. But this sum, which almost doubles the previous annual rate of mass transit expenditures and includes funding for operating subsidies and buses, is far short of what is required to make mass transit an attractive alternative for the millions of Americans who must forego automobile travel if air quality and community environmental needs are to be met.[6]

Funding is only a prerequisite for performance. It does not guarantee it. To achieve the magnitude of traffic reductions necessary to restore clean air in U.S. cities and to save energy will, as indicated previously, necessitate increasing the share of work trips taken by mass transit from 14 per cent to about 35 to 40 per cent. Within a few years, roughly a threefold improvement of the passenger-carrying capacity of mass transit systems is required. Significantly, the most ambitious mass transit system now under construction—the Washington, D.C., Metro system—will reduce traffic at full implementation by only 5 per cent, or less than one third of the city's needed traffic reduction if it is to have clean air.

But the real transit goal cannot be expressed solely in simple numerical terms, because it is also a qualitative goal. It means a commitment to substantial upgrading and expansion of transit service. It means shifting capital investments away from projects that serve the

[6] There are eleven cities in the U.S. with a population of two million or more. Six have mass transit systems, although New York's is hardly adequate. Nonetheless, if the other five cities, which include Los Angeles and Detroit, built systems similar to Washington's Metro system, at a $4-billion-per-system cost, federal assistance to the cities at an 80 per cent federal share would cost another $16 billion in 1974 dollars. In addition, another twenty-two cities with over a million in population are in need of transit help.

automobile and toward those that serve transit. It means managing the urban street network for the benefit of transit instead of cars. It means adjusting price incentives so they favor transit instead of the car. And it means planning future urban land use to minimize the need for vehicular travel and maximize the ability of transit to serve people's travel needs.

How can this be accomplished? The first thing is to incorporate the goals into our thinking—and to start taking them into account in planning. Federally funded transportation planning—which has long been highway-oriented—should embrace air quality, energy, and service to the elderly and poor as criteria weighed more heavily than adding highway capacity. We must give up our pursuit of the mirage of congestion-free traffic, too often at the end of the latest highway proposal. We must set rigid rules: for example, major airports should not be funded with federal dollars unless they are linked to the central city by mass transit.

There is a Gresham's law of transportation as well as of money: bad transportation drives out good transportation. Or, in the urban context, expansion of relatively inefficient systems—highways—has encouraged more reliance on automobiles and discouraged the more efficient systems—mass transit.

Assume for the sake of argument that transit is given a chance. Skeptics would counter: "There are only two problems with transit, the federal budget can't afford it, and even if it could, nobody would ride it." The skeptics are correct because they reflect experience with existing systems, and these are generally lousy.

To illustrate just how bad the situation is, consider a hypothetical transit system in Smogtown, U.S.A. Probably Smogtown transit has these characteristics: about a third of the people live six or more blocks away from the nearest bus stop. Only half live within three blocks. In any case, the bus probably does not go where the potential rider wants to go, even if he has reasonable access. Most transit systems are heavily downtown-oriented, but only a small portion of total trips go downtown, and many trips are not even radial. Even if transit happens to connect the traveler's home with his desired destination, it probably isn't very attractive, because the bus ride takes twice as long as the equivalent car ride. And if, as is likely, parking is free at the other end, the bus probably costs more than the car. If, in spite of everything, a person still wants to take a bus, he may well need to hire a transit planning consultant to plan his route and supply a schedule. Naturally Smogtown has an average transit ridership of about 14 per cent.

A heavy burden of proof is on those who think transit can be efficient. There is, fortunately, more to the hope that ridership can increase by threefold than a transit planner's calculation. Ridership on high-quality transit systems confirms transit's potential. It has already been noted that the Shirley Highway express bus service carries about 40 per cent of its potential riders. This compares with 29 per cent before the express service started and 20 per cent for the Washington area as a whole. If the highway carried these commuters in cars, three additional lanes would be needed. A similar bus way has been successfully implemented along the San Bernardino Freeway between El Monte and Los Angeles. In Toronto, 50 per cent of downtown trips use transit and in cities like Chicago and New York, where auto use is difficult, the figures can exceed 80 per cent.

But these are only isolated cases on isolated corridors. The challenge is to put all the pieces together for an entire system, to design, implement, and manage the urban transportation system so that transit has high ridership, low costs, and, most importantly, priority over the car. The decisive requirement for a mass transit renaissance is that priority be given to incentives in favor of mass transit users. Time is money in the transportation business. Special bus lanes and traffic treatment coupled with automobile disincentives such as malls and auto-free zones, and on-street parking limits, must be implemented on a broad scale. Eliminating subsidized employee parking, which causes average parking costs to be about seventy-five cents, or less than half commercial rates, would be a major step. These reforms, supplemented by transit subsidies, can open the way for transit. A variety of recent transit innovations are evidence that it can be done. In Seattle, a better bus system was funded through a sales tax. It brought both express service, which raised ridership 33 per cent, and free rides downtown. Dayton and Birmingham instituted free downtown bus service in 1973. A subsidy that lowered San Diego's fare from forty cents to twenty-five cents increased patronage 72 per cent. South in Atlanta a city sales tax of 1 per cent bought a fifteen-cent bus ride and helped increase ridership 20 per cent. A sales tax on 0.5 per cent resulted in a big improvement in Denver's bus service and helped increase ridership 35 per cent in two years. Boston and San Francisco have ordered 275 trolley cars, the first manufactured in the United States in twenty-three years. Dayton, Ohio, is planning a full-scale trolley system.

Already data on mass transit ridership is reflecting the impact of these changes. In 1973, for the first time in twenty-three years, the number of Americans riding transit systems did not decline. Also, in 1974, aided by the energy crisis, transit showed a significant gain (7 per cent). These gains were sustained in 1975. This achievement, made even with a drop in New York ridership (30 per cent of the national total) is a welcome harbinger of what the next twenty-three years might bring.

TYING LAND USE
AND TRANSPORTATION TOGETHER

A sustained effort to reduce automobile use must encompass land use. Already half of our homes are located more than three blocks from a transit stop; 30 per cent are six blocks or more distant from a bus or train. The growth of suburbia since World War II has placed so many residences beyond the reach of mass transit that transit's potential market is only half the population. Land-use planning responsive to the need to reduce traffic would have as its goal the development of our cities along transit corridors or in satellite communities easily served by transit or with businesses and residences located near one another. Powerful tools, long unexercised, are available to accomplish this goal.

First, the highway is the chief man-made determinant of urban shape. Urban form in turn determines the need for travel. Despite these obvious relationships, thinking and analysis on where roads should be built has been nonexistent. Obvious questions have never been answered. For example, do circumferential highways generate more traffic as a result of their influence on land-use patterns than radial highways? Are they the cause of perimeter prosperity at the expense of downtown decay? One suspects they do, but one could not find the answer from the U. S. Department of Transportation. If they do, why have so many beltways been funded? But are corridors an alternative? If corridor development is too dense, pollution, perhaps sulfur oxides or particulates, or even automotive pollutants, can exceed health standards. How far can corridorization proceed?

For some cities it may be too late to redirect already-powerful growth forces. As each day passes without answers to these tough questions and the implementation of policies consistent with the answers, more cities fall into the category of the unsalvageable.

New York City exemplifies a city fossilized by narrow-minded highway construction. Robert Moses, the city's powerful public works architect for thirty-five years, believed and practiced the mystical religion that the *next* highway would solve the congestion problem. In a penetrating analysis of Moses' influence, Robert A. Caro described the situation as follows:

> Watching Moses open the Triborough Bridge to ease congestion on the Queensboro Bridge and open the Bronx-Whitestone Bridge to ease congestion on the Triborough Bridge, and then watching traffic counts on all three bridges mount until each was as congested as one had been before, planners could hardly avoid the conclusion that "traffic generation" was no longer a theory but a proved fact. As more highways were built to alleviate congestion, more automobiles would pour onto them and congest them, thus forcing the building of more highways— which would generate more traffic and become congested in their turn, in an inexorably widening gyre, with awesome implications for the future of New York and of all urban areas.[7]

Gresham's law of transportation operated in New York City with a vengeance. Moses opposed any expenditures for transit. He even refused to make a minor alteration in a highway plan that would have allowed mass transit to serve New York's airports. He employed abundant toll revenues to construct more highways. The highways attracted more cars and spawned more dispersed land-use patterns. Transit ridership declined. More trains were late and commuting coaches deteriorated. Riders abandoned transit for cars. Fares went up in futile attempts to resuscitate the service. More riders were

[7] *The Power Broker: Robert Moses and the Fall of New York* (New York: Alfred A. Knopf, 1974).

driven to Moses' roads. The turning point occurred in the 1950s. Toll revenue was vast, and, with the supplement of Highway Trust Fund monies beginning in 1956, New York City had the resources to rebuild its mass transit system as well as extend its highway network. But from 1955 to 1962, according to Caro, it added not one mile of transit, yet completed 206 miles of highways and began construction on another 265 miles. New York City is now probably locked in the death grip of its highways.

Toronto, Canada, by contrast, has saved itself by a vigorous program to improve mass transit. Riders on the Toronto system number 600,000 per day and are growing in number. Compare this sum to Washington, D.C., a city with a slightly larger population and about the same land area, where only 175,000 ride each day. Toronto transit is cheap—twenty-five cents—safe, clean, modern, and reliable.

Washington is today at a threshold not much different from that passed by New York City in the mid-1950s. In this regard, it is representative of many cities that have increased dramatically in size since World War II—Dallas, Indianapolis, Baltimore, Atlanta, Miami, Phoenix, Houston, and Denver. These cities face a choice. Continued reliance on the automobile will seal their destiny as cities where human-scale living is difficult, if not out of the question.

It may already be too late to save Washington. Beltway strangulation may have reached the terminal point. Projections of area-wide travel follow inexorably from the projected land-use pattern, itself preordained by an evolving beltway-oriented land-use pattern. The Washington-area population is projected to grow by 50 per cent over the next twenty years. The vehicle population will rise 100 per cent. And per-car miles traveled can be expected to rise—they always have. If travel doubles, the region must cope with twice today's traffic. Even this estimate does not account for the fact that households and jobs will grow faster than population, generating even more trips. Here is how the land-use pattern in Washington will dictate travel: 60 per cent of the area's trips now originate in the suburbs; in 1994, 75 per cent will; because one out of every two downtown trips is on mass transit, compared with one of every five suburban-downtown trips, and because the average city trip distance is three miles, compared with seven miles from the suburbs to downtown, it follows that travel will increase by at least 100 per cent. If land-use patterns do not change, in twenty years Washington will suffer New York's problems, or Los Angeles's. The only way to avoid this automobile trap is to cease building highways, devote the area's resources to mass transit, and give transit priority on the existing streets.

If Washington should look to Toronto as an example of a North American city that has successfully integrated transportation and land-use planning, so should all major U.S. cities. The province of Ontario, with more authority than our states, imposed region-wide government on Toronto in 1953, increasing the area of the city from 35 square miles to 240 square miles. This area is today so well served by 696 miles of public transit that transit reaches to within two thousand feet of the homes of 95 per cent of the population. Twenty-six miles of subway track are fed passengers by hundreds of miles of bus, trolley, and train lines. Toronto has also relegated the automobile to a secondary role in the city's mobility.

Of the larger U.S. cities, not all have neglected transit. Chicago is an interesting case where its border, Lake Michigan, prevented the construction of a beltway. No Robert Moses emerged to bridge the lake with a midwest version of the Verrazano-Narrows Bridge. Instead, the city promoted radial development along rail lines and radial highways. Today Chicago's Loop survives as the center of the second largest metropolitan area in the United States—with seven million people. The city of Chicago and Cook County may have learned one important land-use lesson: the city's fate is in someone else's hands. The Regional Planning Commission for Northeast Illinois, spanning six counties, can either destroy Chicago by promoting circumferential growth or nourish Chicago by promoting zoning, highway, and mass transit design to promote radial growth.

Philadelphia in the 1960s refused to join other cities in their rush to wrap themselves in beltways. Today its downtown core is relatively prosperous. It is well served by mass transit, including the successful Lindenwold Hi-Speed Line, linking 43,000 southern New Jersey commuters to the downtown area designed by William Penn nearly three centuries ago. Demonstrating the vitality of transit-based land-use patterns, residential growth along the Lindenwold has exceeded by three times the surrounding auto-served areas. Boston has also nourished its core and supported mass transit. Los Angeles has not. In the 1930s a decision was made to give the automobile rather than streetcars priority at intersections. The mass transit priority rule was broken, with results which in the late 1940s ushered in the smog age.

If today's major cities, today's Congress, and today's political leaders ignore the role of transit in shaping growth, which in turn shapes our transportation preferences, the transportation lifestyle change that is a prerequisite to the attainment of environmental goals for many Americans cannot occur. Some have alleged that our freedom is threatened by actions to reduce automobile use. That kind of freedom was aptly characterized by the late Janis Joplin when she sang, "Freedom's just another word for nothing left to lose."

7.

SHAPING LAND USE
AND GROWTH

We can look out our home, office, or car windows and see the reasons why a call has gone out for land-use reform. Practically the only "balanced" community one can see in America is Colonial Williamsburg, tastefully restored with Rockefeller money near Virginia's coast. A blight has stricken our cities in the form of a cold, heavy ugliness. Our suburbs are a monotony the Soviet socialist economy would point to with pride. Along our ribbons of roadways the blight is a never-ending mural of garish, tasteless signs, asphalt plazas, and cantilevered concrete. It is difficult to imagine a contented human being living in such surroundings, much less any form of wildlife as common as a rabbit or dove. Rats, pigeons, and starlings are thriving. A spreading awareness that the origins of our disorientation lie in our neglect of our land environment has helped trigger the land-use rebellion. Labeled the "Quiet Revolution" by a 1971 Council on Environmental Quality report, the revolution today is vociferous and visible.

THE NOT-SO-QUIET REVOLUTION

Like most revolutions, this one has a colorful nomenclature of battle sites: Ramapo, St. Petersburg, Petaluma, Boca Raton, Oregon,
Boulder, Fairfax, Montgomery, and San Jose. In 1971 in the city
of Boulder, Colorado, the voters among its 70,000 residents nearly
passed a proposal to limit Boulder's size to 100,000. Since then Colorado has decisively rejected America's classic growth-is-good politics.
Colorado voted out its powerful congressman Wayne Aspinall, a
long-time defender of resource development interests and chairman
of the House Interior Committee. It rejected in 1973 an opportunity
to host the 1976 Winter Olympics, and in November 1974 it elected
a proenvironment governor, Richard Lamm. Oregon, like Colorado,
is a mecca for outdoors-oriented Americans. Oregon's past governor,
Tom McCall, led an effort to forestall the "Californication" of his
state. Over three fourths of Oregon's recent growth has come from
immigrants, many from California. Oregon's slogan, "Come visit us
but for Heaven's sake, don't stay," is befitting of the nation's elev-
enth fastest growing state.

Other antigrowth efforts are more localized. Ramapo, New York,
holds the distinction of being the recipient of one of the nation's
landmark court decisions in support of its plan to regulate growth.
The New York Court of Appeals refused to overturn Ramapo's 1969
plan to ration permits for new housing in accordance with the community's capital program to install sewerage, parks, roads, and
firehouses. This initiative by Ramapo's citizens, among the wealthiest
in the United States and living thirty-five miles from Manhattan, has
set an example for controlled growth which hundreds of cities are
now trying to emulate.

Petaluma, California, tried, failed, and then succeeded. In June
1973 its citizens approved by four to one an ordinance to ration
growth over five years at a rate of five hundred dwelling units per
year. From 1960 to 1974, the population of Petaluma, located just
forty miles from San Francisco and previously a quiet farming community, doubled to 31,000 as it was transformed into a "bedroom
community." Petaluma citizens set their quantitative limit on housing

growth at about 6 per cent per year based on an estimate of the projected capacity of the city's water-supply and sewage-treatment facilities. In striking down Petaluma's ordinance at the request of four land and real estate developers, the U. S. District Court judge ruled it unconstitutional to regulate "population growth numerically so as to preclude residents of any other area from traveling into the region and settling there." The judge said that every city must take its "fair share" of the population explosion. In another landmark ruling, the Ninth U. S. Circuit Court of Appeals reversed the lower court and upheld the Petaluma action. The prevailing opinion strikes a responsive chord in all who have yearned for a simpler community life: ". . . the concept of the public welfare is sufficiently broad to uphold Petaluma's desire to preserve its small town character, its open spaces and low density of population and to grow at an orderly and deliberate pace."

The most Draconian no-growth action by a locality was taken in March 1974 by the St. Petersburg city council. It voted to set a mid-1974 population limit of 235,000—25,000 below 1974's population —in effect evicting 25,000 people. The Council quickly reversed itself two weeks later, recognizing the unconstitutionality of its expulsion plan. Across the state a few months before, Boca Raton had voted a ceiling on its population, becoming the first U.S. city to limit its size. Whereas the city's zoning would have allowed it to grow from 40,000 population to 150,000, the voters decided to set a 105,000 limit. Like Oregonians, these Floridians, having witnessed the rapid development of nearby Miami and Fort Lauderdale, were seeking to "pull up the gangplank." Other cities have taken more subtle approaches to limiting growth. Fairborn, Ohio, is one example. According to a 1973 ordinance, developers must give up 8 to 20 per cent of their land for parks and open spaces or, if the city agrees, pay an equivalent cash value.

The nation's two wealthiest counties in terms of median family income are Fairfax County, Virginia, and Montgomery County, Maryland, both Washington, D.C., suburbs. A recent census update confirmed that Montgomery County grew at about four times the national average from 1970 to 1974. Not surprisingly, these Washington suburbs have been the sites of some of the toughest no-growth battles. Fairfax in January 1974 tried to declare an eighteen-month "emergency" moratorium on development in order to fashion a comprehensive growth plan, but its attempt was struck down by a county court. Both counties, polluters of the Potomac River, have experienced repeated sewer moratoriums. Under a county facilities ordinance, Montgomery County requires developers to prove the availability of adequate police, school, road, fire, water, and sewer services before receiving a building permit. And recently the county down-zoned 40 per cent of its area.

The growth controversy goes beyond these cited cases into hundreds of communities. One EPA study indicates that 160 cities in Ohio and Illinois alone were under sewer-hookup moratoriums, which prohibit further growth by denying home builders access to sewage-treatment plants and collection systems. Another forty sewer bans have been identified in Florida. And in New Jersey's densely populated Passaic Valley region, over thirty of the area's 112 communities were under a moratorium of some type in 1973. A Department of Housing and Urban Development survey in 1973 identified more than 250 jurisdictions around the country subject to moratoriums on permits for building, water or sewer connections, subdividing, or other essential steps toward growth.

Hostility to growth is not limited to piecemeal development but goes to new towns as well. Loudoun County, Virginia, recently rejected a developer's $112 million new town proposal for 11,000 people. This rural county west of Washington, D.C., was not persuaded by the commitment of the largest U.S home builder, Levitt and Sons, to pay directly to the county $1.3 million to cover the projected difference between the anticipated tax revenue and the county's cost of providing services such as roads, schools, and sewers. Previously, a county circuit court had upheld the county board's 1971 determination that developers had to make provisions to foot the bill for public services that would necessarily accompany new residents. The county's ultimate rejection went farther—to nonfinancial costs such as community congestion and environmental degradation. One county supervisor, a merchant, put it this way: "If you're used to driving for thirty minutes, and one day, because a lot of people come in, it takes you an hour and a half, that's a cost."

The significance of these land-use conflicts is that they are manifestations of a grass-roots movement against development. The
growth psychosis of the 1950s and 1960s is not selling. While the
areas mentioned will be remembered in the land-use archives, the
people responsible will not. They are nameless, faceless Americans
acting from a common fear that what they have seen happen down
the road will happen at, near, or around the place they call home. It
is this characteristic of the revolution in land-use lifestyles that
makes it so promising. People are fed up.

NEW FEDERAL LAND-USE POWER

On June 11, 1974, the U. S. House of Representatives voted 211
to 204 to defeat a national land-use bill sponsored by Representative
Morris K. Udall. The Senate had twice passed almost identical legislation, fashioned by Senator Jackson, the last occasion by a wide 64
to 21 margin. The frustration caused by the House's defeat was
heightened by the circumstances. For almost two years before the
environmental backlash of the winter of 1973–74, before the Nixon
victory of November 1972, and before Watergate, President Nixon
had touted land-use legislation as his number-one environmental priority. Representing the President, then Secretary of the Interior
Rogers C. B. Morton welcomed the January 1974 House Interior
Committee passage of Representative Udall's bill with a press release
of effusive praise. But before the full House acted on the bill, President Nixon reversed himself. He retreated after a tutorial from Arizona congressman Sam Steiger on the bill's alleged threats to private
property rights. Nixon evidently heard something which two years of
deliberation on the bill had failed to expose. He joined with Steiger
and his Arizona colleague Republican minority leader John Rhodes,
the U. S. Chamber of Commerce, the Liberty Lobby, and the American Conservative Union in backing a weaker Steiger bill.[1] Nixon's
compliant Secretary Morton administered the coup de grâce on the
eve of the final House vote by announcing he no longer favored the

[1] The Udall bill was backed by the UAW, AFL-CIO, National League of
Cities, U. S. Conference of Mayors, Governor's Conference, National Association of Counties, National Association of Realtors, and every significant environmental group.

Udall bill he had found so voteworthy four months earlier. CEQ chairman Peterson and EPA administrator Train refused to change colors overnight. Senator Jackson and Congressman Udall charged the White House with impeachment politics. If indeed the land-use bill was sacrificed to placate potential anti-impeachment supporters, it was another Nixon historic first—the first time land, long the collateral for practically everything, had served to secure anti-impeachment votes.

The defeated bill had sought to provide financial support to strengthen state land-use planning efforts. It identified five kinds of land use meriting "more than local concern":

• development in "critical" environmental areas such as beaches, wetlands, historic sites, and wildlife areas;

• large urban developments such as industrial parks, major suburban subdivisions, and shopping centers;

• major second-home and recreation lot subdivisions on rural land;

• regional public utilities such as waste-disposal plants; and

• major public projects such as airports, highway interchanges, and recreational facilities.

The promised federal support was small—$100 million per year for six years. Intervention was benign; states which did not undertake such planning would not get their share of the money. No other sanctions over state action were stipulated. The Senate had defeated amendments calling for federal withholding of highway construction funds if planning was not accomplished, and the House never broached the issue.

The failure of the legislation was mourned by environmentalists as a major setback. And indeed it was. But in many respects the defeat of the land-use bill was like bolting the barn door after the horse had escaped; the federal government already had extensive authorities to control land use. These authorities are so far-reaching that they exceed government's wisdom and expertise to exercise them. Many states have moved to involve themselves deeply in land use. So have numerous local governments. The national failure is great, but it is one of leadership and direction toward a national land use and growth policy rather than one of inadequate authority. It is also a failure of intellect. The polarization of issues, no-growth versus laissez-faire development being a chief example, is evidence of the sterility of our knowledge about the choices. In the land-use bill debate, a U. S. Chamber of Commerce lobbyist intoned that land "is a basic element in our economic system." Environmentalists will retort that it is a basic element in our ecological system or, as Will Rogers observed, "Land is the one thing nobody is making more of."

Few would contest the categorization of land as a "dominant commodity" as characterized in Chapter 1. In the absence of land-use decisions responsive to environmental needs, our cities, coasts, recreational resources, and rural America can be ravaged. Because of negligent land-use controls, beaches erode, wetlands die, lakes become eutrophic, acid rivers are sterile of fish and botanical life, wildlife species are wiped out, and suburbs are built in patterns which require excessive reliance on the environmentally destructive automobile. All these things happen because land-use policies do not recognize land's ecological role.

Equally foolish would be policies which fail to account for land's essential economic role. No-growth policies fall into this category. For environmentalists to point to the abuses of a negligent land-use policy is not enough. They must specify and support land-use patterns which permit environmentally acceptable economic growth. A lifestyle which balances the economic and ecological roles of land is by necessity a compromise lifestyle. Trade-offs will be made. In some instances, there will be a diminution of the ability of the developer and private property owner to profit from their land holdings. In others, the desire of environmentalists to dedicate areas to open spaces and unspoiled scenic vistas will give way to necessary housing, plant siting and resource development. Fortunately, America has the resources and the technology to make these trade-offs without seriously jeopardizing the attainment of either its economic or environmental goals. Whether it has the will and wisdom to do so remains to be demonstrated.

It is not yet widely appreciated that the federal government has recently acquired broad authority to control land-use-caused environmental abuses in practically every area addressed by the abortive Jackson-Udall land-use legislation. A portion of these authorities are mandatory. The rest are discretionary, to be exercised by the executive branch if it chooses. These authorities mark a turning away from the bankrupt policy of land-use planning through highway construction. Since World War II, federally sponsored highways have been the precursors of land development. They dictated mobility patterns and residential preferences. Patrick Moynihan aptly described these conditions: "We already have a national growth policy. It's called the interstate highway program."

Curtailing New Highways Future failures in highway-related land-use policies, unlike those of the past, cannot be blamed on a lack of recognition by federal legislators of the highway's capacity for environmental destruction. Appropriate regulatory procedures for controlling highway construction in an environmentally responsible way have recently been put in place. The Federal Highway Act, the National Environmental Policy Act, the Clean Air Act, and the Noise Abatement and Control Act can be used to control evironmentally damaging highway projects funded by the federal government. The Highway Act and NEPA provisions require consideration of environmental effects before highway construction can begin. The Secretary of Transportation can prevent unacceptable damage by refusing to approve projects. He has similar responsibilities and authorities with regard to airport construction. The Clean Air Act provides another way to control highways, whether federally or locally funded. If traffic on proposed major highways will cause national standards for carbon monoxide pollution to be violated, EPA must oppose their construction. In cities with a smog problem, new highway construction which increases congestion and pollution must be opposed as a violation of NEPA and local traffic reduction plans required by the Clean Air Act.

EPA is attempting to implement "indirect source" and "parking management" regulations. An indirect source is a facility which attracts traffic. Any commercial or industrial facility, any sports stadium or public parking lot with a parking capacity of one thousand spaces, must demonstrate it will not cause a violation of air-quality standards. Within the sixteen large cities needing major traffic reductions to meet air standards, any such facilities with more than 250 spaces must be reviewed to ensure automotive-related emissions do not violate air quality at the immediate site, or region-wide as a result of "traffic generation" and resulting smog-causing hydrocarbon emissions. These regulations, which states and localities can adopt and administer themselves in lieu of operating under the federal government's control, provide land-use authorities with the opportunity to guide the siting of facilities in a manner consistent with mass transit availability and the degree of carpool and even bicycle utilization.

In their entirety, these authorities for controlling highway and parking construction are sufficient to give local agencies the tools to accomplish the first objective of land-use planning: putting the land-use horse before the transportation cart. If planners want to develop transportation corridors or balanced satellite cities and can show the environmental need to protect air quality, they have the power to do it. Such a reform would permit, and indeed require, developers to plan real estate development in units consistent with orderly growth. Rather than highways becoming the leading edge of growth, thus guaranteeing excessive automobile emissions, or rather than uncoordinated residential development spawning traffic and congestion that politicians must relieve by voting funds for more highways, development and transportation can evolve within the framework of an area-wide land-use plan designed to reduce auto dependency.

Siting Industry   After highways, the second major land-use determinant is industrial development. The authorities of the federal government extend to the land-use aspects of new industrial facilities, including key energy plants such as oil refineries and power plants. EPA's recently promulated nondegradation regulations mandate land-use-related siting decisions for all major industrial plants. Included are power plants, smelters, oil refineries, steel mills, and municipal incinerators, among others.

To ensure that any decision to locate such a facility is consistent with land-use plans, each state must divide and classify its land according to the three use categories established by EPA. The first category is reserved for areas with pristine air. The air-quality standard for these areas essentially precludes the siting of any major industrial facility. National parks, mountains, coastal plains, and desert clean-air regions are expected to be identified by the states as Class I regions. Class II regions, where air quality can deteriorate only slightly, are areas where growth can occur, but only through the siting of facilities controlled with the best technology and located where atmospheric conditions are not prone to inversions or stagnant conditions. Giant facilities, for example power plants above 1,000 mega-watts or oil refineries larger than 150,000 barrels per day, are ruled out, as are groups of smaller facilities. Class III is for areas where large-scale industrial development is necessary to extract concen-trated raw materials or where the grouping of industrial facilities has an extraordinary economic or energy benefit. Air quality in these areas can be permitted to deteriorate up to the national air-quality standards that protect health and property, but may not exceed such levels.

Before this policy was initiated, EPA concerned itself with the dirty air in the one-quarter of the nation already suffering from the consequences of inadequate industrial pollution-control and land-use decisions. Now every state must be covered entirely by a land-use plan that incorporates air-quality considerations. Aspen, Colorado, can be designated a Class I region. Pueblo, Colorado, a steel and in-dustrial center, can be designated Class II or III, depending on state and local preferences on how much clean Colorado air should be sacrificed to facilitate economic growth. Like almost every major de-cision EPA has made, its plan to prevent significant deterioration of clean air quality provoked both the Sierra Club and industry to sue the agency. Both failed and Congress has legislatively strengthened EPA's approach.

EPA has instituted another planning procedure to identify long-range automotive and industrial pollution problems in 150 fast-grow-ing areas throughout the country. Each area is required to project the level of plant and automobile air-pollutant emissions and as-sociated air quality for ten years. If such projections indicate air quality will be violated, they will trigger alterations in plans to con-trol traffic generation and industrial facility siting.

Protecting Rivers and the Coastal Zone   The third area where land-use planning must prevail is the coastal zone, also addressed by recent federal legislation. The 1972 Coastal Zone Management Act funds coastal zone planning in thirty coastline states. The bill con-tains little authority to do more than plan. The Nixon Administration intentionally delayed its implementation by refusing to fund it fully. But planning for coastal protection is already well advanced on the basis of state authorities. California, Hawaii, Oregon, Washington,

Delaware, Massachusetts, Connecticut, North Carolina, Maine, and Florida are among the states launched toward land-use controls to protect beach access, wetlands, estuaries, and coastal wildlife areas. The Coastal Zone Management Act is intended to assist the planning efforts of the coastal states.

As in the case of highways, where federal intervention has too often been part of the land-use problem rather than part of the solution, the Corps of Engineers' dredging and channeling activities in coastal zones have often encouraged helter-skelter development. What is needed is less federal involvement of this type, not more.

Federal land-use authorities are also much in evidence in water-quality planning. Already local communities have been forced by federal clean-water agencies or have taken advantage of federal or local authorities to ban sewer hookups. This is the nuclear deterrent to land-use abuses. Like the Air Force Minuteman missile, it cannot be used often or it loses its credibility. Nonetheless, the Water Pollution Control Act amendments of 1972 require that every municipality obtain a federal permit to discharge pollutants into navigable waters. If development outpaces the capacity of the treatment works required to meet national standards protective of water quality, development must stop. As a practical matter such "sewer bans" usually last up to two years while treatment works are being completed. But in some areas land-use controls will need to be exercised to limit the number of dischargers where even the most advanced treatment technologies cannot remove a high enough share of the pollutant discharge to protect the water. In other cases federal funding for sewer-treatment plant capacity beyond that justified for the present population may be limited to an amount consistent with the ability of a region's environment to sustain its air and water quality in the face of fast growth. EPA recently exercised this authority in a manner designed to put localities on notice that ineffective land-use plans and capitulation to developer wishes will not be supported by federal financing of 75 per cent of the cost of sewers and treatment plants. Ocean County, New Jersey, sought EPA's approval and funding for a waste-water-treatment plant to serve a population of 390,000 by 1990, compared with a current population of 140,000. EPA cut the plant size to service 250,000 people because its analysis showed that the use of automobiles by a larger population would cause violations of air standards. Federal authorities are available to control the quantity of land developed by limiting treatment capacity. The full impact of such authorities on regional growth is not yet understood or appreciated.

Another water-related federal authority, section 208 of the Water Pollution Control Act, provides localities with authority to be exercised at their discretion to control the siting of facilities that can jeopardize water quality. Between 1976 and 1978 major metropolitan areas will complete "section 208 plans" to identify areas where pollutant runoff problems such as heavy metals from streets, fertilizer from farmlands and lawns, or simply excessive dirt and silt, damage water quality. Already in Oregon, land adjacent to the Willamette River has been zoned to preclude development which will damage the river and its shorelines. Section 208 plans may also identify areas where additional growth may not occur, given the ability of existing treatment technologies to treat increased loads and still permit recreation and quality fishing in local rivers. When such an assimilative capacity barrier is encountered, zero-discharge treatment options such as land disposal systems may be the only alternative until better treatment technologies, approaching and encompassing complete recycling, are devised.

Too often federal authorities are viewed as a panacea for our problems. Land-use problems demonstrate that federal intervention by the Federal Highway Administration and the Corps of Engineers, for example, needs to be tempered rather than extended. NEPA, the Clean Air Act, and the Water Pollution Control Act amendments of 1972 all restrain such intervention. On the other hand, increased involvement by the federal government in regulating the location of shopping centers, parking lots, and industrial facilities cannot help but be viewed as only a temporary assist to state and local land-use planning efforts. If perpetuated, these federal activities will be counterproductive or ineffective. The real loss, and irony, of the defeat of the Jackson-Udall land-use bill in the House is that, by providing additional resources to the states, it would have hastened the day when federal intervention in specific siting decisions can give way to state-developed and state-managed land-use plans that provide an appropriate general framework for public debate and involvement in the key land-use decisions.

STATE LEADERSHIP

California's Coastal Zone Conservation Act, passed by a state-wide referendum in November 1972, is the nation's most far-reaching coastal zone planning activity. One state-wide and six regional commissions were empowered to approve all development within a thousand yards of the ocean. They have prepared and submitted to the California legislature a land-use plan for land up to five miles from the ocean along California's 1,067-mile coastline. The thrust of coastal commission decisions augurs well for coastal land-use planning. Preservation of agricultural zones in the face of developer interest has received high priority; improved public access including public transit to coastal areas is a common theme; a desire to protect the habitats of the salmon and other species against logging, landfills, and other threats is in evidence; and a reluctance to clutter the coast with power plants, oil rigs, and other energy facilities has been demonstrated. California is following Delaware's lead. In 1971 Delaware banned further industrial facility siting within two miles of its hundred-mile shoreline. This prohibition remains intact despite pressures from a Du Pont-led consortium to overturn it.

State-led coastal land-use activities extend from the state of Washington to southern California, around Florida, and from North Carolina to Maine. With only a few gaps, they demonstrate that land-use planning is under way to protect sensitive coastal and wetland ecologies against development and industrial abuses. But the fast-growing southeastern United States extending along the Gulf of Mexico remains unprotected. Pressures to build second and retirement homes along the unique barrier islands of South Carolina received recent impetus when the sheikdom of Kuwait paid $17 million for the ten-by-three-mile Kiawah Island. Additional state authorities will be needed to protect the U.S. southeastern shoreline.

Protection for the entire 53,677 miles of U.S. coastline will be a task requiring constant public vigilance and participation. But by any measure, the last three years have witnessed an encouraging list of state land-use planning initiatives. If efforts continue, additional federal authorities seem unwarranted although federal funding is still needed. The lesson of these coastal land-use initiatives is their testimony to a powerful motivation in favor of land-use planning: the collective private interest of the many who want guaranteed access to unspoiled beaches and coastal resources against the private interests of a few developers and potential homeowners. If a similar collective interest in land-use planning in our urban and suburban areas can be demonstrated by environmentalists and growth-policy advocates, land-use planning will be quickly advanced.

Besides planning led by the coastal zone states, comprehensive land-use planning is under way in Colorado, Vermont, Maine, Hawaii, North Carolina, Florida, Arizona, Nevada, and Oregon. In at least twenty other states land-use planning covers important environmental resources such as wetlands, flood plains, coastal marshlands, and special river areas, for example the Hudson River. About a dozen additional states control the siting of energy facilities. In 1974 alone, new strip mining laws were enacted in nine states. The Council of State Governments in a 1974 report summarized the status of state land-use reform as follows: thirty states were considering comprehensive land-use planning legislation; twenty-one states were attempting to fashion long-range goals for their population and resources, including six states with population commissions working on the task; and ten states had adopted resolutions on stabilizing their populations. After this report was issued, the defeat of the federal land-use bill caused about ten states to back off from considering comprehensive land-use planning.

Nonetheless, land-use planning has become within the last four years a growing state and federal activity. Only now are a few agencies going beyond mere plans and beginning to actually influence land-use decisions. Adapting to these new conditions, under which local zoning is no longer the only restraint on development and economic profit is not the only criterion, will be an essential requirement of the era of environmental lifestyle change.

TO SUBURBIA

The suburbs have been, with the shopping center and the express highway, among the few beneficent innovations of the automobile era. Suburbia has given us privacy, spaciousness, and a sense of home in a fast-moving world. Our small yards, where we pasture our children and on weekends regain a measure of adult sanity, are our private meccas. We have escaped the alienation from the oppression, humdrum, and filth of the industrial revolution that Marx feared. But suburbia is taking its own toll. It has spread so far and wide it has lost its center or sense of community. We cannot enjoy it; all our hours are spent getting to or from work or driving the children to their distant school, sports, or social activities. Before suburbia, adult social relationships and camaraderie were enjoyed in the cafes, night spots, movie houses, and churches of our cities. Now it is vainly sought from television set or in the shopping center parking lot.

HOW CITIES DIE

At the same time suburbia has offered much and delivered much less, our cities have experienced a desperate decline. Like last year's bird nests, it is difficult to imagine them ever being inhabited again. Life in some cities is held together by a port, or capital sunk in industries too great to be abandoned, or a seat of government, or a commercial cog or two like a bank or stock exchange. Some survive merely by the good fortune of having been at the intersection of highways linking suburbs. However, cities contain the last vestiges of our civilization and culture. For all their suffering, if they are extinguished our civilization will vanish with their universities, their ethnic communities, their art treasures and cultural inheritance. We do not have a London or Paris. But without a Boston, Philadelphia, Charleston, or Washington, D.C., of what value would our cultural and political inheritance be? Without a New York, Dallas, Chicago, Kansas City, or St. Louis, what would become of our commercial acumen? Absent Pittsburgh, Detroit, Gary, and Cleveland, where would we renew our industrial strength?

Some of these cities have already succumbed, bled to death by fleeing suburbanites and industries and dissected by highway corridors. New York City and Detroit exemplify this genre. The final crushing blow to these cities ironically is dealt by their own governments. As the costs of crime, corruption, powerful unions, and cleanup burdens like trash removal escalate, the tax burden on the middle class rises. The middle class leaves, prospective middle-class workers take jobs elsewhere, and the city goes broke. An assessment by the Community Council of Greater New York of the plight of New York's middle-income family in the year prior to October 1973, the month in which the Middle Eastern cartel helped kick off the world's inflation, demonstrates how big-city costs can become unbearable. Over the twelve months, the cost of goods and services rose by 10.6, per cent, the highest percentage rise in seventeen years. But the four-person family needing $13,543 per year to live modestly saw its income tax payments, Social Security deductions, and state disability payments, added together, make a 25.2 per cent jump, or more than double the record inflation rate.

In mid-1974 New York City reported that it lost 24,000 manufacturing jobs a month over the January–April period, bringing the four-year total of jobs lost to a quarter of a million, or about equal to the jobs gained through the entire decade of the 1960s. Manufacturing industries cannot afford New York City's high rents, high energy costs, high transport costs caused by congestion and costly energy, and high business taxes. Manufacturing employment had been declining in New York City since the 1950s. But these declines were offset, until 1969, by gains in service-industry employment. Since 1969 service employment has been dropping too. Corporate headquarters have redeployed to Stamford, Connecticut, Houston, and Washington, D.C. Companies, like their employees, cannot afford New York City.

Detroit is an even more extreme example of big-city decline. While New York lost 6.4 per cent of all jobs between 1969 and 1973, Detroit lost 19.4 per cent, followed by Baltimore with 11.3 per cent, Dallas with 9.7 per cent, and St. Louis with 8.9 per cent. The birthplace of the automobile's planned obsolescence is now experiencing it.

Our civilization could possibly survive the decline of New York City and Detroit. For that matter Newark, St. Louis, and Dallas would not be unduly missed. But if we believe in the city as the repository of our civilization, if only to nourish our suburbs culturally and employ our bureaucrats, some future for the city must be defined. Besides, in 1970, 64 million Americans lived in central cities, not much fewer than the 76 million who lived in suburban cities and towns. These proportions reflect a dramatic reversal of the past: in 1940 the city population numbered 43 million, compared with only 26 million in suburbia.

Our most acute environmental problems are in the central cities. Trash, high carbon monoxide levels, dirt-filled air, and polluted water characterize urban blight. The decline of our cities means these problems will get worse and the cities will not have the economic base to correct them. Most environmentalists think of environmental policy in terms of trees and fish. But protection of human health is its first objective, and the urban population suffers most from pollution. An intelligent land-use policy could reduce the toll. The uninhabitability of the central city and thus the exodus of the middle class owes a great deal to poor land-use practices.

Ironically, zoning was first conceived in New York City in 1916. Retailers erected zoning barriers to stop encroaching industry. Dirty industry was to be cordoned off so residences and retail establishments would be spared. Later this "nonconforming" use character of zoning led to the separation of all types of activity, for example retail from wholesale, multifamily from single-family dwellings. Thus the concept of a mixed or balanced community was the enemy of zoning. At the same time, zoning boards never could resist the lure of piecemeal commercial interests. Any single commercial establishment that identified a street corner or plot on a busy road was able to persuade the zoning boards that its presence would expand the tax base and so on. By this process the community aura of city existence was eclipsed by ugliness. Finally, when consideration was given to placing the single most important land use in twentieth-century America, the highway, zoning boards deferred abjectly to state and federal officials.

SUBURBIA'S FLOTSAM

Moving outside the city, the automobile cut a path to the suburbs lined with unsightly fast-food stores, motels, gasoline stations, tire stores, auto and trailer sales lots, and drugstores. This collage, from suburb to city and suburb to suburb, accented in asphalt, is known to land-use planners as "strip development."

Among the perils of strip development are other automobiles. Data from a 1972 Virginia State Highway Department study of traffic safety on U.S. route 1 from Washington, D.C., to Richmond compared with that on parallel interstate route 95 shows that travel along the strip-developed U.S. 1 is three times as likely to kill you and four and a half times as likely to injure you as faster travel on the parallel interstate. Mixing commuter and interstate travel with stop-and-go shopping and MacDonald hamburger hopping is murderous. Thus lives have been saved by the interstate highway system because the average distance between interchanges is four miles and signs are not allowed to obscure or divert driver vision.

Multiple-strip development is the best way to characterize a long list of new centerless towns. Los Angeles, Phoenix, Denver, San Jose, and Albuquerque fall in this category. Another land development problem common to these cities is "leapfrog sprawl." An area develops only to be surrounded by land held by speculators or abutting the less attractive parts of the community—its body shops, junkyards, or trailer camps. A few miles down the road a new community blossoms. Each makes sense on its own terms, but in cities like Phoenix, together they preclude the preservation of open spaces, whether desert or farmland, and increase dependence on the automobile because densities are too low or centers are too dispersed and haphazard to support mass transit. Phoenix has 2,327 people per square mile, compared with 24,922 in New York and 6,207 in Los Angeles.

The environmental problems of these cities, strip- and leapfrog-developed alike, and the close-in suburbs of cities like Atlanta and Washington, are different from old-town pollution. Most evident is oxidant or smog pollution caused by the automobile-dominated patterns. You take your car to get a pack of cigarettes or the newspaper. Millions of short trips, stops, and starts spill unburnt gasoline vapors into the air. Emissions are usually at least twice as high from a cold engine and at slower speeds. Engine start-up multiplies them as much as tenfold. Higher energy consumption, which in turn has its own environmental impacts, is another manifestation of suburban growth. A study of the New York City region found that on the sparsely populated (1,000 per square mile) fringes of New York

City, per capita yearly energy consumption was 190 million BTUs per person. This compares with annual usage as low as 100 million BTUs in the center city, where densities are 35,000 persons per square mile. Higher suburban energy use is due to such factors as increased reliance on the automobile and fewer multifamily dwellings.

Water pollution problems are more subtle. Many of our urban streams and rivers are polluted by "urban runoff" of silt and dirt. Before large land areas were paved, a two-inch rainfall took six hours to reach the nearest water body. Now the same rainfall takes half an hour. Before, when it merged into the stream or river it was relatively clean, having been filtered by land seepage. Now it arrives laden with dirt and bacteria eroded from parking lots, streets, and bare land. The effect of such filthy water on water quality is as severe as the more widely recognized problems created by discharges from large, overloaded treatment works. An estimated four billion tons of sediment washes annually into our streams because of land misuse. Dirt keeps the sunlight from supporting water plant and fish life. Rivers like the Potomac are so silt-laden that only the roughest forms of aquatic life, like the carp, can survive. Runoff water, because it contains vegtation, food, and animal wastes, has a high biochemical oxygen demand, a characteristic which, as the wastes are broken down in water, consumes oxygen. If these wastes take up the oxygen supply in rivers and streams, there is inadequate oxygen for fish life. Other constituents of runoff from streets and parking lots, identified by EPA, are nutrients such as phosphates, nitrogen, and nitrates (which nourish aquatic plant growth to the point that the plants demand so much oxygen that fish life is again jeopardized); disease-bearing intestinal (or coliform) bacteria; heavy metals, including zinc, lead, mercury, chromium, and copper; and pesticides such as DDT and aldrin-dieldrin eroded from lawns.

Before suburbia, two characteristics of the urban landscape helped cleanse rain runoff. One was seepage through permeable ground, both forest and agricultural. The other was urban wetlands, now replaced by concrete stream channels and downtown shoreline landfills held in place by concrete girdles. Wetlands are natural treatment plants. Half-submerged wetland plant life takes up nutrients and filters out dirt with top efficiency. In one group of seven states—

Arkansas, California, Florida, Illinois, Indiana, Iowa, and Missouri —46 per cent of the wetland areas, or over 17 million acres, have been destroyed.

Without wetlands or permeable soils, water rushes headlong to the nearest river. Underneath the land surface, the ground water supplies are not renewed. Thus, suburban runoff creates two other problems besides water pollution: ground water depletion and flooding. Long Island, New York, and Santa Clara County, California, are two areas which have experienced severe depletion of ground water, causing wells to dry up and, in some cases, land to subside. Before the 1950s, Santa Clara County and its chief suburban centers, San Jose and Santa Clara, were verdant agricultural areas nourished by a mammoth underground storage basin. The Santa Clara Valley was known widely for its prune, pear, apricot, and nut orchards. Sprawl has depleted the water supply and displaced the orchards. The homes so mindlessly built in the floodplain are frequently flooded by spring and winter rains. Coping with these subtle stresses on the surburban ecology is among the chief tasks of environmentally responsive land-use planning.

WHY IT HAPPENED

More overt is the problem suburban growth has created for treatment of human wastes piped by sewers to thousands of treatment plants. A metropolitan area cannot be named that has not fallen behind in providing adequate waste-water treatment. Oddly, the dispersal of our population to suburbia caused a concentration of the pollution discharges to our rivers and streams. Suburbia is usually too closely developed for septic tank use. While highways have determined urban shape, sewers have been a willing accomplice. They connect suburbia with old downtown treatment plants where capacity and the degree of treatment have lagged far behind levels necessary to protect water quality. Not only has practically every one of the 90 million Americans born since World War II placed a demand on a treatment plant, so have about 15 million migrants to our cities and additional millions in annexed towns and villages previously dependent on septic tank disposal systems. Between 1940 and 1973 the total U.S. population increased 62 per cent, while the number of people requiring waste treatment increased 135 per cent. Until the late 1950s the sewered population grew at about the same pace as the total U.S. population, but from then until the early 1970s, the sewered population jumped as a reflection of suburbanization.

This shift in living patterns greatly complicated the environmental problem. The accompanying chart shows the effect of increased treatment of sewage wastes on total pollution discharges, taking into

TOTAL PUBLIC WASTE-WATER TREATMENT PLANT
DISCHARGES BY TYPE OF TREATMENT*

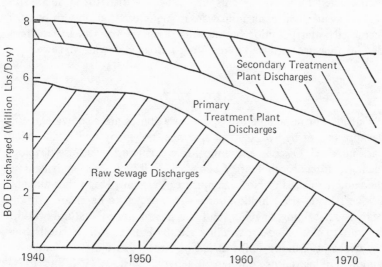

* Conventional treatment of human wastes is by "primary" and "secondary" treatment. Solid constituents of the waste which flows through city treatment plants are screened out as the first step in the primary treatment process. Then large tanks hold the sewage until additional solids fall out by gravity. Primary treatment removes from 30 to 50 per cent of all pollutants. Secondary treatment removes 85 per cent by mixing the waste streams from the primary process with air via sprinklers or aerators. Oxygen nourishes aerobic bacteria which feed on the minute solids and with such solids, fall out in holding tanks in the form of sludge. Because the bacteria multiply at a fast pace, portions of the sludge, called activated sludge, are intentionally fed back into the plant after the primary treatment stage. Secondary effluent is then chlorinated or disinfected to remove harmful bacteria called fecal coliforms and discharged. In the most advanced "tertiary" phase, chemicals are added to combine with and remove pollutants that remain after secondary treatment.

account the large increase in the number of persons who required sewage treatment.

The top line represents the total amount of sanitary biochemical oxygen-demanding wastes (BOD) discharged from public sewage treatment systems. This total is segmented into three areas showing the contribution from systems employing various levels of treatment. Despite the fact that BOD from discharges of raw sewage was reduced by a factor of six between 1940 and 1974, the total amount of BOD discharged from all treatment systems fell only marginally. The wastes of so many additional suburbanites were added to the load treated by sewage plants that "success" had to be defined as staying even. Suburbanization was, in many cases, a prescription for increased water pollution because the discharge from these new residential areas was diverted to already overloaded downtown sewers.

RURAL BENIGN NEGLECT

Outside our populated areas, land-use abuses are also evident. But because few of us live in rural America, not many understand what has happened. Of course, the most important rural land-use development is the encroachment of suburbia itself. An area equivalent to the combined sizes of New Hampshire, Vermont, Massachusetts, and Rhode Island—19.7 million acres—is expected to be cleared by the year 2000. Mining, logging, and the destruction of natural wildlife habitats to clear land for farming are the most notorious rural land-use concerns. Mining ranks ahead of airports as the most land-consumptive industrial or commercial activity. Between 1930 and 1971, 1,470,000 acres of land were disturbed by coal mining and slightly more than this amount again by other mining activities. All types of mining have destroyed a total of 1,687,288 acres of wildlife habitat and polluted 281,116 acres of water. Until recently, shrinking acreage in cultivation in the United States spared further destruction of wildlife areas by farming. Now large areas of states such as North Carolina, even areas never before farmed, are being cleared by large corporate farmers, including Italian and Japanese firms. Soybeans, the only major crop boom since the war, provide evidence of what is in store for rural wildernesses not yet set aside in protected areas:

from 1950 to 1969, 4.1 million acres of forested wetlands in the lower Mississippi Valley and southern Florida were drained and cultivated in soybeans.

Approximately another million acres in rural land are cleared of timber each year. Clear-cutting techniques have cut wide swaths through our national forests. All standing vegtation is leveled by this technique, rather than the more sensible but more costly practice of cutting only the mature trees. A recent landmark decision by the Fourth U. S. Circuit Court of Appeals may end this practice. The court found that clear-cutting of the Monongahela National Forest in the Allegheny highlands of West Virginia is illegal. This decision effectively ends the Forest Service practice of allowing lumber companies to clear-cut national forests.

By comparison with suburban land-use policy, preservation of rural lands has achieved a measure of success. The most visible evidence of this is the increasing prevalence of certain forms of wildlife such as the beaver, elk, and wild turkey. Even the buffalo, alligator, snowy and great egrets, sea otter, and golden plover are making a comeback. Some credit for these successes goes to our national parks and national forests and to areas protected by the U. S. Fish and Wildlife Service. Together these entities administer about a quarter of a billion acres of U.S. land. In 1964 the Wilderness Act established a National Wilderness Preservation System to protect the natural state of a portion of these lands. If wilderness areas now proposed for inclusion in this special category are approved by Congress, roughly one sixth of these national lands would be protected from miners, trailers, and the automobile. Less successful but still important is the designation of eleven rivers and river segments as part of the National Wild and Scenic Rivers System. Established by the 1968 Wild Rivers Act, this system could be used to protect wild portions of many of our rivers that are still unspoiled.

Recent decisions against major dam-building projects are another encouraging sign of rural land-use sanity in America. The governors of New York, New Jersey, and Delaware voted to scrap, after thirteen years of controversy, plans to build the Tocks Island dam on the Delaware River. This action saved the last unspoiled area in proximity to densely populated northern New Jersey. Also defeated were plans to build the five-hundred-foot-high Hells Canyon dam across the Snake River. For over twenty years northwestern power companies have fought to turn the nation's deepest water gorge (7,900 feet versus the Grand Canyon's 5,500 feet) into a hundred-mile lake along the Idaho-Oregon border. A key factor persuading the governors of the bordering states to oppose the dam was its expected destruction of salmon and steelhead runs and breeding grounds.

An emerging threat to our rural environment is the second home. Our desire to place our own habitat far from suburbia and deep into nature's wilds poses a threat to valuable national lands not protected by federal ownership or control. Wetlands are dredged and filled for waterfront home sites. Between 1956 and 1965 over a third of the productive coastal wetlands in California, Florida, and New York were lost to development. Isolated forests and mountain areas are dissected with roads to attract the tired and harassed urban and suburban dweller for a weekend or summer vacation.

NEW PERCEPTIONS OF GROWTH AND LAND-USE RIGHTS

The environmental abuses that underlie citizen discontent are not, at least consciously, the chief impetus to land-use reform. Taxes are. Citizen outrage against growth is a form of tax rebellion. Traditionally, a new industry, a commercial establishment, or neighbor has been viewed as an asset to the community. More income earned meant more spent. A bigger market would enrich the existing residents. Establishments were enticed into town by tax breaks and other inducements. To many this old Chamber of Commerce growth philosophy is literally bankrupt. The new residents have not paid their way. The sewage-treatment plant is overloaded and the river is unswimmable. The schools have deteriorated. Crime rates are up. The roads are bad, and they are clogged. The air is dirty and the community is noisy and unsightly. As if all these developments are not in themselves an indictment of growth, perhaps in some cases offset by new-found wealth for those able to sell real estate, escalating local taxes added a further insult. Yes, replacing a farm with a subdivision increases the tax base. But it also places new demands on the public coffers that may not be covered by additional tax revenues. In its headlong rush to develop and "sprawl" in the 1950s and 1960s, America incurred a fiscal as well as an environmental deficit. Both have come due. It will take us the balance of this century to pay them off.

Decisions on land use involve our most treasured rights. The automobile, which was not around when America was founded, is not mentioned in the Articles of Confederation. Land is. The rights to move freely about the United States and to own property were viewed by our forefathers as essential prerogatives of the citizen. The courts have agreed that the Articles of Confederation are encompassed by the Constitution although they are not mentioned. Partly because land has been so abundant in America and because land-use abuses have been limited to "next door" concerns, pressures to control land use have rarely reached above the local government level. In 1926 the U. S. Supreme Court upheld the constitutionality of zoning in *Village of Euclid, Ohio* v. *Ambler Realty Company*. By the end of 1927, forty-five states had enacted zoning-enabling laws. Today about five thousand local jurisdictions "zone."

Land was precious to America's settlers because its control in Europe was a dominant factor in the economy and in the hierarchical society they were fleeing. But in the modern U.S. economy, agriculture employs less than 5 per cent of the population. Now that America has passed through the agriculture phase, another land-related phenomenon has proven integral to personal development: mobility. About one sixth of all Americans move to a different residence each year. And one sixth of all commuters travel more than thirty miles each day to their jobs. From the South to the industrial heartland and from the East to California have been two well-trodden roads to economic betterment in America. Now the journey is from the North to the South and West, where new jobs are available. Mobility is job access. Mobility is an opportunity to get a "new start" somewhere else. Mobility allows industry to renew its plant and equipment unencumbered by old processes and habits. Within communities, mobility to adequate housing is a cherished goal for every young family, particularly those raising children who need suburbia's space to afford a dwelling large enough for their needs and wants. Mobility was and is an essential part of the American opportunity and the American success.

No-growth policies therefore can be a roadblock to the path of opportunity in America. Even more difficult is that pulling up the ladder or gangplank can be a form of racism. It can be a type of snobbery of the rich, the "haves" over the "have-nots." Spokesmen for no growth or controlled growth may be seeking to keep out blacks, the poor, or unfamiliar ethnic groups. A response to these motivations has been an occasional coalition between developers and civil rights groups against no-growth ordinances. The environmental movement is vulnerable to an embrace by racists or the rich. It is largely middle- and upper-middle class and overwhelmingly (about 96 per cent) white. A Sierra Club survey of its members identified only 7 per cent as "blue collar" workers. The vast majority of Sierra Club members are teachers, students, managers, executives, and professionals.

The dilemmas of growth versus the environment, of mobility versus social protectionism, and of an open society versus a racially or class-dominated one represent serious challenges to an informed and successfully managed growth policy. Devising successful policies to shape growth means coping with three sets of concerns. First is preference and rights which are the most basic aspect of land-use policy in a free society. They encompass the right to profit from land, the right to mobility, and the right of access and opportunity regardless of race, sex, or class status. Second is the issue of economic growth. America must grow by building factories, shopping centers, and oil refineries if it is to employ its people and offer them the challenges of a more diversified and rewarding existence. Land must be used in this process, but used carefully and restored if the third land-use consideration, environmental preservation and protection, is to receive its proper weight. Thus a triangular land-use policy of preference, growth, and the environment must be fashioned. By definition, such policies will be compromises worked out in the political process.

Americans are not confident this is occurring. A 1973 *Christian Science Monitor* survey found the public skeptical of the integrity of local zoning officials and demanding that such officials openly disclose their real estate holdings and hold open meetings. Sixty-two per cent believed zoning decisions were not arrived at fairly. Zoning is often viewed as another smoke-filled-room operation. A 1973 Gallup poll found 55 per cent of those surveyed did not think their government was handling growth policy adequately, while 29 per cent rated local efforts as excellent.

Part of the confusion results from the citizen schizophrenia over the underlying issues. Even Oregonians hesitate to choose between growth and the environment. Polled in 1971 by Louis Harris and Associates, they answered as follows: 32 per cent wanted a new plant even if it produced a large increase in pollution, and 55 per cent wanted it if pollution increased slightly. In sparsely populated eastern Oregon, the same figures were 50 per cent and 69 per cent, respectively. The state's then unemployment rate of 6 per cent, and up to 14 per cent in spots, helped produce this strong progrowth response. Deep down, Americans do not know what they want. One poll finds three out of every four Americans want to see future growth take the form of private homes spread more or less evenly throughout a region rather than clusters of apartments built with open space in between. Another poll, in an apparent contradiction, finds only 5 per cent agree with the statement that the "government should continue to facilitate low-density suburban patterns of development; this is what people want." This second group of respondents favor more government involvement in land use, including more compact urban settlements, more mass transit, and growth in the form of planned new communities with open space.

A NEW AMERICAN WAY WITH LAND

An intelligent public dialogue is a starting point for a national land-use policy to shape growth. What are our choices? Can we all drive? Can we all live on one-acre plots? Are there too many of us in our cities, or have the patterns of growth needlessly yielded excessive automobile traffic? What are the facts?

It must be honestly conceded that many of the facts are not known and most of the alternative choices we face have not been developed. It will take at least a decade to provide the citizen with the facts he needs to choose intelligently. But already much is known that is not reflected in national or local actions.

Changing Demography Looking to the future, land-use planners must weigh a new set of developments that will shape the housing and land-use preferences of Americans for the next twenty-five years. The crystal ball has been turned upside down. Instead of the sharply rising school-age population of the past (the nineteen-and-under age group grew by eight million in the 1960s), we can anticipate in the 1970s an increase of only three million. On the other hand, the twenty-five-to-thirty-year-old age group will rise by eleven million in the 1970s, compared with only two million in the 1960s. Overlap this demographic reversal with a description of its housing and locational manifestations. There will be fewer children pulling families to suburbia. More working women will favor close-to-job living. Less demand for housing room for large families and the higher prices of near-work-place housing will favor high-rise and townhouse living.

Two other characteristics of this changing outlook are important. One is that the number of households will skyrocket. More people, men and women, even college-age adults, prefer to live alone. The rate of household formation in the 1975–85 period will exceed by one third the rate of the 1950s and 1960s; over 27,000 new households will be established each week. Every month will see the addition to our landscape of an urban-suburban complex equivalent to a Fort Lauderdale, a Youngstown, or a Riverside.

New Preferences Secondly, most of these additions will be within automobile commuting range of our major urban complexes, or standard metropolitan statistical areas (SMSAs). A recent study in the state of Washington showed that about one half of those surveyed want to live within a fifteen-minute drive of the city limits. An earlier study in Wisconsin found that people prefer to live outside the city but within thirty miles of it. Today's young adults, in part because of their higher educational background and their desire for the diversity of city life, have a stronger preference for near-urban living than their parents did.

In a sense, the foregoing preferences are expressed by survey respondents who view their choices in terms of today's alternatives. It is well established that since the war the best jobs, the best opportunities for higher income and achievement, have been available near San Francisco, Los Angeles, Washington, D.C., Chicago, and the other major metropolitan centers. At the same time, surveys have found that almost two thirds of all Americans long for the rural areas or a small town or city. This longing is no doubt reinforced by the deterioration of the urban environment. As our economy matures to become more service-oriented, and as improved interstate highway transportation permits the dispersal of manufacturing activities to take advantage of lower-wage rural labor, some Americans are realizing their wish to avoid big-city life altogether. This is the startling finding of a 1973 census update: high population growth rates of 4.2 per cent were recorded in nonmetropolitan counties (those with no urban centers of 50,000 or larger), compared with a rate of 2.9 per cent for metropolitan counties. During the 1960s, the growth rates were —4.4 per cent and 17.0 per cent, respectively—a dramatic reversal. The areas of fastest rural growth constitute a priority list of the nation's most attractive, yet unsettled rural environments: the Ozark-Ouachita Mountains, the eastern slope of the Rockies from Idaho to New Mexico, upper Michigan, eastern Kentucky and Tennessee, North Carolina's Piedmont, Georgia, and the Gulf and Carolina coasts.

The advantages that have favored these regions—climate, recreation, low taxes and abundant low-wage labor—have favored the entire South, the sunny portions of the Southwest, and the eastern slope of the Rockies. The entire area has been labeled the "sun belt." Through the mid-1970s the population of the West and South has grown at four times the rate of the Northeast and North Central states. No state in the North Central region grew faster than the national average 1970–75 growth rate of 4.8 per cent, and only Maine, New Hampshire, and Vermont in the Northeast exceeded the national rate. In the West, the coastal states' growth rates have dropped, with the exception of Oregon. High growth is occurring in Idaho, Wyoming, Colorado, New Mexico, Arizona, Utah, and Nevada. The thirteen fastest growing metropolitan areas in the United States from

1970 to 1974 were all located in only four sun-belt states: Florida, Texas, Arizona, and Colorado.

Even farming, boosted by lucrative farm prices in the early 1970s, showed a slight gain in population in the 1972 farm census, the first gain since the 1945–47 period. Today there are 9.6 million farm residents. It will be enough if there is no further drop from the historic 1910 peak of 32 million; there may even be a gain if America realizes its capacity to feed more of the world's hungry people.

Environmental Benefits With one exception these demographic developments and the expressed preferences of Americans for new living choices are favorable to the goals of environmental improvement in the 1976–2000 period. Even for some cities, there is hope that a younger working population will revive the lethargic downtown areas vacated by their parents. In Boston there is already evidence that this is occurring. From 1963 to 1973 Boston's gain in service jobs exceeded its loss in manufacturing jobs, reversing a decline that began in the 1950s when industry fled to the South and services to suburbia. The city's population has grown by 2 per cent per year since 1970, compared with annual rates of decline of 1.4 per cent in the 1950s and 0.8 per cent in the 1960s. Boston's recovery has been facilitated by major public investments in mass transit and downtown renewal. Some cities will duplicate Boston's success; others, such as St. Louis, Baltimore, Newark, New York, and Detroit, will probably fail. At least in the 1980s and 1990s, demography and personal preference will give some cities a chance.

A second land-use implication of these trends is the emergence of what might be called the suburban activity center, or satellite, or mini-city. Replacing the homogenous sprawl of the 1960s there will be, in major metropolitan areas like Washington, D.C., Denver, Houston, and Atlanta, suburban cities that meet the needs of proximity to major urban areas of a million or more while maintaining populations of 50,000 to 250,000. These adult-oriented in-cities will be practically self-contained, with service employment, shopping centers, and high-rise and townhouse residences. They will be linked by mass transportation and "fast buses" to the urban core's financial, governmental, or entertainment complex, five to twelve miles away.

Atlanta's Buckhead-Lennox area, with its high-rise apartments and condominiums, its fashionable department stores, including Saks and Nieman-Marcus, and its numerous theaters, tennis courts, and restaurants, is typical of this new genre.

The energy crisis will reinforce this rollback of the spread city toward more compact and urban subcenters. Already outer fringe town developments have gone bankrupt under the dual pressures of the energy and housing crisis of 1974–75. But even with abundant financing, the energy cost of travel will continue to rise. New suburban developments beyond fifteen miles from main job centers and not served by mass transit will have difficulty surviving the Arab embargo.

The unfavorable implication of these patterns of development is the almost certain revival of the second-home boom. Just as close-in living has its attractions keyed to urban life, so is the need for a second residence enhanced by the new preferences of adults. They want a mountain, coastal, or lake retreat as an escape or status symbol. And they can afford it. The wife will often work and the smaller families will be free of the income drag of a large brood of children. There will be longer weekends and vacations to get away. Now there are five legal three-day weekends per year, and vacations, which now average 1.7 weeks per year, will rise to 2.5 weeks per year by 1990. Thus, careful control of second-home developments must be a principal environmental concern.

Overall balance will be the chief characteristic of land use development for the next twenty-five years. In contrast to the past, when practically all growth centered in the suburbs, future growth will be divided among central cities, mini-cities, suburban areas, and even the revived rural counties of America. The total environmental impact of these developments will be more manageable because of their dispersed impacts. Mini-cities, unlike suburbia, can be served by mass transit, and growth in the South and in rural areas will place demands on transportation systems often not already overburdened by the automobile. At least these developments will give public officials more time to implement anticipatory policies to shape growth in environmentally acceptable patterns.

A LAND-USE POLICY AGENDA

New tools and procedures are needed to respond to this opportunity. In a variety of areas reforms are necessary: public policy toward private property must emerge from the zoning age to recognize and reduce the social costs of uncontrolled development; new transportation thinking must reflect the hard-earned knowledge we now have on how transportation shapes land-use patterns; land-use planning, too long a "coloring book" exercise in optimum development for the planner's sake, must define and incorporate key land-use–environmental-transportation relationships so that public officials can see more clearly the consequences of piecemeal development decisions; new-cities concepts for old cities and new ones need perfection and demonstration; finally, the region-wide public needs to be informed and given a choice in determining land use through an open and clearly articulated land-use planning process.

New Views toward Private Property Of all the necessary land-use reforms, most fundamental is the requirement to modify our attitudes and policies toward private property. The Fifth Amendment to the Constitution reads: "nor shall private property be taken for public use without just compensation." For two centuries private property rights have rarely been usurped to protect public interests, because in truth the public interests were rarely threatened. Zoning has been the chief vehicle to sort out conflicts where industrial land, for example, encroaches on residential or commercial territory, and it has been an accomplice in making room for major roadways and public facilities. Now congestion, air and water pollution from suburban and urban concentrations, and the need to provide open spaces and to protect floodplains add up to a substantial public interest that land-use practices must recognize.

The public is attuned to these needs. A 1973 survey by the *Christian Science Monitor* found 77 per cent of the respondents agreed that in cases of a demonstrable public interest, private property "rights" should be curtailed, and 58 per cent favored paying compensation based on present-use values rather than on potential developed-use value. Only 2 per cent believed there should be no encroachment of private property options.

What some fear is that the "taking issue," as the public right to curtail private property use has been labeled, will be abused, that vague public policies will preclude property owners, including the old and poor, from selling to developers. The clumsy manner with which local governments have set crude population ceilings and implemented sewer moratoriums and similar no-growth measures is justification for such fears. Owners fear their land will be "down-zoned" or, if development is altogether excluded, for example to provide open spaces, land could be "wiped out" in property-value terms. While courts have consistently upheld zoning limits that deprived owners of major real estate gains, they have also grown impatient with growth "pauses" and similar tactics that in a wholesale manner take private land off the free market.

Justice Louis Brandeis in a Supreme Court Dissent a quarter of a century ago saw a constitutional justification for "taking":

Restriction imposed to protect public health, safety, or morals from dangers threatened is not taking. . . . the property so restricted remains in the possession of the owner. . . . The State merely prevents the owner from making a use which interferes with paramount rights of the public.

A variety of methods to "internalize" the environmental consequences of development have recently been introduced. These constitute "taking" in the Brandeis sense. Already mentioned are ordinances requiring developers to set aside up to 20 per cent of their parcels for parks or open spaces, or in some cases to pay into a fund to support public facilities. More direct growth costs such as roads and schools can be internalized through a charge for developers. California and a few communities require developers of major projects to complete an impact statement to permit the community to assess the environmental and social consequences of development and to "charge" the developer or reduce his project accordingly.

Trusts and Taxes An exciting recent land-use innovation is the environmental trust, established by six states thus far. The Maine

Coast Environmental Trust and the Maryland Environmental Trust, established by state legislative action, are quasi-public bodies empowered to obtain environmental or conservation easements from property owners in exchange for property tax relief. Owners of eight thousand acres of Maine coastline have given up for a specified number of years or indefinitely the right to develop their land more intensively. A Maryland farmer has done the same thing on a farm owned by his family since 1663. This convenient method of relieving property owners of the tax burden that has forced others to sell to developers involves no direct costs to the state other than for a small staff and the foregone land tax revenues. By concentrating such easements in ecologically sensitive areas such as wetlands and watersheds, major environmental gains can be achieved without the controversy and delays attendant to most land-use decisions.

A private organization, the Nature Conservancy, has pioneered a wholly private approach. From private sources it has mobilized a $4 million fund to purchase 732,000 acres of land. Major corporations have transferred large land holdings, including North Carolina's Great Dismal Swamp, to the Conservancy's ownership. Often property tax reductions by local governments have facilitated these transfers.

Another innovation is the Land Bank. Tax revenues or development fees are paid into a fund that can be used to compensate property owners for environmental easements or to offset down-zoning or wipe-outs. Favorable court treatment to public taking often turns on whether "just compensation" is provided. Also, public instruments are needed to capture windfalls that accrue to property owners at the general taxpayers' expense. For example, subway siting consequently enriches those holding adjacent property. These windfalls should be taxed at higher rates than normal profits from property sales. Finally, as long as the community is dependent on real estate tax revenues for two thirds of its revenues, city promotion of development is assured. More general taxes, on income or sales for example, should replace real estate taxes as the principal source of urban funds.

In short, we are entering an era of experimentation with a variety of new incentives for and against land development. Localities have an extraordinary degree of flexibility. But their past failure to utilize zoning authorities to accomplish environmental goals is reason to doubt that much will be accomplished without state involvement and federal guidance.

THE DIMENSIONS
OF THE FEDERAL ROLE

Federal guidance can provide a broader framework for local land-use decisions, demonstrate tax and other alternatives, and help guarantee the achievement of overriding societal goals such as the protection of public health from environmental abuses. It can also play a vital role in identifying the relationships between land use and transportation and between land use and the environment.

A Fair Share of Growth   A "fair-share" growth policy is a federal policy action long overdue. Localities troubled by no-growth sentiment have received no guidance from the federal government. It is clear that no-growth is no solution. A fair-share policy would make population growth at a minimal annual rate for all localities a national requirement if the demand is there and environmental limits permit such growth. Part of a fair-share policy is a legally enforceable civil rights assurance that controlled or no-growth policies cannot be employed as racial or social barriers. In addition, a fair-share growth policy should outline what America's land-use needs are, including how many people will need homes, where they prefer to live, and the scope of commercial and industrial land needs to sustain economic growth.

Finally and above all, such a policy would accommodate needed local flexibility in growth decisions. While no-growth would not be tolerated, slow-growth would—at the price of reduced federal support for public facilities such as schools, roads, and sewerage. Local governments should have a major input, responsive to local growth needs, into the formulation of a fair-share growth goal. Average-growth cities would aspire to grow at the average annual rate, and high-growth areas would maximize the growth of their populations. Only residential and commercial growth would be guided by the growth policy. Already environmental requirements, particularly those for air-quality nondeterioration, are in existence to shape industrial growth. The issuance of permits for home building and associated zoning decisions would be the control measures to determine local growth. Areas not opting for a particular growth rate would be classified for high growth.

Highways and Land Use Beyond establishing this fair-share growth framework, the federal government must upgrade the land-use input into decisions on the highway and waste-water-treatment construction projects it finances. The Department of Transportation owes America a monumental intellectual debt: to tell us how highway and mass transportation funding influences land-use patterns. With such knowledge, our federal transportation expenditures can be directed by state and local planners from traffic-creating beltways toward traffic-reducing road designs supportive of satellite cities. Such cities should be linked, where appropriate in large urban complexes, by mass transportation. The twin goals of a transportation policy must be to reduce traffic by promoting land-use patterns that permit jobs, shopping areas, and homes to be located in close proximity to one another or, as an alternative or complement, to permit the use of mass transit on highly traveled corridors. Urban and suburban highway placement since the mid-1950s has done neither. This same emphasis must find support at the state and local levels, where reducing reliance on the automobile or reducing the road-induced incentives for sprawl have received no attention worthy of note. By contrast to U.S. developments, which devote 25 to 30 per cent of the land area to streets, British-planned new towns allocate only 13 per cent to streets and railways.

Federal funding for waste-water-treatment works and sewers can also help shape land-use patterns. The federal government can withhold construction funds from projects that will result in environmentally damaging growth. It can use the same authorities to force a locality that needs funding to add enough capacity to serve its "fair share" of the nation's population growth.

Federal Help for State Planning Federal support is also necessary to strengthen state and local planning efforts. The defeat of the land-use bill will delay until its eventual passage the funding of state land-use planning efforts. Meanwhile, the EPA is spending more than the amount called for in the land-use bill to support area-wide water-quality planning by councils of governments and other broad-based planning units. This effort, if properly executed and supplemented by other region-wide planning focused on transportation, housing, clean air, and recreation needs, should help overcome the sterility of the recently dominant and ineffectual "master planning." Land-use master planning to the year 2000 exceeds our ability to anticipate developments like the energy crisis and overreaches the decisions of the day, just as zoning underreaches them. Rather, the specification of key environmental relationships should become the chief function of land-use planning. What is the region's environmental carrying capacity? How many vehicles can the air stand? How much pavement will reduce the ground water supply to inadequate levels and allow excessive runoff pollutants to adjacent surface waters? What transportation and land-use development patterns will minimize travel? Where can mass transit succeed? What criteria should major development projects meet? Where can industry locate? The grandeur of master planning found its reward in the size of the document. New York City's late 1960s effort ran to six volumes and cost $425,000 to print. Future land-use planning should measure its success in the number of developer, sewer, and highway decisions it influences and ultimately in the success of the urban region in attracting residents and jobs while meeting environmental standards. Another criterion of planning success is the degree to which the public is brought into the decision process and informed of the growth consequences and alternatives.

Protecting State and Local Prerogatives Just as there are numerous opportunities for federal involvement in land-use planning, there is a point beyond which federal involvement is destructive of local initiative and potentially a threat to the widest possible scope for individual choice. It was noted earlier in this chapter that under court order EPA has promulgated regulations implementing the Clean Air Act that could involve federal officials in the approval of any development with more than a thousand spaces for cars, whether it be a hotel, a country club, a townhouse development, or a shopping center (churches were exempted in a moment of bureaucratic grace). Federal involvement to such a minute level of detail is inappropriate because federal officials are in no position to make the correct local assessment. Moreover, land-use plans to provide the appropriate guidance should be put together on a region-wide basis; piecemeal federal involvement is more likely to undermine than to promote such comprehensive local planning. The sooner states and localities assume the responsibility—and the passage of the land-use bill will hasten the arrival of that day—the better for land use.

Federal studies can help localities to view their problems in a national perspective and to adopt quickly successful measures tried in other communities. Recently three agencies—CEQ, EPA, and HUD —supported the preparation of a report titled "The Cost of Sprawl." For the first time localities can document the comparative costs of various development patterns. The report contains a comparison of a low-density sprawl community with a planned high-density community. Each covers six thousand acres (nine square miles) and has 33,000 residents. The sprawl community consists mostly of single-family dwellings scattered uniformly over the area. In the planned community, half the land is vacant. Ten per cent of the housing is clustered single-family units; 20 per cent is townhouses, 30 per cent is garden apartments, and 40 per cent is high-rise apartments. The cost to construct the planned community is 56 per cent of the cost of its sprawl counterpart, a $227.5 million difference, because there are fewer structures and more common walls, less land is utilized, and there are fewer miles of roads, sewers, and utilities. About half of the sprawl energy requirements are needed in the planned city. Electricity for heating is less and so is gasoline for travel. Missing, of course, is the most essential input: the individual preferences of 33,000 people may warrant more than the one thousand single-family homes out of ten thousand housing units. Also, occupants of the more confined planned community are more likely to purchase second homes on dredged-filled wetlands. The federal government helps when it provides such information to assist local planners, but its involvement is not productive if it acts to regulate on the basis of such information or believes that without local input it has the whole story.

Another study by University of California ecologist Dr. Kenneth

E. F. Watt shows that 25,000 people typically spread over ten square miles could reside in six thirteen-story apartments covering one five-hundredth of the same area. Of course, such a study is a trivial contribution and would be taken seriously only by Soviet planners of the 1930s. Today's Soviet planners have at least advanced to the point that they are "test modeling" four types of single-family dwellings. It is not planning's job to dictate people's lifestyles. Its function is to project the full long-term implications of our collective lifestyle choices and, where the public health is endangered or vital parts of the ecosystem are placed in jeopardy, to set appropriate limits or disincentives on lifestyle choices.

THE ENIGMA OF A SUCCESSFUL CITY

It is an odd commentary on the capacities of modern society that we have yet to determine what makes a city work. We know what does not work. We pledge not to "Californicate" or Manhattanize our cities. The principal innovation of the post-Levittown era is the shopping center, itself a travel-saving improvement over strip development, but hardly a community. We have reinvented the row house and call it a town house. But somehow in designing cities or so-called "new towns" we always forget something. In the United Kingdom there have been repeated efforts, dating from Sir Ebenezer Howard's turn-of-the-century "garden cities," to establish "new towns." These efforts have largely failed. Apparently the goal of attracting sufficient business activity to employ the resident population has been consistently undermined by Britain's sluggish economy and the economic dominance of London. But near Washington, D.C., two new communities—Reston, Virginia, and Columbia, Maryland—have attracted employers as well as residents. These towns were financed by private enterprises, respectively owned now by Gulf Oil and Connecticut General Life Insurance Company. Columbia has attracted 32,000 residents and 20,000 jobs, some held by out-of-towners. But Columbia and Reston have the same Achilles heel: they both are automobile dependent. To a substantial degree, even these upper-class bedroom communities need mass transit to survive in an energy-short age. They need transit and lower priced residences to attract all income groups (Columbia's average family income is $19,000 per year).

Congress sought to create a large number of similar "new towns" when the 1970 Housing Act authorized federal loan guarantees to help finance private profit or nonprofit sponsored efforts. Both new towns in town and new satellite towns were contemplated. To date the record is dismal. Initially the Nixon Administration withheld support for new towns. Then fifteen applications were approved. Recently, one of these, Grananda, on the outskirts of Rochester, New York, went bankrupt. The largest of these new towns is The Woodlands, designed to house 150,000, about thirty miles from Houston. It too is in financial trouble. Others followed. In early 1975 the U. S. Department of Housing and Urban Development terminated the new towns program.

One of the approved projects is Cedar-Riverside in Minneapolis, Minnesota. This is a "new town in town," and is designed to reclaim a hundred acres and settle 30,000 people in a downtown urban community. It features the restoration of old buildings, the installation of a second-floor-level pedestrian transport system above traffic and parking, and a diverse community of theaters, shops, and mixed housing types. This new town can draw inspiration from its surroundings. Minneapolis and its sister city, St. Paul, already are evidence that cities have a future. Their innovative government has, since a 1971 state law linked six counties into a Twin Cities region-wide council with land-use powers, showed that sprawl can be controlled and the city center nourished.

Taking shape on Roosevelt (formerly Welfare) Island in New York City's East River is a new town planned for 21,000 families. It will have no automobiles but will be linked to Manhattan by a Swiss-designed cable car, and local travel will be by bicycle or electric bus. It remains to be demonstrated that this high-rise, in-town new town can avoid crime, financial problems, and New York City's dismal future.

These notable projects may eventually bear fruit. We await the entrepreneur who does for towns what the shopping center has done for shopping. Perhaps the energy crisis will spark a new insight that drastically alters our urban and suburban landscape. More likely is a slow and difficult restoration of the city as a cherished center of cultural and economic activity, surrounded by satellite or mini-cities of mixed composition linked by mass transportation. Some people will escape this environment altogether and return to the most attractive spots in rural America. Things will get better. Land use in America can only improve.

TOWARD
ENVIRONMENTAL GROWTH

In Oxford, England, in June 1860 a great debate occurred between the esteemed bishop of Oxford, Samuel Wilberforce, and an upstart scientist and disciple of Charles Darwin, T. H. Huxley. A year earlier Darwin had published *On the Origin of Species by Means of Natural Selection*. The Bishop's famed rhetorical excursions on behalf of religion moved Oxford's skeptical academics to label him "Soapy Sam." He unwisely attacked Darwin's theories in a public Oxford forum only to have his arguments leveled by Huxley and thus became the object of the crowd's ridicule. Just over one hundred years later, a debate with pretensions at least as extraordinary as those of the Oxford confrontation has been occurring on a worldwide scale.

THE DOOMSDAY DEBATE

This doomsday debate is over two of the central faiths of advanced societies held consistently and fervently since the commercial revolution of the sixteenth century and the nineteenth century's industrial revolution. First is a faith in economic growth as society's beneficent *deus ex machina* bringing us wealth, power, leisure, and a worthy challenge for daily living. The second faith dates back to Newton, Bacon, and other discoverers of man's scientific ability to dominate or at least to understand and improve nature: our belief in technology as man's companion in productivity. If growth has been our religion, technology has been the prayerbook, Bible, and hymnal all in one.

Now we are told it is not so. Growth is bad because the way it inevitably occurs fouls our air, rivers, even the biosphere—our very cocoon. If it continues, life on earth may die of suffocation, poisoning, cancers, and we will suffer birth defects and starvation.

The most articulate spokesman for the technology-is-bad viewpoint is biologist Barry Commoner, director of the Center for Biology and Natural Systems at St. Louis's Washington University. Commoner's book *The Closing Circle* (1971) has done more to educate us about ecological problems than any book since Rachel Carson's *Silent Spring* of a decade earlier. His homey rules—for example, "Everything is connected with everything else," and "There is no such thing as a free lunch"—translated ecological sophistications, previously wrapped in impenetrable jargon, into kitchen and cocktail party vernacular.

Commoner's view is that ecological problems became serious after World War II because the nature of growth in the postwar era took an odd turn. He cites increased reliance on aluminum, the advent of high-compression-engine cars, the throwaway bottle, synthetic petrochemicals, the fertilizer industry, phosphate detergents, and DDT to buttress his argument that recent ecnomic growth has caused the proliferation of unnatural materials. Normally, natural ecological processes break down wastes into recyclable elements through biodegradation. But nature's waste disposal system is clogged and stalled by new synthetic products. Also, to produce them requires a greater expenditure of our scarce natural resources; for example, the aluminum and petrochemical industries are energy guzzlers.

With such a collection of ecological devils, it was incumbent on Commoner to identify a conspiracy or Great Perpetrator, and he has fingered the private-enterprise system as the culprit. Profit-making firms introduced and oversold synthetic-fibered clothing in place of wool and cotton fabrics, phosphate detergents in place of soap made from natural fats, the throwaway bottle to replace the returnable one, and truck transport in place of more energy-efficient rail shipment.

Commoner finds no, or relatively little, benefit to the people's welfare resulting from these products and he has documented, as have others, the extraordinary ecological harm they have caused.

Commoner's solutions are provocative if not archaic. He would nationalize the railroads, and establish communal lawnmower centers so machines could be shared; he would nationalize the petroleum industry; he would re-establish beer taverns to centralize drinking to reduce the beer-can disposal problem; and he favors communal baths in the Japanese tradition as an energy-saving measure.

Commoner's assessment of our ecological ills is anecdotal and populist. Unfortunately, it is inconsistent on its own grounds, and because he has continued to press it in the face of contrary government and private-sector performance, it is devoid of prescriptive value.

While he locates the origins of severe ecological stress in the post-World War II era, it is well known that the regional ecological problems with which he is primarily concerned were more acute before World War II, when low-grade coal and night gas were our sources of heat and light rather than oil and electricity, and when open-hearth steelmaking and coal-powered steam locomotives were spreading filth in our industrial cities. Even occupational hazards singled out by Commoner, such as the recently exposed liver cancer caused by working in polyvinyl chloride plants, have at most affected hundreds. They cannot be compared with factory diseases of the industrial revolution which affected hundreds of thousands. Moreover, his nostalgia for old factors of production like wood over today's aluminum overlooks the fact that our forests would be bare if we had continued to rely on wood.

One of Commoner's more curious post-World War II technology culprits is the automobile, but it predates the war by a generation. He identifies the high-compression engine of the late 1940s as the ecologically damaging automotive development because its higher combustion temperatures caused higher levels of nitrogen oxides emissions. But, compared to smog and carbon monoxide pollution, nitrogen oxides are not a serious air-pollution problem. What is new about the automobile in the postwar era is that there are so many of them and we drive so much. That's a problem of lifestyle, not technology. Moreover, even if Commoner were willing to shift the origins of our ecological difficulties to the early twentieth century, when the industrial revolution reached its peak and the automobile was invented, he would have another difficulty. Numerous critics have observed that had we relied on the horse to improve our mobility in the twentieth century, our major cities would be buried under tons of horse manure and our rivers would be reeking cesspools.

For all the difficulties with his arguments and his solutions, Commoner has identified an important area of ecological abuse in focusing on the synthetics and new products industries. More than three hundred chemical compounds are introduced into the marketplace each year. But by any measure our efforts to cope with these abuses have met with success. The major sources of mercury pollution have been all but eliminated. After the imposition of very stringent emission limitations, the production of PCBs (polychlorinated biphenyls) is being terminated. The courts have ordered the Reserve Mining Corporation to discharge its asbestos-bearing tailings on land rather than into Lake Superior. Already air discharges of asbestos, mercury, beryllium, and polyvinyl chloride are controlled by the Clean Air Act and a long list of pesticides and heavy metals are controlled by the 1972 Water and Pesticides Control acts. The pending Toxic Substances Control Bill, would force preintroduction tests of new chemicals.

If Commoner is anecdotal, his colleagues in global doomsaying Dennis and Donella Meadows, in their computerized study *The Limits to Growth,* have oversystematized the process and implications of growth to the point of absolute sterility of empirical content. Published by the Club of Rome in 1972, *Limits* has become to some a refutation of conventional wisdom as devastating as Darwin's *Origin of Species.*

The *Limits* computer model runs on four key assumptions: (a) population grows exponentially; (b) industrial production and its associated pollution grow exponentially; (c) natural resources will be consumed at an exponential rate; and (d) technology, whether to control pollution or mine additional natural resources, grows linearly. In particular, the study projects that far into the future pollution-control technology can be expected to cut pollution to only 25 per cent of 1970 levels, on a per unit of production basis.

Fed into the computer, these assumptions produced several growth-caused world collapse scenarios. One might be called the "Resource Exhaustion System Collapse Scenario." It projects continued growth until limited natural resources are exhausted—for example, coal in 150 years. Industrial production halts and highly mechanized agricultural output which is dependent on industrial production also collapses. The world starves. Another scenario assumes resource-saving technology permits growth to continue but rising pollution eventually poisons the environment so that we either stop growth or die. Under either scenario these bleak results are expected within about 150 years. *Limits* concludes: (a) GNP and population growth must stop; and (b) comprehensive planning must be employed to enforce an "equilibrium" no-growth state.

Accompanying these developments would be far-reaching societal changes such as massive income redistribution. Otherwise, income differences in multiples of 150 would remain common between poor and rich countries without the safety valve of continued improvement which has allowed the majority of the world's population to enjoy higher levels of consumption from the steadily growing world pie of wealth. More standardized and routinized living would be in order.

The many critics of *Limits* saw its results as the product of computer modeling propelled by poor history and poor economics. Several problems with the analysis led to this suspicion. First, the *Limits* model assumed an annual world population growth rate of 2.1 per cent, with the world's population doubling every thirty-three years. Already the U.S. population growth rate is about 0.7 per cent, and, if present two-child family birth rates continue, it will be zero per cent in the year 2037. Canada, Denmark, Finland, Germany, Sweden, Austria, Hungary, Poland, Japan, and others have fertility levels which will lead to zero population growth rates in the near future. A recent World Bank report on fertility data found that "of the 66 countries for which accurate data are available, as many as 56 show a decline." Second, we have no proof that technology will not continue to make natural resources, or substitutes therefore, available at an exponential rate. It has thus far, and resource-developing gains continue. Third, market pricing is not incorporated in the *Limits* model. Thus, unlike the real world, technology is not spurred forward to produce new materials to substitute for those exhausted. Nor are there incentives or regulations in the model to further reduce emissions per unit produced. The *Limits* model does not reflect the inevitability that higher resource costs will increase prices of goods and, therefore, dampen demand and output growth. Finally, there is no basis for the assumption that pollution reductions are limited to a once-and-for-all 75 per cent reduction from 1970's emission rates. Our experience thus far is that every fifteen years technological gains have halved the pollution rate. That is equivalent to a 75 per cent reduction every thirty years. Such a performance would be adequate to keep pace with a 4.5 per cent economic growth rate, comfortably more than one fourth above the post-World War II growth rates in the U.S.

Thus, on several fronts, the assumptions put into the Club of Rome computer model appear to be in conflict with what is actually going on around us. The entire doomsaying theology is based on a simple logic of bad growth. Population increases. More goods are produced. New technologies are introduced to produce more goods. The new technologies are dirtier than the old ones. Therefore, the environment gets worse at an accelerating rate. The facts are available to refute the two essential links in this sad logic. Technology is getting cleaner, not dirtier. And the number of additional people economic growth must serve is decreasing. Moreover, the United States is experiencing changing consumption habits and a rising preference for leisure because America's population is aging and because Americans are becoming to some degree economically satiated. These developments relieve the pressure on cleanup technology and thereby on the environment.

CAN CLEANUP TECHNOLOGY OUTPACE GROWTH NEEDS?

Now that programs are under way to abate pollution, it is possible to add empirical content to the *Limits* concept and see whether exponential growth of "bads" will inevitably outrun the linear growth of "goods" as *Limits* postulates.

First, the nation's air- and water-pollution abatement laws, with their technologically based standards, are requiring industry to reduce pollution 85 to 95 per cent. To be conservative and allow for implementation slippages, let us assume an 80 per cent pollution reduction is achieved by 1990 instead of the 85 to 95 per cent reductions that are actually planned by 1978–80. Thus, in just a few years, efforts already under way will exceed the 75 per cent reduction predicted for the next two hundred years or more by *Limits*. In other words, if there are absolutely no new technological efforts made toward further cleaning our environment, we will not be in trouble until the year 2012; assuming a 4 per cent annual economic growth rate which doubles the economy every seventeen years, and assuming the abatement program seeks its reductions from 1972 levels of emissions, by 1990 pollutant levels would be 40 per cent of 1972 levels. Not until the year 2012 would 1972 pollutant levels be reached.

The same refutation of *Limits* is possible if we take a couple of specific industry-growth and pollution-abatement projections. The accompanying chart shows the growth in water pollution from the paper industry. Effluents into water from the paper industry currently contain about ten million tons per year of biochemical oxygen-demanding pollutants (BOD). BOD competes with fish life for oxygen

PROJECTED PAPER-INDUSTRY POLLUTION

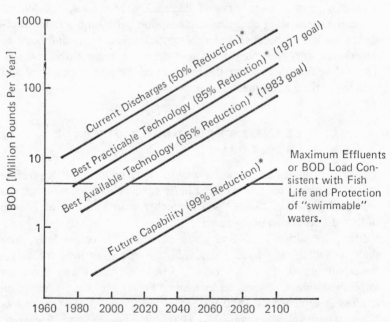

* This reduction is in the pounds of effluents (BOD) per ton of paper product.

in the water. Until recently it was winning rather than the fish. By 1977 and 1983, the law will require successively higher degrees of treatment by the paper industry. As the chart indicates, "best practicable technology" represents the 1977 effluent standard and the "best available technology" line is the 1983 effluent standard. The amount of discharge after the 1977 level of treatment is reached is a good approximation of the discharge that can be allowed without damaging fish life or making our rivers unswimmable. Therefore, given present technology and likely future growth rates, water quality will not be violated by the paper industry before the year 2010. The "future capacity" line on the chart indicates the effectiveness of a technology which is currently available but prohibitively expensive. The task is to develop more efficient and more cost-effective methods of pollution reduction for the paper industry within the next thirty-five years. There are already signs that this has been accomplished. A new treatment process now in operation in Canada completely eliminates water waste discharges from pulp and paper plants.

It is noteworthy that the foregoing results are based on an analysis of abatement results achieved primarily through end-of-pipe treatment rather than process change. The latter approach to abatement, which utilizes wholesale revamping of the production process as opposed to simple additions of treatment technologies at the end of the pipe or stack, offers the potential for even more dramatic reductions in pollution per unit of output. The cost to industry in selecting one or the other of these types of treatment is not what it may at first appear.

A recent EPA study found that water pollution from a copper mill could be reduced at an investment cost of $500,000 and a $156,000 annual operating cost through the use of end-of-the-pipe technology. A much lower cost of $141,000 in investment and $74,000 per year for operating would result if a production process change were made that reduced water use in the industry by 90 per cent. An annual cost saving of $163,000 resulted from implementing the process change.

Similar breakthroughs may be in prospect for air-polluting industries. Anaconda announced on January 4, 1973, that it is building a new smelter in Montana that will eliminate all sulfur dioxide emissions and be cheaper to build and operate than today's production processes. A few days later, the Aluminum Company of America announced it had developed a new smelting technology for aluminum which is air-pollution-free.

A recent article in *Science* magazine attempts to explain such periodic bursts in technology. Responding to a market or regulatory need, new technologies emerge, are improved, then become static in performance. If there is added pressure for better performance, a new technology is developed which repeats the same sigmoid evolution but begins at the ultimate performance level of the obsolete technology.[1] Environmental legislation in the United States is designed to exert the pressure on industry for better performance. New engineering approaches are being taken. Industries are trying total recycling systems, "closing" their operations to the environment, or in other cases learning to operate off each other's wastes. This legislation is working far better than it needs to to keep the doomsayers well behind us.

SMALLER FAMILIES AND LOWER GROWTH RATES

If vigorous legislative action and industry performance have proved the technology assumptions of the doom forecasters wrong, the reproductive decisions of millions of Americans have broken the back of their computer model.

During this century's first seventy-five years, the nation's population nearly tripled from 70 to 210 million. The next seventy-five years to the year 2050 look considerably different. Currently, we are experiencing a decreasing birth rate. The three-child family is being replaced by the two-child family, and rather than tripling the population, which a repeat of the past seventy-five years would bring, we expect, if present trends continue, a comparatively meager 25 per cent increase in population. What is more, we expect zero population growth, where the number of deaths balance the number of births, by about the year 2037.

On December 4, 1972, a sort of Victory for the Environment Day arrived. On VE Day, the American people attained a fertility rate

[1] See C. Starr and R. Rudman, "Parameters of Technological Growth," *Science* 182 (Oct. 26, 1973): 358–82.

which, if perpetuated, would eventually yield a zero population growth (ZPG) rate. The average fertility rate per family had fallen to 2.1 children. Because today there are so many more childbearing-aged families in the United States than there are older people, our population continues to grow. It would take an average of 1.2 children per family to achieve ZPG immediately. That is out of the question except in the minds of a few ZPG enthusiasts who want to take the decision to bear children out of our hands and impose a mandatory program of population control.

Since 1972, the fertility rate has dropped further to 1.9; while there are some signs it could drop to 1.8, it appears to be levelling off and may even rise slightly.[2] If it were to reach the 1.8 level, by the year 2000 the U.S. population would be 250 million, as compared with 264 million if the 2.1 eventual replacement rate is sustained.

The reasons for this reduced population growth rate are only remotely environmental. The big-family era after the war may have been a one-generation lag from the era when a large family size was essential to the farm production unit. Also, children in this country, just as in India or Southeast Asia, are a form of social security, providing their parents with a source of income and affection beyond their productive years. The advent of social security legislation has reduced this incentive for large families. The role of women has also changed. Familial bliss has lost appeal for some. Census data for 1973 showed 38 per cent of the women twenty to twenty-four years of age were single—up from 28 per cent in 1960. And after marriage, work is more important. In 1973, 41 per cent of married women held jobs.

Technology has had a positive effect too. The birth control pill sells like aspirin to those who can afford it and can be obtained free by those who cannot. Data for 1973 show even 68 per cent of Catholic wives between the ages of eighteen and thirty-nine were using contraceptives. Also in 1973, there were an estimated 850,000 steri-

---

[2] According to June Sklar and Beth Berkov, "The American Birth Rate: Evidence of a Coming Rise" *Science* 189 (Aug. 1975): 693–700, 1973 and 1974 fertility data for California and nationwide show that long-delayed but wanted births by women of the young childbearing ages (twenty to thirty-four years) are beginning to take place and will probably cause the fertility rate to rise.

lizations of men and women and 700,000 legal abortions. Even though reported abortions hardly approach the number actually performed, recent data for Washington, D.C., showed that more pregnant women opted for abortions than for deliveries.

Fewer people mean less environmental stress. However, population size is a crude measure of this stress. More important are two other factors. First, the composition of the gross national product has a large impact on the environment. The shift of demand from manufacturing to less environmentally abusive service industries will help. In 1970 for the first time, more Americans were employed in services than in manufacturing. Second, the preferences of Americans for leisure and the projected aging of the population can reduce environmental stresses by reducing the need for growth.

Our natural resources are affected doubly by economic growth. On the one hand, resources are required to establish for additional Americans a level of wealth and income at the existing standard of living; on the other hand, resources are consumed to raise the standard of living of the rest of us by the additional annual increment we expect. Since 1900 the real gross national product has had to grow an average of 3 per cent per year, doubling every twenty-three years, to keep pace not only with a rapidly increasing population, but also with aspirations for a higher standard of living. Over the past decade, this pace has jumped to 4 per cent annually to meet the dual demands of an increasingly higher population growth rate. Looking ahead, the lower population growth rate, according to calculations made in 1970 by the U. S. Commission on Population and the American Future, will reduce the expected gross national product in the year 2020 from a level of 100 per cent to 78 per cent. Put another way, the GNP growth rate will fall from 4.0 per cent to 3.1 per cent.

Next, this calculation must be adjusted to recognize that the environment is helped if a large part of increased productivity is used for leisure-time activities and a higher proportion of disposable income is spent on services. For example, if an assembly line worker processed ten automobiles per hour in 1970 and fifteen per hour in 1980 without increasing his forty-hour week, he would produce 50 per cent more automobiles and collect the commensurate extra income to spend for half again as many goods and services. That is not going to happen. Instead, the laborer will work a seven-hour day using a portion of the productivity increase for leisure activity. Also, more of his increased earnings would be directed to services than in the past.

The effect of this change on the year 2020's GNP is to drop it all the way to 54 per cent of the high-population, high-manufacturing employment projection. Thus, the changing composition of GNP toward services and the rising preference for leisure have about the same dramatic effect on lowering the GNP as does the projected lower population growth rate. Combining the two effects drops the per year GNP growth rate to a low 2.4 to 2.5 per cent.

THE EFFECT OF AGE

One more calculation is essential. What is the impact of a change in the age composition of our population? Young and old people, when considered as population sectors, exert different pressures on the environment. Children demand relatively little from the environment: food, clothes, and shelter. Older people also place relatively modest demands on the environment. The largest impact occurs when people enter the labor market; incomes spiral, as do needs for automobiles, houses, and the equipment for the new work force entrants. A tremendous strain is placed on the nation's resources and, consequently, on the environment. We are currently at a point where people born during the baby boom of the late forties and early fifties are entering the labor market. Not until 1987 will the number of twenty- to thirty-nine-year-old war babies peak.

The impact on the environment of the changes in size of each age group is the sum of the environmental demands of each. As is obvious from reviewing the population growth figures, the environmental demand due to population increase will peak sometime between 1987, when the number of people in the most demanding twenty-to-thirty age group peaks, and the year 2037, when the total population peaks.

To estimate the expected effect, let us introduce a unit of measurement and call it the environmental demand unit (EDU). As expected, available data tell us that when people enter the work force they consume the most. As shown in the table, the largest increases in family income and expenditures take place when the age of the household head is between twenty-five and forty-four years old. After age fifty-five, his or her family's expenditures and income decline precipitously.

INCOME AND CONSUMPTION INDICES BY HOUSEHOLD HEAD AGE GROUP (DOLLAR EXPENDITURES NORMALIZED TO EIGHTEEN-TO-TWENTY-FOUR AGE GROUP)*

Age of Head of Household	Income	Housing	Clothing	Autos
18-24	100	100	100	100
25-34	141	130	166	114
35-44	255	130	233	114
45-54	272	115	233	128
55-64	206	92	133	86
65-74	127	77	66	57
75-	75	54	33	14

* Compiled by James N. Heller, Energy and Environmental Analysis, Inc., from U. S. Department of Commerce, Bureau of Labor Statistics data.

Based on this and other data, the following environmental demand units (EDUs) can be assigned to people in each of the four following age groups: one to nineteen years, EDU 1.0; twenty to thirty-nine years, EDU 2.0; forty to fifty-nine years, EDU 1.5; and sixty years and above, EDU 0.5. The accompanying chart is a plot of the environmental demand of these age groups projected to the year 2050. The chart was constructed by multiplying the size of the population in each age group for each year, by the environmental-demand-unit weighting factor appropriate to that group. Under these assumptions, peak environmental demand due to population increases occurs near the year 2010. This is 27 years earlier than the 2037 estimate based on a crude population analysis. That is good

ENVIRONMENTAL DEMAND OF POPULATION BY AGE GROUP

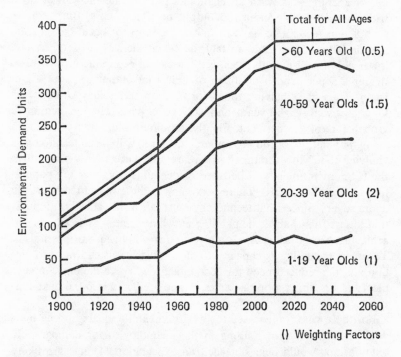

() Weighting Factors

news. But the bad news is that through 1980 the most severe environmental demands can be expected. Beyond 1980 the rate of growth of EDUs drops to below the 1900-1950 rate.

INDUSTRIAL POLLUTION-FREE GROWTH

The upshot of this analysis is that economic growth and environmental improvement are compatible goals. We saw earlier that cleanup technology has demonstrated a "halving time" of fifteen years. In other words, every fifteen years technology is improved so as to be able to reduce pollutant discharges by 50 per cent. For example, if one hundred pounds of pollutants are emitted to the air and water for every one thousand tons of output, fifteen years from now only fifty pounds will be emitted. Thus, cleanup technology is capable of keeping pace with an economic growth rate of 4.5 per cent, which would double industrial output in fifteen years. But we have found that economic growth is not going to occur at a rate approaching 4.5 per cent. In fact, based on the shift to services and lower population growth rates, we can expect economic growth rates nearer 2.5 per cent, a doubling of industrial output in twenty-eight years. Thus, the "halving time" for cleanup technology could be as long as twenty-eight years and still keep pace with an economic growth rate of 2.5 per cent. Finally, accounting for the impact of an aging population on environmental demand will push technology's "halving time" to over thirty-five years and place the date at which the U.S. environment will be freed of demands from a rising population to as early as 2010. There is nothing in these facts to support the doom-sayers. Since what technology must do to stay ahead of population is less than half as demanding as what technology is capable of achieving, the occasion is certainly one for optimism, not pessimism. Together, technology's capacity to clean up the wastes from production and the reduced need for economic growth give the environment plenty of breathing room as far as can be predicted into the next century.

For those who want to see the environmental apocalypse one hundred years from now, nothing in the technological or demographic relationships would bear out such an expectation. Things are likely to get better before they get worse, at least. Meanwhile, per capita income can continue to rise. All this assumes, of course, that the vigorous regulatory program to reduce industrial pollution is carried forward relentlessly.

ATTACKING LIFESTYLE POLLUTION

Lifestyle pollution is another matter altogether. Lifestyle changes come into the picture not as a reform to forestall doom from pollution but as a measure to make the environment pleasant for us all and health- and life-giving for the perhaps 5 to 10 per cent of our population who are sick, infant, or infirm. Earlier the automobile was cited, along with energy and land use, as an example of lifestyle pollution. The automobile cannot be controlled sufficiently to clean the air in our largest cities. Even the planned 95 per cent reduction in automotive emissions to be achieved in a decade will not be enough for the cities with air-quality problems as serious as Los Angeles's and Denver's. If we are pessimistic and estimate that an 85 per cent reduction on average will be achieved throughout the car population because of disconnects and malfunctions of emission controls, in the 1990s increased travel will push city-wide emissions to the levels prevailing in the early 1970s. While technology allows us to be optimistic about industrial cleanup, it does not permit full attainment of environmental goals because it cannot solve the problem of lifestyle pollution.

Traffic reductions are necessary to curb our auto-dominated way of life. To achieve complete cleanup in some cities, traffic will have to be reduced by 20 to 50 per cent. Obviously, if half of the cars were banned from the road overnight, large-scale economic dislocations would follow. But generally, if the 20 to 50 per cent reductions are implemented over a ten- to fifteen-year period (see Chapter 6) severe local economic impacts can be avoided through the application of creative mass transportation solutions in concert with supportive land-use measures. National economic growth need not be inhibited. In the very worst cases, such as the greater Los Angeles area, where the patterns of development are so automobile-dependent, there may be a real choice between growth and the attainment of environmental standards, but not between growth and continued pollution at today's levels. And the resulting levels of pollution will not cause the population to suffer epidemiclike losses. Pollution levels will get better in the Los Angeles Basin, even if air standards protective of the most vulnerable portions of the population are not met. Such an achievement may not be worth bragging about, but it surely is not a disaster meriting the no-growth solution prescribed by the no-growth advocates.

Enough has been said in this book to free its refutations of no-growth theories from the accusation that it has embraced economic growth as we have known and worshipped it for at least a century. America is already changing its commitment to unfettered growth.

Industry no longer has a free license to pollute our skies and rivers in the name of "progress." Communities are demanding that industries be good neighbors or no neighbors at all. U.S. federal regulations are as tough as any in the world and we can be proud of our willingness to set a high standard. The American concept of growth is fading into a concept of leisure. Soon the "cowboy economy" like the Western will be remembered in the movie houses as a delightful, sometimes difficult, adolescent stage in America's development. We will laugh at the boiling smokestacks and scarred land. We'll have a dig-'em-up as well as a shoot-'em-up past.

The rise of the service economy is itself a form of economic satiety for the world's wealthiest people. Close on its heels is a preference for leisure, the outdoors, perhaps even a modicum of the simple things of life. What must be done is to replace the drift toward these values with a conscious policy of environmental growth. We must finally and completely commit ourselves to an environmental lifestyle. We must end lifestyle pollution by modifying our automobile, land- and energy-use habits. The choices are hard choices. But, they are signposts on the path to environmental growth, reachable by the end of this century. Such growth will be a dynamic economic condition, not a static economy. It will give us the ability to cope with our social ills, to continue to increase our income and opportunities, to sustain our technological leadership, and to continue to provide leadership throughout the world. It can give us all these and a clean environment too.

INDEX

About the Author

Robert L. Sansom, a former Fulbright Scholar, Rhodes Scholar, and White House Fellow, was an aide to Henry Kissinger from 1968 to 1971 on the National Security Council staff. From 1972 to 1974, he served as assistant administrator in charge of air and water programs with the EPA. He is the author of *The Economics of Insurgency,* and presently runs Energy and Environmental Analysis, Inc., a Washington-based consulting group which he founded.

DATE DUE